DATE DUE

Volunteers on the Veld

C&C

CAMPAIGNS & COMMANDERS

GREGORY J. W. URWIN, SERIES EDITOR

CAMPAIGNS AND COMMANDERS

Volunteers on the Veld

Britain's Citizen-Soldiers and the South African War, 1899–1902

Stephen M. Miller

University of Oklahoma Press : Norman

ALSO BY STEPHEN M. MILLER

Lord Methuen and the British Army: Failure and Redemption in South Africa (London, 1999)

Library of Congress Cataloging-in-Publication Data

Miller, Stephen M., 1964–
Volunteers on the Veld : Britain's citizen-soldiers and the South African War, 1899–1902 / Stephen M. Miller.
p. cm. — (Campaigns & commanders series ; v. 12)
Includes bibliographical references and index.
ISBN 978-0-8061-3864-0 (alk. paper)
1. South African War, 1899–1902. 2. Military service, Voluntary—Great Britain—History. 3. Soldiers—Great Britain—History. 4. Great Britain. Army—Recruiting, enlistment, etc.—South African War, 1899–1902. I. Title.
DT1900.M55 2007
968.04'831—dc22 2007006506

Volunteers on the Veld: Britain's Citizen-Soldiers and the South African War, 1899–1902 is Volume 12 in the Campaigns & Commanders series.

The paper in this book meets the guidelines for permanence and durability of the Committee on Production Guidelines for Book Longevity of the Council on Library Resources. ∞

1 2 3 4 5 6 7 8 9 10

Contents

Illustrations

All illustrations are courtesy Anne S. K. Brown Military Collection, Brown University Library.

Maps

Acknowledgments

There are a number of people I would like to thank for their assistance in researching, writing, and completing this book. I am grateful to my colleagues at the University of Maine, in particular Alex Grab, for reading part of the manuscript, and Scott See and William TeBrake, who as chairs of the History Department made sure I had the financial support I required to attend conferences and get important feedback on sections of this manuscript. A special thank-you to Suzanne Moulton and Ulrike Livingston for staff support. I would also like to thank the University of Maine, which provided a summer faculty-research grant that made it possible for me to travel to the United Kingdom. For their suggestions and support for this project, I acknowledge Ian Beckett, Matthew Hughes, John Laband, Fransjohan Pretorius, E. M. Spiers, Keith Surridge, Bruce Vandervort, and Ian van der Waag. I am indebted to Gregory Urwin, for approaching me to write for the Campaigns and Commanders series; to Charles Rankin, editor-in-chief of the University of Oklahoma Press, for all his assistance in making sure this project made it through production; and to Kevin Brock, for his editorial assistance.

I would also like to thank the staff of the libraries and archives used in my research, including the British Library, Corporation of

London Records Office, the Guildhall Library, the Imperial War Museum, the Liddell Hart Centre for Military Archives, King's College, the National Archives, the National Army Museum, and in particular Stuart Hadaway at the Worcestershire Yeomanry Museum. Peter Harrington at the Anne S. K. Brown Military Collection, Brown University Library, did a wonderful job in providing the illustrations that accompany this text, and Mike Hermann, senior cartographer at the Canadian-American Center, University of Maine, created the maps. I must also acknowledge the assistance of Fogler librarian Mel Johnson and the staff at the University of Maine's Interlibrary Loan Department. Thanks to the *Journal of Military History* and the *Journal of the Society for Army Historical Research* for granting permission to use parts of my published articles in this book.

Finally, I would like to thank my family and friends for the emotional support they provided during this long, arduous journey. I could not have finished this work without the help of my friends in Late for Work (Rob Baldwin, Larry Corbett, Eric Gallandt, Jamie Heans, Larry Leblanc, Fred Leigh, Jamie Moreira, Martin O'Connell, and their families), Peter Cook and Leslie Gould, Michael Lang and Susan Pinette, and Rob and Allison MacCormick. Finally, with much love, I wish to thank my sons, David and Max, who have taught me so much about life; B.P.M., S.S.M., and M.V.M.; and most of all my wife, my everything, Jessica P. Miller. This book is dedicated to my parents, Malcolm and Frances Abrams, and to Patricia Keogh.

Volunteers on the Veld

Introduction

In the final months of the South African War, Lt. Gen. Lord Paul Sanford Methuen and his "Kimberley Column" were making yet another drive across the western Transvaal. Methuen had been conducting British operations in the northern Cape Colony and the western Transvaal for over a year and a half. It was a zone of the war that both Lord Horatio Herbert Kitchener, the commander in chief of British forces in South Africa, and his predecessor, Lord Frederick Sleigh Roberts, had deemed nonessential to overall British strategy and to achieving final victory in this prolonged struggle. But it was an exceptionally large area to control, and Methuen rarely had more than three thousand men to maintain order, relieve isolated garrisons, protect and repair lines of communication, and hunt down the enemy. Indeed, Methuen often found himself doing little more than chasing shadows.[1]

Despite the many obstacles, the British managed to maintain relative calm in the districts of the western Transvaal through late 1900 and 1901. Trekking across the veld almost daily, Methuen met with repeated success. His troops confiscated stock, destroyed crops, and periodically caught up with the enemy and captured Boer burghers. British tactics of counter-insurgency, which included the destruction of selected farms and the construction of a network of blockhouses, at last seemed to be taking their toll on the enemy. Boer ammunition supplies were running low, and remounts were harder to find. Civilians were increasingly reluctant to support the guerrillas.

Yet Methuen was far from confident. For one thing, one of the most talented Boer commanders, Gen. J. H. de la Rey, "The Lion of the West," remained at large, and there was nothing to suggest that he and his "bitter-enders" were ready to lay down their weapons anytime soon; indeed, de la Rey was still in the process of refining his guerrilla tactics.[2] The other potential problem was the quality and quantity of his troops. The most recent reinforcements lacked experience, and Methuen questioned their resolve in battle. They were a far cry from the first batch of Imperial Yeomanry he had received early in 1900.[3] In late February 1902 he sat down and wrote a letter to Lt. Gen. Ian Hamilton, Kitchener's chief of staff. In it Methuen listed his mounting difficulties: there were not enough men to maintain order or to conduct decisive operations; the men he had were overburdened and were increasingly ill of health; the Boers were free to strike at will; and the Imperial Yeomanry he was receiving as reinforcements were inferior to the departing troops.[4] But he never sent this letter, for he knew how Hamilton's reply would read. Methuen would be told that he would have to make due with the resources he had, and in no time at all, his inexperienced men, or so Hamilton would have assured him, would become hardened and resolute soldiers as good as any the Regular Army could provide.

On 2 March 1902 Methuen left the town of Vryburg and headed east. This would be his final trek through the western Transvaal and his last attempt to capture de la Rey. His Kimberley Column numbered roughly thirteen hundred men. Although the force included three hundred seasoned regulars of the First Battalion Northumberland Fusiliers and the First Battalion Loyal North Lancashire Regiment and two sections of Royal Field Artillery, the bulk of the column consisted of Volunteers raised in South Africa and Imperial Yeomanry raised in Great Britain. Their quality was mixed at best, but Methuen was gambling on the power of numbers. His plan was to rendezvous with two of his subordinates in the village of Rooirantjestfontein, just south of Lichtenburg. This would bring the size of his command to close to four thousand men—certainly a force much larger than anything de la Rey could muster.

On 6 March, still more than twenty-five miles from Rooirantjestfontein, the British force skirmished with Commandant L. J. van Zyl's burghers. Although the Boers were chased away without much difficulty, Methuen's suspicions about the quality of his men were realized—the volunteers and yeomen had panicked.[5] The general, however, had no choice but to continue his journey as planned. His force could only be effective in stopping de la Rey if it were enlarged and buttressed with more experienced regulars. His intelligence indicated that de la Rey's commando was some distance to the south and that van Zyl did not pose any immediate threat. In addition, his own communication with his subordinates, Lt. Col. H. M. Grenfell and Col. A. N. Rochfort, had ceased. Methuen had to assume that the two would do everything they could to make it to the meeting site. He could not leave them in the lurch, so he proceeded as planned. His force crossed the Great Hart's River and moved to Tweebosch, where his men and horses could find water.

At 0300 hours the next day, Methuen headed out of camp with a slow-moving oxen convoy. One hour later a more mobile second column followed. As the day broke, everything was going as planned. The second column had made up ground and was only a mile behind the first. But unknown to Methuen, Van Zyl had alerted de la Rey of the situation immediately upon his encounter with the British. Boer reinforcement arrived that same night. De la Rey's force, more mobile and, as the day's events would show, surprisingly confident, now outnumbered the Kimberley Column. At 0500 hours de la Rey's burghers struck the rear guard of the second column. Both British columns halted—and panicked. The Khoisan drivers of the oxen convoy abandoned their vehicles and ran for cover at the sound of the first shots. The wagons could not be moved. Methuen hurriedly gave orders to defend them and at the same time prepared to reinforce the column under attack.

Ninety minutes later, as the Imperial Yeomanry arrived to strengthen Methuen's failing right flank, de la Rey ordered his commando to charge. British soldiers were not accustomed to seeing Boers fire from their saddles. Traditional Boer tactics were more akin to those of imperial mounted infantry: they rode forward, dismounted and hid their horses, and fired on foot. To make things worse, many of Methuen's troops were green and had never experienced any kind of fighting at all. The second column, made up mostly of volunteers and

Imperial Yeomanry, broke. The scene was one of chaos. Leo Amery, in his *Times History of the War in South Africa,* reports, "The horde of fugitives swept along the left flank of both convoys, crossed the river, sucked into the current of flight the 86th [Company Imperial] Yeomanry and Cape Specials, who had not fired a shot, and never drew reign till they reached the top of a rise some three miles away."[6] Although the regulars managed to make a heroic stand and the artillery gunners fought until almost the last man, the battle was lost. Three hours later a twice-wounded and exhausted Methuen ordered the raising of a white flag. De la Rey had not only eliminated the main British presence in the western Transvaal but also captured a British general in the process.

This important encounter of the South African War remains underappreciated and sometimes is overlooked altogether by military historians and pundits alike.[7] The reasons for this are many. For one, the war's end, coming only a few months later, overshadowed all of the events of 1902. By the time the battle of Tweebosch was fought, the outcome of the war, many have argued, was inevitable, and so the interest of scholars naturally has shifted away from examining the closing battles of the war and toward investigating the process of negotiation and settlement. Second, just as Roberts and Kitchener viewed the western Transvaal as an unimportant backwater, historians have followed suit. The administrative capitols and the larger population centers of the annexed territories were not to be found in that region, nor the lucrative gold veins of the Witwatersrand and the diamond mines of Kimberley. Thus Methuen's defeat, some have argued, merits no more than a sentence or two in any retelling of the war.

Third, the obscurity of the battle reflects that of its defeated general. The study of World War I has eclipsed most scholarly and public interest in the South African War. Had the British officer in command been Douglas Haig, Herbert Plumer, John French, or some other veteran who went on to greater fame in 1914, Tweebosch probably would have been given a chapter in some postwar character study and received more overall attention. But Methuen came out of retirement in 1915 only to hold an administrative post in Malta. Although once a household name, he has been largely ignored since 1918.

Fourth, the focus of most military histories of the South African War have been on its first year, when the British orchestrated traditional set-piece battles and the Boers, for the most part, responded in kind. The encounters were large, the casualty rates were high, and the purpose seemed clear. By mid-1900, however, the nature of the war had greatly changed. Knowing they could not compete with the British utilizing conventional tactics as the disparity in manpower grew, the Boers radically altered their strategy and engaged in a campaign of insurgency. From this point onward, it becomes much harder for a historian to define and illustrate the course of the war, and many writers have not even tried. Unfortunately, as a result, the significance of the South African War as a modern guerrilla struggle has been lost to generations of readers.

Finally, the battle of Tweebosch has been largely ignored for the past century, I believe, also because of the "irregular" nature of the majority of its combatants. Although the Boer commando system relied on men hastily thrown together lacking in both discipline and regimentation, the British system did not.[8] Indeed, in the nineteenth century Great Britain relied almost exclusively upon its Regular Army to furnish troops for overseas service. Auxiliary forces, like the Militia, Yeomanry, and Volunteers, often mislabeled as "irregulars" by their detractors, were used primarily for home defense—and many believed them incapable of even carrying out that task.[9] And yet by mid-1900, the British had become dependent on these troops in South Africa, particularly on the periphery in places like the western Transvaal. Although at the time the performance of Methuen's troops at Tweebosch was front and center in the debate over the use of auxiliary forces at home and abroad, by the end of the decade, the battle was purged from the British historical memory and written off not as a failure of the Regular Army, but as a failure of ill-trained, undisciplined, irregular troops, an occurrence that the military reforms of 1907 promised would never happen again.[10]

There is currently a significant gap in the existing literature of late Victorian military and imperial history. While the Regular Army has received great attention, Britain's "citizen" army, the Yeomanry, Volunteers, and Militia, has been almost completely overlooked.[11] Recently, thanks in part to the influence of the "new military history" on war studies, some historians have turned their attention to subjects other than strategy and tactics. Yet their focus has remained centered on the Regular Army. The connection between the auxiliary forces and Britain's imperial mission has yet to be fully examined. Who were the men who filled the auxiliary ranks? Why were so many of them shipped overseas to fight in South Africa? Why had the British effort to win the war become dependent on their performance? These are only a few of the important questions that this work addresses.

Popular and scholarly treatments of the South African War have consistently emphasized the first phase of the conflict, from its outbreak in October 1899 to the lifting of the sieges of Kimberley, Ladysmith, and Mafeking, the last of which occurred in May 1900.[12] The contribution made by British auxiliary forces during this period was minimal and, therefore, has been mostly ignored. Studies of these services in the Victorian period, notably Hugh Cunningham's *The Volunteer Force* and Ian Beckett's *The Amateur Military Tradition,* have emphasized institutional change rather than operational history.[13] New edited collections stressing social aspects of the South African War have largely and purposely ignored the British soldier altogether.[14]

This project seeks to redress the imbalance in the literature by concentrating squarely on the British Volunteers of the South African War. It examines such issues as motivation for enlistment, the use of citizen-soldiers in a guerrilla war, and the effects of combat on the men themselves. It utilizes new approaches to historiography to elucidate the ways in which popular culture, education, religion, sports, entertainment, and the media shaped imperial attitudes. But it also draws from traditional approaches, and much of the narrative relies on firsthand accounts of veterans as told through their letters, diaries, and memoirs. Their stories help us better understand contemporary concepts of duty and honor, the role of discipline and leadership, peer pressure and male bonding, and the demoralizing effect of fighting a long, drawn-out war without clear objectives and direction.[15]

In 1899, Great Britain stood alone as the only major European power that had yet to implement some form of national service. Yet until the South African War, there seemed to be very little reason to do so. Although voluntary enrollment in the Regular Army never numbered as high as the War Office would have liked, the needs of home defense and empire were met through a variety of successful, inexpensive measures. The advocates of the "Blue Water School," who believed Britain could be safeguarded by the Royal Navy and wanted to limit the growth of the army, were in ascendancy. Compulsory military service, a very unpopular idea among the public since the days of the Restoration, was deemed unnecessary and extremely costly. As an alternative, the War Office supported the growth of voluntary associations—auxiliary forces like the Militia, Yeomanry, and Volunteers—to strengthen home defense. Overseas, Indian- and African-raised regiments supplemented the regular units in their numerous expeditions and military encounters during the Victorian Age.

When the South African War erupted in October 1899, most Britons were confident that the outcome would be favorable and come swiftly. Although the government received overtures recommending the inclusion of auxiliary forces to complement the regular units in the field, neither officials nor the public believed that it was necessary or prudent to accept these offers. The Regular Army, they assumed, possessed more than ample resources to defeat a "bunch of farmers." The Boer offensive, unleashed at the onset of the war and resulting in the sieges of Kimberley, Ladysmith, and Mafeking, dictated British strategy for several months. In response to political pressure and to sustain morale at home, Gen. Sir Redvers Buller, the British commander in chief, chose to divide his forces in order to relieve the beleaguered garrisons.[16] This strategy failed when, in early December, three British divisions were stopped cold in their tracks. The unimaginable had occurred: a bunch of farmers not only had prevented the world's leading imperial power from carrying out its will but also had humiliated its professional army over the course of a single week.

As a result of "Black Week," the War Office warmed to the idea of supplementing the Regular Army overseas with able-bodied volunteers. It asked for and accepted offers from Militia regiments, Volunteer corps, and irregular units raised by county notables; it also called for the establishment of the Imperial Yeomanry. In all, more than 100,000 men voluntarily left Britain as part of these auxiliary forces to fight in South Africa.[17]

When the war broke out, nearly one out of every four men living in the Great Britain and Ireland had some sort of military experience. Many volunteers did not even consider the merits of enlisting; they instinctively acted and transferred from one military institution to another. Some joined because of peer pressure; others had family problems and sought temporary escapes. Many went to seek out a new life or to fulfill their sense of adventure. And, of course, several risked their lives by going to war simply because they could not find work at home.

Researchers up to the 1970s focused on patriotism as the sole motivator of British recruits in the South African War. This was challenged by Marxist and labor historians, who emphasized the importance of economic factors such as underemployment and seasonal recruiting patterns. Most recently, scholars have opened up new fields of investigation by exploring the importance of cultural factors such as music halls, popular art, children's literature, and invented traditions. To completely understand British citizens' motives for enrolling in the auxiliary forces, it is necessary to synthesize relevant aspects of the economic, political, and social history of the late Victorian era to determine what multiple and overlapping forces shaped the decision-making process.

Chapter 1 attempts to do just that by examining late Victorian society and situating the auxiliary forces as social institutions in the history of Great Britain and of British imperialism. It concentrates on militarism, patriotism, muscular Christianity, and the role that class had in determining a particular outlook toward the military and volunteerism. The chapter also addresses British fears of invasion and the interconnection of the core and the periphery. In general, it paints a broad picture of British society focusing on the forces that affected enrollment in the Volunteers, Yeomanry, and Militia.

The focus of chapter 2 is on the Anglo-Boer conflict from immediately prior to the outbreak of hostilities through the opening months of the war itself. During this period, representatives of the auxiliary forces first made offers to contribute manpower overseas and the government reached its final decision to employ such units in South Africa. The discussion here is centered on the nature of the South African War and its importance for Great Britain and its people. It also looks at the individuals and pressure groups that advocated for the employment of the auxiliary forces.

Motivation for enrollment in the military during wartime cannot be explored simply in terms of class or individual circumstances but must be situated within the history of each unique conflict. While it is true that the state can always find a limited number of men to risk their lives and volunteer for service during wartime, it is important to explore why, at this particular time, the outpouring of support was so great. Is it a fact that volunteers understood this distant war to be a grave threat to the well being of Great Britain? Did civilians view South Africa or its people somehow differently from other imperial concerns? If so, were these the reasons for the overwhelming response to the government's call for help in December 1899?

The third chapter examines recruitment during the winter of 1899–1900, with particular emphasis on the Imperial Yeomanry and the Volunteers. For many Britons who lived through both the South African War and the World War I, it was surprisingly the former conflict that aroused greater feelings of discomfort. The British military was very busy during the last quarter of the nineteenth century. The government sent units on so many expeditions to so many different locations that, no doubt, even some cabinet ministers had a hard time keeping track of them all. And although there were a few scares, notably the Anglo-Zulu War of 1879, and a few defeats, like the First Boer War of 1880–81, ultimate victory in these campaigns was commonplace. This led to complacency among government officials, military officers, and the citizenry. Black Week hit Britain like a mighty thunderbolt from the sky, awakening the nation from its conceit and forcing it to respond in a unique way to the challenges posed by the Boer republics. The public's response to the government's call to arms to meet the needs of home and empire was loud and enthusiastic. Recruiting offices of the auxiliary forces were flooded, and in just a few months, citizen-soldiers joined the professional "Tommy Atkins" in South Africa.[18]

This chapter also looks at the men who enlisted in the auxiliary forces and volunteered for duty in South Africa. It provides a social analysis of their backgrounds (that is, class, age, regional ties, and military experience), examines the drills and methods of training they endured, and how the recruits took to their newly regimented lives. Another important aspect of this examination is how communities embraced and supported their locally raised units and then sent them off to war. But most importantly, chapter 3 examines the motivation for enlistment. Although there were a variety of economic and social factors that influenced soldiers' choices, this study demonstrates that the need for psychological fulfillment found in the expression of patriotism was the most typical reason for enlistment in the Volunteers and Imperial Yeomanry during the war.

Most of the men who signed up and contractually committed to a limited engagement of one year or the duration of the war had never been out of the country before; indeed, few had traveled farther than the nearest pub.[19] Active volunteers shared their experiences with their friends and families through letters. After the terms of service had been fulfilled, those who returned home shared their recollections in person and through written narratives. Tales of combat, though often limited by actual experience in the field, overshadowed other kinds of tales, for example, witnessing the warm sun rising on the veld on a cold winter's day, escorting prisoners to the Cape Colony, or listening to the bleating of a confiscated herd of sheep. How the men expressed themselves about their military service is the subject of chapter 4.

Some of the earliest tales, and those best documented through letters sent home, describe assemblage, barracks life, and the voyage to South Africa. Although usually overlooked in histories of the conflict, these experiences offer much insight into the world of the volunteers. It was through these events that the men were introduced to military discipline, drill, and of course each other. And it was during this process, long before they saw the enemy for the first time, that these citizen-soldiers were first subjected to one of the greatest hardships of war—being away from home and family. Life in Britain, in transit, and at sea was filled with both wonderment and tedium. Examining these experiences shows how vital they were in constructing esprit de corps and preparing the men for war.

Chapter 5 continues the story of the volunteers after they disembarked in South Africa, examining how they were employed at the end of the conventional phase of the conflict and through the important period of transition to irregular warfare. As large numbers of auxiliaries began to arrive in Cape Town, Port Elizabeth, and Durban in early 1900, the conventional phase of the South African War was coming to its end. The Boers, due to Britain's overwhelming advantage in manpower, a disparity that they could only expect to worsen, abandoned the strategy that had not only brought about the unqualified successes of Black Week but had also shown its limitations at the battle of Paardeberg in February 1900.[20] They shifted away from maneuvering the British into fighting set-piece battles and toward engaging them in a protracted guerilla struggle. Although it took several months to fully appreciate the need to make changes of their own, the British eventually adjusted their strategy, with Lord Roberts approving such counterinsurgency measures as wide-scale farm burning and the relocation of civilians to concentration camps. As a result, the volunteers, making their way into the soon-to-be annexed republics in mid-1900, did not face the enemy on the pitched battlefield but instead were posted to isolated blockhouses and ordered to protect lines of communication and guard prisoners.[21]

Few of the men who volunteered in the wake of Black Week could have anticipated this new type of struggle. Indeed, even the volunteers raised in 1901 and 1902 envisioned war in the conventional sense. Chapter 6 continues the examination of the auxiliary forces in the field and focuses on the volunteers during the guerrilla phase of the South African War, especially how they now viewed their military role and their attitudes toward the enemy, combatants and noncombatants alike. These men had a very difficult time making sense of the changes, and few understood the role they played in the evolving struggle. Indeed, even their officers, many of whom had served in the Regular Army, were not entirely sure of what they were doing and how British command was using them to win. Increasingly, the volunteers grew confused and exasperated, and they longed for the comfort and security of home.

Chapter 7 weighs the pros and cons of using citizen-soldiers in the South African War, assessing their performance and looking at how the public and the government viewed their contribution to the war effort. Even before the first volunteers had returned to Britain, there was a vigorous debate over their use. Letters to newspapers either lauded or criticized their performance. Many questioned whether the men were being used properly in the field. Military reformers challenged the War Office on issues ranging from the proper forms of drill and training to the equipment best suited to volunteers' needs. After the war the debate continued. For much of 1903 and into 1904, a royal commission heard testimony on the Militia and the Volunteer force. Demands to reform the auxiliary services grew louder, and perhaps inevitably, the discussion became part of a larger debate on national service. A series of Conservative secretaries of state for war, Lord Lansdowne, William St. John Brodrick, and H. O. Arnold-Forster, could not satisfy the critics nor make any headway with the opposition in Parliament. Eventually, it was a Liberal secretary, R. B. Haldane, who brought about a radical solution in 1907, completely overhauling the auxiliary forces with the creation of the Territorial Force. Great Britain would enter World War I in

1914 with a very different military system than that with which it went to war in 1899. The Victorian auxiliary services—the Volunteers, Yeomanry, and Militia—were consigned to history.

Yet in 1902 Lord Kitchener needed these forces to win the struggle in South Africa. It proved to be an anxious dependency. When he received the news of the disaster at Tweebosch, he was distraught. The year had not started well, and more and more politicians back in London were growing impatient for a quick end to the fighting.[22] Even if the poor performance of the volunteers had raised new doubts, what other choice did Kitchener have but to continue to rely upon them?[23] The Regular Army and colonial contributions could not satisfy the manpower needs—only the Volunteers could. The newly raised Third Contingent of Imperial Yeomanry was just beginning to form at Aldershot, Edinburgh, and the Curragh. In a few months they would start their journey to South Africa. If the war was to be won immediately, however, the volunteers in the field would have to do.

The history of the British auxiliary forces in the South African War is not just a story of a string of incidents like Tweebosch. It is also a story of great successes. Overall, the volunteers performed admirably. In a time of need, they answered the call to arms, left kith and kin to risk their lives in a distant land, and in the end played a large role in their country's victory. When it was all over, the volunteers returned home to large crowds of supporters who had not forgotten their contribution. While some remained very critical of their performance, most praised them. The South African War was a pivotal event in the history of Great Britain, its empire, and its military. Citizens were transformed into soldiers; conventional war gave way to low-intensity conflict; and as the nineteenth century ended, the twentieth century ushered in modern warfare.

Maps

Great Britain and Ireland, 1899

South Africa, 1899

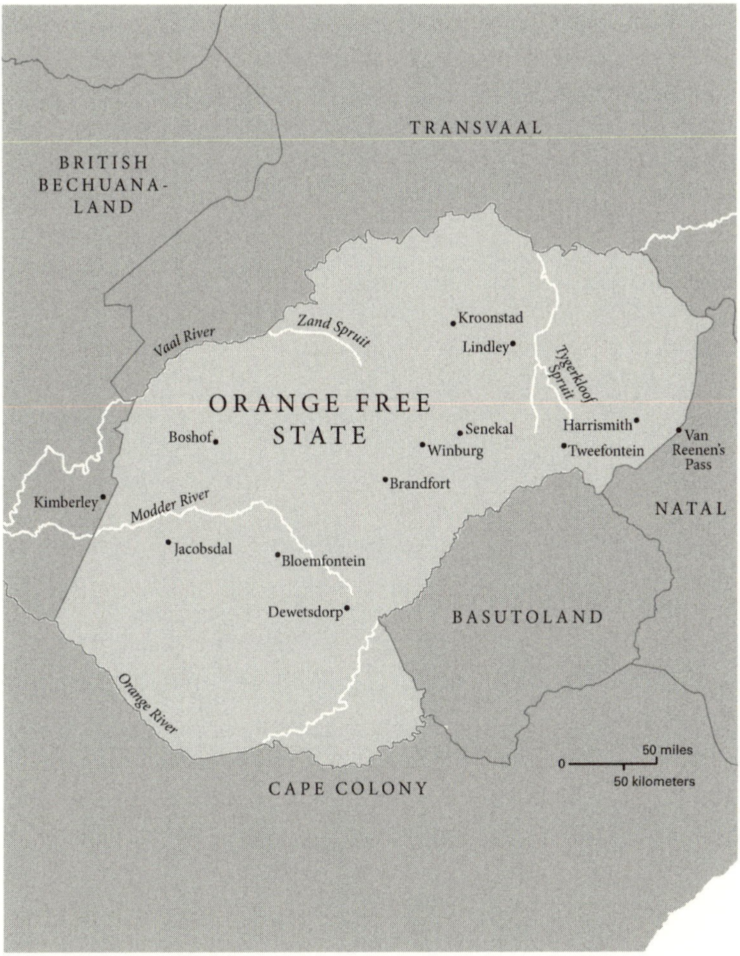

The Orange Free State, 1898

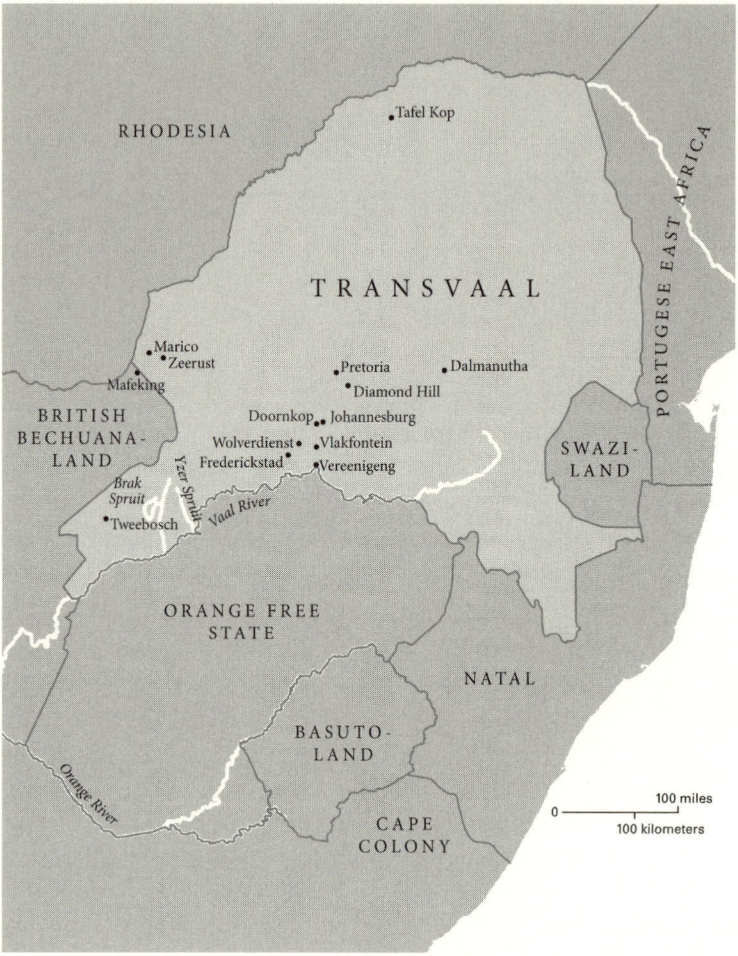

The Transvaal, 1899

1

The British Volunteer Force

In an 1878 article in the London serial *The Nineteenth Century,* John Holms writes: "The army appears to be the only institution in the kingdom which is outside of the people. They know nothing of it, take no interest in it, and express no opinion on it."[1] Although things would change by the end of the century, Holms, an avid military reformer and a Liberal member of Parliament from Hackney for seventeen years, knew what he was talking about. In the aftermath of the Crimean War, Great Britain's Regular Army was unpopular. The war with Russia seemed only to highlight many of its shortcomings: incompetent leadership, deficient medical support, and questionable training. The Cardwell Reforms of the early 1870s were beginning to sweep away some of the most problematic features of a broken system, but the army remained stigmatized by dishonest recruiting measures, poor terms of service, and a lack of discipline that resulted in its exclusion from a variety of public spaces.[2] Public spectacles of drunkenness were all too common a sight both at home and abroad, and perhaps as many as one-third of the home force was stricken with venereal disease.[3] It is no wonder that the public distanced itself from the army. "Tommy Atkins" was hardly someone to invite over for dinner to meet the family.[4]

And yet at the same time the Regular Army was being shunned by the public at large, increasing numbers of young men were entering the auxiliary forces as Volunteers, Yeomanry, and Militia. This apparent paradox, a nation disregarding its formal military force while embracing its informal one, was easily explained by contemporaries. Benjamin Disraeli once quipped, "We are not a military nation, but we are a martial race."[5] Gen. Lord Garnet Wolseley echoed this sentiment in 1887 when he declared, "We may not be a military nation but without doubt we are the most warlike people on the earth."[6] Britain in the late nineteenth century was becoming militarized not in the traditional sense of growing its military budget, readily turning to its military to support its foreign policy abroad, or merging state and military interest, but rather in cultivating and developing a heightened martial ethos among its citizens. The auxiliary forces played the most significant role in fusing the will of the state and the drive of the people.

As Ian Beckett has shown, late-Victorian society was much more militaristic than mid-Victorian Britain.[7] It "was made up of a renewed militarism, a devotion to royalty, an identification and worship of national heroes, together with a contemporary cult of personality, and racial ideas associated with Social Darwinism. Together these constituted a new type of patriotism, which derived a special significance from Britain's unique imperial mission."[8] The interests of the nation and the empire were fused, and the army, like the navy before it, became a symbol of power used to expand and defend Britain's global position.

This imperial mission was inculcated in children through a variety of modes, including Sunday sermons, aggressive advertisements, after-school instruction, and weekend participation in any of a wide array of "paramilitary" organizations such as the Boys' Brigade, the Church Brigade, and the Jewish Lads' Brigade. But it was the school setting, with its curriculum including quasi-military drill, that Matthew Arnold and others identified as the nation's primary cultural transmitter.[9] M. D. Blanch has noted, "The evidence suggests that a significant part of school time in the period 1880–89 was spent in transmitting nationalistic and imperialistic values to children."[10] By the end of the century, few children could have left school without developing a strong sense of nationalism, a belief in Anglo-Saxon racial ascendancy, and unquestioning support for the imperial mission.[11]

Literature proved to be one of the most effective vehicles in the propagation of the imperial mission in late Victorian society. It was highly sensationalized and portrayed an invidious distinction between the morally good Briton and the evil Other. Children's literature especially presented war as glamorous, the pursuit of the imperial mission as heroic, and patriotism as a responsibility for all.[12] Patrick Dunae writes that *The Boy's Own Paper,* which was devoted to propagating the imperial mission, was the most important and influential juvenile periodical ever published in Great Britain.[13] Through the effective employment of sympathetic and heroic young male protagonists, literature produced by G. A. Henty and others like him helped legitimize the use of violence in defense of the moral good. All graduating teens, working and middle class alike, thus were exposed to the ideals attached to the military and the empire: loyalty, duty, self-help, and patriotism.

Since the turn of the century, when John Hobson identified the role of the music hall in spreading the "fervor of jingoism" throughout working-class communities, the influence of music halls on late Victorian society has been the subject of ongoing debate.[14] Whether the militarism and imperial language of these venues was initiated by the propagandist or was a response to public demand, there is no doubt that large numbers of middle- and working-class attendees accepted the message they had to offer. Music-hall entertainment featured exotic tales of army life, daring exploits of the rank and file, and the patriotic extolling of a Christian civilization pitted against savage foes. The play *Tommy Atkins,* which put the common soldier at center stage, was one of the most successful plays in music-hall history.[15] But it was perhaps the "Absent-Minded Beggar," Kipling's ode to the volunteer recruit in the South African War, that proved to be the most influential message resounding from the stage. This ballad, commissioned by the *Daily Mail* and set to music by Sir Arthur Sullivan, raised more than £250,000 for soldiers wounded during the South African War.[16] It had an immediate effect on men like H. L. Birkin, who volunteered for the Imperial Yeomanry in 1899 after the call was put out for able-bodied men in the wake of the disasters of Black Week.[17] Kipling almost single handedly restored the strong ties between civilians and soldiers and put Britain and its army back together again.[18] Thanks to the "Absent-Minded Beggar," Tommy Atkins became a national hero for the first time since Waterloo.

The military was resplendent in late Victorian society. Britons eagerly followed the newspaper coverage of their numerous and successful campaigns. Boys' clubs and contemporary literature helped disseminate militarism and patriotism to all classes. Schools, with their increasingly nationalistic textbooks and martial drill, served to reinforce the values that the government and churches deemed important.[19] Cadet corps at universities and public schools proved to be some of the best recruiting grounds for future volunteers. But it was the growth and popularity of the auxiliary forces—the Yeomanry, Militia, and especially the Volunteers—that did more than anything to legitimize militarism and bridge the gap between the armed forces and the people. Auxiliaries became a point of community interest and civic pride, an aide to the military authorities, and an outlet for entertainment. As Capt. W. H. Jones declared at the Royal United Services Institution on 10 March 1898, "If the Volunteers had never done anything else, we owe them a debt of gratitude for one thing, that they have brought military knowledge to the people much more than it was before they existed."[20]

Of the auxiliary forces, the Militia was the oldest. Although considered Great Britain's "constitutional" force, the service had fallen into disrepair by mid-century. Its numbers had been cut drastically since the end of the French wars, and the ballot, the means used to raise a vibrant force, had been suspended since the early 1830s.[21] In theory the Militia was to act as a democratic counterweight to the authoritarian Regular Army, protecting Britain from the abuses of a despot. But in the nineteenth century, the Militia had more or less turned into a branch of the Regular Army. With the difficulty of recruiting soldiers for the Crimean War, the government passed regulations allowing for the active recruitment of militiamen. As a result, the Militia became a feeder for the Regular Army, with nearly 33,000 militiamen joining its ranks during the Crimean War.[22] Although the Earl of Derby's Militia Act of 1852 attempted to resuscitate the force through the promotion of voluntary enlistment, its numbers were severely depleted in the 1850s.[23]

In response to growing public concerns in the aftermath of the Crimean War and the Indian Rebellion, Jonathan Peel, secretary of state for war in 1858–59, set up a royal commission to evaluate the state of home defenses.[24] A discussion concerning the state of the Militia naturally occurred. Ultimately, Peel did not think the

Militia could obviate Britain's vulnerability to invasion, and regardless a return of the ballot would have been very unpopular and expensive. Although Peel's successor, Sidney Herbert, considered reopening this politically risky option, in the end the Militia remained practically dormant as the Volunteers became an increasingly attractive option for strengthening home defense.

A decade later Edward Cardwell returned state attention to the Militia. With his localization scheme of the 1870s, each Militia regiment was linked to its county's Regular Army regiment. At the same time, the county lord lieutenants were stripped of their command of the Militia and control transferred to the Crown. In 1881 the full process of this "territorialization" was completed under Hugh Childers.[25] Thus, the service was completely subsumed by the army. Not only did many Militia regiments lose their long-cherished designators (often reorganized as the "Third" or "Fourth" Battalion of the county regiment), but because of their closer association with the Regular Army, declining public interest, and the lack of a clear role, they began to lose much of their individual character. For most Britons, the militiaman became merely Tommy Atkins on the weekend.

The reputation of the Yeomanry, or volunteer cavalry, was far worse than that of the Militia in the first half of the nineteenth century. Whereas the Militia, at least in theory, was established to provide the citizenry with the means to protect themselves from the abuses of monarchical power, the Yeomanry was established to suppress Britons if the local authority deemed them riotous or tumultuous. The Yeomanry was to act as an arm of the county magistrates. And indeed they acted, most notoriously at St. Peter's Field in Manchester in 1819 and in Bristol in 1831, killing scores of their countrymen.

The origins of the Yeomanry date to the French wars of the 1790s. Since each man was required to supply a horse and saddlery, its membership mostly consisted of tenant-farmers and agricultural laborers.[26] This feature of the Yeomanry did not change until the South African War. Control of such forces lay in the hands of the lord lieutenants, though there were occasions in which the home secretary bestowed command to military district generals. Because of this lack of central authority, Yeomanry corps, like battalions of the Militia, often developed in their own way, absorbing their county flavor and taking on the personalities of their commanders and subscribers. The number of men in a troop, the number of troops in a regiment, and even the relationship of troops within a regiment differed considerably from county to county. It was not until the 1870s that real reforms were enacted to standardize and professionalize the service.

The size of the Yeomanry was never great. There were fewer than fifteen thousand at mid-century, and the force actually shrunk over the next few decades, only to witness a dramatic increase during the South African War.[27] The construction of a modern police force removed their raison d'être, and thanks to the expansion of the railway network, the Regular Army could be readily employed without depending on the services of the local Yeomanry.[28] Some regiments disappeared altogether, while others fell dangerously below establishment. If a unit could boast full strength, it was only because of the devotion of local principals. Ultimately, the Yeomanry suffered a worse fate than the Militia, not so much subsumed as ignored. Mid-Victorian governments apparently had given up on this force.

As private and public interest in the Militia and Yeomanry dissipated, awareness of the Volunteers began to surge. Ironically, it was neither the debacle of the Crimean War nor the drama of the Indian Mutiny that led to the birth of the Volunteer Movement; rather, it was the fear of the unknown. France's construction of a port at Cherbourg and its development of an ironclad fleet, rumors of its alliance with Russia, and the political fallout after Orsini's failed attempt to assassinate Napoleon III with an English-made bomb led to a sudden wave of Francophobia and panic within Great Britain. Questions began to arise over whether the Royal Navy could safeguard Britain. To many, a French invasion seemed imminent, and Britain's land forces were stretched dangerously thin. Alfred Lord Tennyson, Britain's poet laureate, summed up these fears of invasion when, in 1859, he wrote the poem "The War."

> There is a sound of thunder afar,
> Storm in the south that darkens the day,
> Storm of battle and thunder of war,
> Well if it do not roll our way,
> Storm, storm, riflemen form!
> Ready, be ready, against the storm!
> Riflemen, riflemen, riflemen form!

Be not deaf to the sound that warns,
Be not gull'd by a despot's plea!
Are figs of thistles? or grapes of thorns?
How can a despot feel with the free
Ready, be ready, to meet the storm!
Riflemen, riflemen, riflemen form![29]

Tennyson's call, "Ready, be ready to meet the storm," was echoed by many others.

The creation of the Volunteer Movement was orchestrated by the middle class and initially served as a vehicle for their political participation. The Royal Navy and the Regular Army were the preserves of the upper class, where rank was more often determined by purchase than by merit. Few could hope to advance without possessing the necessary political and military contacts. The middle class found no favor in these institutions. Nor was the Militia ever a serious option either. Even more so than the Regular Army, the Militia was dominated by rural elites. The middle class hoped that through the apparatus of the Volunteers they could demonstrate their commitment to the state. Not only could the force help deter invasion, but it could also supplement the Regular Army and the local police in a domestic emergency. Its existence could also provide political muscle against the advocates of compulsory service, a prospect the middle class as a whole detested.

In 1859 Derby's short-lived second government reluctantly gave in to middle-class pressure and an effective press campaign spearheaded by the *Times*, accepting the services of the Volunteers.[30] Derby, Disraeli, and the Earl of Malmesbury, the foreign secretary, were fearful that the growing conflict in Italy could lead to a general European war.[31] British home defenses needed to be strengthened anyway. Since the Volunteer force required no government funding, there was little risk involved. The alternatives, notably an extension of the Militia, which would have been costly and potentially could have disrupted the labor force, were not attractive. Any such move would have been a very risky political gamble.[32]

Just a few weeks before Derby's government stepped down, Peel issued a circular to the lord lieutenants. Utilizing an 1804 act (44 George III, c. 54), the lord lieutenants received authorization to form Volunteer rifle and artillery corps. These remained under the control of the lord lieutenants of the counties until 1871, when command was centralized under the War Office. Each corps was subject to service in the event of "an actual invasion, or appearance of an enemy in force on the coast, or in case of rebellion arising out of either of those emergencies."[33] Members needed to provide their own weapons and equipment during drill. They were also required to attend twenty-four drills a year to be returned as effectives, who were exempt from the Militia ballot. Any volunteer could resign in peacetime after having provided fourteen days' notice.

Lord Palmerston's second government, which followed Derby's, was more interested in the Volunteers' social function than in their ability to defend the nation. Palmerston never thought much of their military value, nor did Herbert. Administering the Volunteers was thus passed on to the Earl de Grey, the undersecretary of state. Grey worked hard to build efficiency and uniformity within the Volunteer corps.[34] This goal was a bit of a challenge, for not only was there no money but also the radical wing of the Liberal Party feared the prospect of a strong, armed body that could assist an overzealous local authority.[35] No one wanted another "Peterloo" on his hands.

At least for the time being, the Liberals had nothing to fear. Often it was the Volunteers who felt threatened by the masses and not the other way around. The force was derided as a "toothless lion" and heckled by onlookers with catcalls of "Who shot the dog?" When their meetings and parades ended for the day, "each individual went home in a storm of chaff, and the clever pencil of John Leech made fun of them in *Punch*."[36]

Despite these rebuffs, the Volunteers continued to grow in size over the next decade. Within three months of its creation, 119,000 men, mostly middle class, had joined the service. By 1868, enrollment was up to 200,000.[37] Many middle-class contemporaries saw membership in the Volunteers as the ultimate expression of loyalty and duty to their country. Certainly the mayor of Leicester did when he pronounced Volunteer participation as "the highest and purest [form of] patriotism."[38] Ian Beckett, a historian of the "amateur tradition," agreed in *Riflemen Form*, writing that "it cannot be denied that the predominant motive force behind the Volunteer movement was patriotism and the sense of duty."[39]

But if patriotism was the major force behind the Volunteer Movement in mid-Victorian Britain, it was a transient one at best, for it could not sustain middle-class involvement after the panic subsided. Although class continued to dominate the direction of the force, once it became clear that there was no genuine French threat, and the romance of dressing up and playing soldier dissipated, professional men, clerks, and businessmen returned to their usual forms of entertainment. Instead, artisans, factory workers, and laborers—the working class—were persuaded to take their places and soon made up the majority of volunteers.[40]

As membership shifted, the importance of the Volunteer force shifted as well. It continued to serve as a focal point for both local and national patriotism, but more importantly, it became a vehicle of social control. Olive Anderson has described British militarism in the late nineteenth century as "not only an affair of unprecedented adulatory attitudes towards Britain's professional soldiers, but also of civilian imitation of military organization, discipline, and paraphernalia, and the diffusion of military sentiments and rhetoric in general."[41] Although most historians eschew far-reaching claims about the strength of militarism in mid-Victorian Britain, few would dispute that it permeated late Victorian society. Militarism became a potent force used by the government and a variety of interest groups to manipulate the people, particularly on issues related to the empire. It would be a difficult task to prove that increased militarism was caused by the expansion of the auxiliary forces, but that expansion certainly can be seen as a symptom of the process. Indeed, social philosopher Herbert Spencer, who had hoped that industrialization would lead to a more democratic and decentralized society and dreamed that militarism would eventually disappear as a result, pointed directly to the growth of the Volunteer forces as one of the "alarming signs of 'rebarbarisation'" in Great Britain.[42]

As the events of the late 1850s spurred on militarism and gave birth to the Volunteer Movement, the events of the 1870s kept Britain on the same path. Writing at the end of the century, John Hobson identified 1870 as the year when "primitive passions" were awakened in his countrymen and the "love of nation [was] transformed into the hatred of another nation, and the fierce craving to destroy the individual members of that other nation."[43] Even more so than the panic of the late 1850s, the Franco-Prussian War unleashed a wave of uncertainty as European state relations changed dramatically. Patriotism was ignited by war fever, and the whole of British society was transformed, Hobson argued, into a gigantic crowd "craving blood."[44] In this transformation jingoism was born. Whether the growth of British militarism can be pinpointed to a specific year is suspect; nonetheless, the 1870s seems an appropriate decade to begin an investigation of the topic. Signs of a burgeoning militancy are evident as the language of patriotism was altered by Disraeli to win over the middle and working classes to his Conservative foreign policy.[45] Certainly by 1878, when the "Dogs of War" were let loose, and the "rugged Russian Bear" had "crawled out of his lair," many had come to embrace an overt, aggressive imperial militarism.[46] According to contemporary social critics like L. T. Hobhouse, this sentiment spread rapidly throughout British society over the next two decades: "All classes alike give way to jingoism, and shut their ears to wisdom and humanity."[47] Likewise, future prime minister Henry Campbell-Bannerman lamented, "But oh! The degraded, apathetic, sport-loving, empty-headed, vulgar lot that our countrymen have become."[48]

Although militarism was spreading to all arenas within British society, it rarely dominated politics in the late Victorian era. Elections generally turned on domestic issues, not military ones. That Lord Rosebery stepped down after his government was defeated in June 1895 over army estimates was symptomatic of the Liberal Party's inability to govern in Parliament and not of any increased importance placed on military preparedness. In governance, civilian authority overtly eclipsed military authority. In 1870, two years after forcing the commander in chief's office to physically relocate to Pall Mall, Edward Cardwell carried a bill through Parliament officially subordinating the position to the secretary of state for war. Twenty years later the Hartington Commission recommended a further reduction in the status of Britain's highest-ranking soldier. And all evidence indicates that it was the civilian War Office that controlled the fate of the British army during the South African War and not the commander in chief.[49]

The War Office's stranglehold on decision making and the weakness of military issues in shaping national politics in general obscure the importance of militarism in late Victorian society. Historians must look elsewhere. British identity during the era of the "New Imperialism," charged with racialism, Social Darwinism, and muscular Christianity, largely defined itself through martial culture. Its heroes, Henry Havelock, Charles Gordon, Frederick Roberts, and

Garnet Wolseley, were soldiers. Its songs, both in the opera house and in the music hall, often centered on themes of war. Its literature was reinvented to promote a masculine code emphasizing chivalry and military honor. Its newspapers enthusiastically reported on the army's seemingly endless clashes with Afridis, Asante, Sudanese, and Zulu. And its streets and parks were often filled with the military spectacle of men in uniforms, reviews, parades, and drills. The twenty years that followed the Bulgarian agitation saw a steady rise in Britain's interest in the military, and martial values became the values of the Victorians.

Palmerston realized the potential of the Volunteers as an agent of social construction, especially as more and more workers joined its ranks. Through this service, expressions like nationalism, expansionism, and militarism could be fostered. Similarly, many in the church viewed the Volunteers as an agent to help spread Christian virtues and the word of God. Leaders in the Anglican Church as well as those in several dissenting churches identified service as a stimulus to self-improvement, a notion that was increasingly popular. Since Volunteer corps were initially funded through private sources, churches expected to play an important financial role at the local level, which would ensure that they possessed a degree of influence over the direction of the movement.[50]

The military, in general, was becoming "Christianized" by the 1860s. A number of Christian societies were seeking converts among soldiers and finding success. Others worked toward the "moral improvement" of barracks life. But it was in the empire that the evangelical mission, riding an upsurge of enthusiasm, met with its greatest success.[51] The colonies became a proving ground for the bible and the sword. As G. F. Wyatt has stated, "efficiency at war represented God's test of a nation's soul."[52] Britain's imperial mission became God's mission, and muscular Christianity was transformed into imperial Christianity.[53] Charles Gordon's accomplishments in China and Henry Havelock's "martyrdom" in India focused an enrapt nation on feats of Christian fortitude and sacrifice. In this way, Christianity, the empire, and the military were joined together.

Religious groups naturally extended their outreach to the Volunteers, helping forge a Christian and militaristic ethos for young men at home. This linkage provided some muscle to Christianity. Religious groups also reached out to cadet corps and boys' brigades, where they attracted Britain's youth. John Mackenzie writes that "deliberate attempts were made to suck working class children into a consciousness of imperial and military destiny."[54] Young boys could "play soldier for Christ," and uniformed Christian youths eventually turned into uniformed Christian adults.[55]

Indeed, William Alexander Smith, the founder of the Boys' Brigade, was confident that his youth organization would produce good Christians as well as popularize military service among the working classes.[56] Smith was distressed over urban working-class conditions. He felt that adolescents were particularly at risk, that they were unproductive and were too readily turning to crime. Through the Boys' Brigade, he would attempt to promote "habits of Reverence, Discipline, Self-respect, and all that tends towards a true Christian Manliness."[57] These habits, he insisted, would keep boys in school, in church, and out of trouble.

Smith believed wholeheartedly that there was no contradiction between masculinity and Christianity. "All a boy's aspirations," he wrote, "are towards manliness, however mistaken his ideas may sometimes be as to what that manliness means. Our boys are full of earnest desire to be brave true men; and if we want to make them brave, true Christian men, we must direct this desire into the right channel. . . . We must show them the manliness of Christianity."[58] But Sunday school was not the proper forum to spread this message, mainly because it was unpopular; church attendance was in decline throughout Great Britain. Smith astutely recognized that the uniform, the dummy rifle, and the military cap would make his message attractive to boys who might otherwise brand Christianity as effeminate. They were also a means of heightening the sense of patriotism and military spirit among working-class youths.

Active in the Volunteer Movement, Smith brought their methods to the boys of Glasgow, first to Sunday schools and then to the Boys' Brigade, which he established in 1883. Most of the officers of these brigades were volunteers, militiamen, and yeomen. A contemporary of Smith's remarked on the connection between the Boys' Brigade and the Volunteers: "To the Volunteer movement we are indebted for this novel and interesting organization which seeks to use military drill and discipline for the religious and moral improvement of the boys in our mission districts and Sabbath schools."[59] The link between physical self-control, taught through drill and discipline, and spiritual wholeness was a common theme of most contemporary uniformed youth organizations such as the Church Lads' Brigade, the Jewish Lads' Brigade, and the Catholic Lads' Brigade, all established in the 1890s. Even though it is often overlooked, muscular Christianity played an essential role in the best known of these uniformed youth organizations, Robert Baden-Powell's Boy Scouts, created after the South African War.

Militia, Yeomanry, and Volunteer officers were also active in the cadet corps. Cadet corps bridged the age gap between the uniformed youth organization and the auxiliary force. Although initially associated with public schools, by the 1880s they had made their way to the working class. Sir Francis Fletcher Vane, founder of the first working-class cadet corps, was an experienced Worcestershire militiaman. For him and other corps leaders, drill and discipline remained the key to building a better British youth: "Healthy physical exercise will make up for narrow soundings; discipline will cultivate the values of obedience and self-control as well as reverence for law and order, and through esprit de corps, patriotism will grow; true patriotism will lead to a just appreciation of the duties of citizenship, and the part which the Anglo-Saxon race is called upon to play in the cause of progress."[60]

John Springhall's research on the First London Cadet Battalion of the 1890s reveals that a great number of cadets continued to serve their country in uniform as they entered adulthood.[61] Like the boys' and lads' brigades, the cadet corps produced many future volunteers, yeomen, and militiamen; they also produced many Regular Army recruits. For working-class cadets, the army was a natural career choice, especially with skilled jobs becoming harder to find at the end of the century.

Even more so than in the cadet corps, it was at the public schools where muscular Christianity and the Volunteer Movement blended to form its most complete expression. Although a career in the Regular Army was open to middle-class cadet-corps graduates, most shunned it, opting for Volunteer service instead. Late Victorian headmasters at Eton and Harrow were committed to turning their boys into Christian gentlemen and patriots.[62] They sent off their graduates to spread the word of Britain's unique mission and, if necessary, to die for the cause. Martyrdom for empire was elevated to a new level. Charles Gordon, in particular, who died at Khartoum while defending the interests of the empire, took on an almost mythical status. As J. A. Mangan has written: "The foremost image of the public schoolboy in empire was defined, and constant: the warrior-patriot. His purpose was noble and sacrificial—to fight and die for England's greatness overseas."[63] The auxiliary forces provided many of Britain's warrior-patriots and "Christian knights" with an initiation into public service.

Church leaders thought it practical and desirable to turn rough and disorderly young men into obedient and disciplined Christians. Middle-class employers agreed. After all, as Walter Houghton points out, "Except for 'God,' the most popular word in the Victorian vocabulary must have been 'work.'"[64] Many invested in the auxiliary forces, in part, to further their interests in the workplace. Drill and discipline there naturally marched hand in hand with drill and discipline on the parade ground.

In his 1905 autobiography, Samuel Smiles, author of such works as *Thrift, Duty, Character,* and *Self-Help,* wrote: "I have often been amazed and distressed to find what a number of helpless and idle creatures exist in this busy world. Some of them think that it is want of 'luck' that attends them; but when I make inquiry, I find that it is oftener carelessness and indifference, idleness and a tendency to viciousness; and very often the break-down of character of these unhappy people comes from their devotion to drink and its sordid accompaniments. It is not so much the want of mental powers as the lack of will and self-help. They will do nothing for themselves, but expect other people to help them."[65] Smiles aimed his doctrine of self-help primarily at young men, the same group likely to join the auxiliary forces. He believed that through hard work and discipline, even the poor could overcome major obstacles and attain an acceptable level of well-being in their lives. Although critics have often attacked Smiles as a shameless promoter of selfishness and greed, his message included a component that he hoped would play out on a grander scale. Individual progress, he argued, was essential to the development of the nation.

As Tim Travers has shown, the term "self-help" distorts its actual nature. Not everyone had the capacity within, Smiles believed, to find moral improvement. Therefore, some sort of guidance was required for those who sought moral regeneration through its principles but did not fully understand the concept.[66] For Smiles, the key lay in education, and the best medium for that was his book.

Although his autobiography makes only a few references to the military, security, or foreign-policy issues, and while his heroes were capitalists such as George Stephenson, George Moore, and Josiah Wedgwood, not soldiers, Smiles did appreciate the value of military discipline: "Wonderful is the magic of drill! Drill means discipline, training, education. . . . These soldiers—who are ready to march steadily against vollied fire, against belching cannon—or to beat their heads against bristling bayonets . . . were once tailors, shoemakers, mechanics, weavers and ploughmen; with mouths gaping, shoulders stooping, feet straggling, arms and hands like great fins hanging by their sides; but now their gait is firm and martial, their figures are erect, and they march along to the sound of music, with a tread that makes the earth shake."[67] And since he knew that compulsion was not an option, volunteer service was the next best thing. After all, their goals were very similar. "One dare scarcely hint, in these days," Smiles writes, "at the necessity for compulsory conscription; and yet, were the people at large compelled to pass through the discipline of the army, the country would be stronger, the people would be soberer, and thrift would become much more habitual than it is at present."[68]

Political, church, and business leaders supported the growth of the auxiliary forces as a means of imprinting loyalty, duty, self-help, and patriotism upon young men in a rapidly changing society and reinforcing a moral code that would benefit an industrial nation. But the men who joined the Volunteers, and to a lesser extent the Yeomanry and Militia, had other concerns on their minds. Motives for enlistment were complex.[69] But certainly the opportunity for leisure was high on the list of many a man who signed up. Especially among groups like the artisans, Volunteer service was seen primarily as recreational.[70] Service meant the occasional weekend away, the excitement of the rifle range and the camp, and the camaraderie of other like-minded men. In short, the battalion or corps acted as a social club.

By the second half of the century, the majority of Britons were living in urban areas. As the standard of living in cities rose, professionals, clerks, and an increasing number of regularly employed workers found themselves with more money and more free time. Consumer goods and services expanded to meet their growing demands. Railways made travel to the countryside and seaside relatively cheap and easy. Music and organized sport became prominent features of late Victorian leisure.

The auxiliary forces could also supply leisure opportunities to their communities. By the 1880s, the British public had become fascinated with military pageantry. On most weekends in London, one could view, if one had wished, more than one regular or auxiliary battalion on display. The presentation of the colors, the changing of the guard, and even regimental drill had become public events. The military began displaying their latest heavy guns and vehicles on these occasions as the people's interest in new technology grew. Attendance at the royal tournament in Islington became more or less ritual for more than 100,000 men and women by the mid-1890s.[71]

Spectators may have looked forward to the annual royal tournament, but most satisfied themselves by observing smaller-scale parades and regimental brass bands at the local level. And it was there that the auxiliary forces played the key role. They served to bridge the gap between the military and the people, not only entertaining the crowds but also enhancing community pride. Newspapers covered their activities, civic groups raised funds for their uniforms and instruments, and the public spaces where they marched brought their communities physically together. Some observers, including the Christian Socialist author Charles Kingsley, even argued that the auxiliary forces, in particular the Volunteers, helped reduce class tensions. Kingsley noted, "By the performance of a common duty, and the experience of a common humanity, these volunteer corps are becoming centres of cordiality between class and class."[72]

Others pointed to the role that the auxiliary forces played in promoting physical fitness. Even though middle-class participation in the Volunteers was short lived, Andrew Wynter, in the London weekly *Once a Week,* credited the organizations "with fostering a love of outdoor life that has been utterly wanting among the great middle-classes for a century."[73] Sir William Hardman identified the Volunteer Movement as a sign of Britain's physical fitness and well being when he wrote: "Muscular Christianity, the Volunteer movement, and alpine climbing are in ascendant. The affected Dandy of past years is unknown. If he exists, he is despised."[74]

The rise of militarism was a prominent feature of British society at the end of the nineteenth century. It adapted well to suit the needs of the New Imperialism. The public embraced their empire, and a large segment of it committed to its expansion. They accepted military force as a means to carve out new territories and pacify older ones, and they supported the deployment of the army around the globe to further that goal. In this climate the uniformed officer and the common foot soldier, both mostly forgotten characters since 1815, reemerged as heroic symbols of Britannia.

Overseas events alone did not restore the army's standing in British society. The image of the soldier was resuscitated in large part due to the development of the auxiliary forces at home. The auxiliary forces served as an important bridge between soldiers and civilians. They made it acceptable to wear uniforms, to parade through city streets, and to drill on public greens. They became focal points of civic interest and pride. They embraced and served to reinforce the values of late Victorian society. And they made it possible for the British public at large to associate those values with all uniformed groups—cadet corps, boys' brigades, and most importantly, the Regular Army.

By the time the South African War erupted in October 1899, the British had ceased to associate its military with the failures of the Crimean War. Instead, they rode a wave of optimism as they watched events unfold in the Cape Colony and Natal. When three British divisions were stopped cold in December and the government responded by calling for volunteers, Britons responded enthusiastically. Within a few weeks, ten thousand men had enlisted in the Imperial Yeomanry, virtually all of the Volunteer battalions had raised active-service companies and readied to set sail for South Africa, and the Militia had opted overwhelmingly to serve overseas. Many more men volunteered to serve, but their offers were turned down. That the auxiliary forces had come to play an important role in late Victorian society and had shaped the belief that uniformed civilians could participate in the country's defense ensured that the public would support their role in the conflict.

2

The Outbreak of War

> The issue now . . . is nothing less than that of British Supremacy over South Africa. It is one from which, when raised, no British Government can flinch. It is one which we can not evade when we are challenged upon it, and it is one we can admit no compromise.[1]

By September 1899, most if not all Britons knew that the possibility of war with the Boers of the Transvaal was likely. Certainly, there were those who thought it could still be avoided and hoped that the two sides could reach an understanding and settle their differences. And there were many who did not appreciate the intricacies of the conflict nor were particularly interested in the current political situation. Nevertheless, Britain's widely circulating and politically active press ensured that the country was mentally prepared for the outbreak of war and encouraged to support it.[2]

The War Office, however, was not as convinced as the editors of *The Times, The Daily Mail,* and other pro-war newspapers that Britain would soon be fighting and that its military needed to be ready. Lord Wolseley, the commander in chief, urged military preparedness but was hamstrung by the government, which failed to listen to his warnings, and could only take limited action himself without its approval. Gen. Sir Redvers Buller, who would command the army in South Africa in 1899, was similarly ignored.[3] But whereas Wolseley had only to worry about the state of the British army, and Buller, a localized conflict, Lord Lansdowne, the secretary of state for war, had to worry about the political and financial ramifications of an early mobilization. Military preparedness would have to be delayed until Lord Salisbury's government was willing to commit to war. When in a strange twist of events the Transvaal and, even more surprisingly, the Orange Free State presidents delivered a forty-eight-hour ultimatum to the British agent in Pretoria, Salisbury was forced to declare war, ready or not, on 11 October 1899.

The South African War was one of Britain's last "small wars."[4] It proved, however, to be much "bigger" than anyone expected. The Second Asante War (1873–74), the expedition to quash the Urabi Rebellion in Egypt (1882), and the Tirah campaign along India's Northwest Frontier (1897–98) were more typical of the challenges faced by the British army. These conflicts were short, brought few British casualties, and cost the Treasury little. If additional British regulars were not available or not warranted, locally raised or colonial troops could supplement the expeditionary force. Volunteers, other than a company of engineers required to provide a specific technical skill, as they did in the Sudan in 1884, for example, were not generally needed. The greatest hurdle in these imperial conflicts, or so many officers opined, was not defeating the enemy in battle but bringing him to battle. Overcoming the logistical difficulties involved in overland transportation, supply, and communication could pose nightmares to regimental officers often moonlighting as staff members.[5] If these obstacles could be surmounted, and they ultimately were, as a rule superior technology more than compensated for any deficiency in numbers.

But the South African War was different. The press often painted the Boers as completely alien (and thus inferior) to the British in racial and religious terms, so cultural negotiation was impossible. For example, the *Daily Mail* stated that the "Dutchmen" were tricksters and cunning, while the *Daily Telegraph* commented on "the seemingly permanent hostility of two virile . . . stocks, each of which is demanding itself a future dominion."[6] But the cultural similarities of the two peoples far outweighed their differences, especially when compared to Britain's recent imperial encounters with the Afridis, Ndebele, and Pedi. Boer generals understood the British military mind and developed tactics and altered strategy to frustrate their opponent's plans. In this they were much more successful than other imperial adversaries.

In technological terms, at least those related to warfare, the Boers again presented mostly similarities rather than differences. Any weapons they could not manufacture themselves, for example, could be purchased from sympathetic distributors in Germany and Austria-Hungary, a luxury Britain's African and Asian enemies seldom could afford. Although quantity was an issue from the beginning of the conflict, and the disparity only got worse once the war began, the quality of each side's weapons was comparable, and indeed the Boers even outclassed the British in some categories. Therefore, this enemy's capability posed a technological challenge unlike any other the empire faced in the late Victorian era. In anticipating yet another small war, the British grossly underestimated their opponent as they had twenty years earlier.[7]

The First Anglo-Boer War (1880–81) may have ended with the Pretoria Convention of 1881 and the London Convention of 1884, but the confusing language and the hostile tone of the settlements, many critics argued in the summer of 1899, had ensured a future confrontation. Why it took nearly twenty years for this second conflict to occur suggests that the real causes of the South African War were much more complex then a mere debate over words.[8]

Great Britain's role in the entire South African region changed dramatically with the discovery of diamonds and gold and the launch of a mineral revolution. Prior to that, British politicians had satisfied themselves with control of the coast and limited direction over the interior. Germany as yet posed no threat to their strategic interests in southern Africa, and the only European power with any influence in the region, Portugal, could be kept in check through light diplomatic pressure. The empire made its peace with the Boers and recognized the existence of two republics, the South African Republic (Transvaal) and the Orange Free State, in 1852 and 1854, respectively. But the development of the diamond industry at Kimberley in the early 1870s stimulated British capital investment and captivated a curious public at home. Cheap local labor and political stability were requisite before large amounts of capital could be risked and large profits could be reaped. Both Liberal and Conservative governments were willing to assist in the development of the budding industry, which led to a restructuring of British interests. The land around Kimberley, Griqualand West, was quickly annexed, and over the course of the next thirty years, most of the region, including Bechuanaland (Botswana), Basutoland (Lesotho), Swaziland, Rhodesia (Zimbabwe and Zambia) and Nyasaland (Malawi) came under British governance. In the process African resistance was crushed, and land, labor, and minerals were obtained at cut-rate prices.

Because the British were more reluctant to use force and (as stated above) technological differences were not as significant, overcoming the white Afrikaans-speaking population of South Africa proved a more difficult task. An attempt to confederate the region resulted in the First Anglo-Boer War with the South African Republic and a humiliating British defeat. Gladstone's second government was more than ready to halt its imperial venture and give up, at least temporarily, its hopes of incorporating the Boer republics into a British-dominated South Africa. But the timing could not have been worse for some British and European venture capitalists concerned about President Paul Kruger's political and social oligarchy and his financial determination in the Transvaal. In 1886 the main reef of the Witwatersrand was discovered outside of Johannesburg. British machinations to incorporate the gold mines as they had done with the diamond mines in Kimberley could not be achieved without the resumption of full-scale hostilities. But neither the Liberals nor the Conservatives wanted another war. Memories of the humiliating defeat at Majuba and the high cost of more than two hundred casualties, not to mention the loss of their colors, were still fresh. Charles Gordon's ill-fated mission to Khartoum and Wolseley's failure to rescue him in 1885 left persistent doubts about Britain's ability to flex its imperial might at will.

These concerns and anxieties over the Boer states and their capacity to influence the region did not erode during the next decade. Liberal and Conservative governments alike, however, continued to rule out war as an instrument of foreign policy. There were other methods available, some of which came at little or no cost to the Treasury. For one thing, as noted above, the British were busy claiming and annexing territory in the region, effectively cutting off the Boers from further expansion into the interior. Some of these ventures, notably those into Matabeleland and Mashonaland, were conducted by Cecil Rhodes's chartered concern, the British South Africa Company, with minimal involvement of the London government. This imperial expansion limited Boer trade options by forcing them to depend on rail lines constructed through British territory to the coast and prevented a much-feared union with German-controlled South West Africa (Namibia).

A second method, and an even more overt attempt to thwart Boer hegemony in the region, was Rhodes's plan to overthrow Kruger's government in Pretoria. This attempt, which resulted in the notorious Jameson Raid of 1895, proved to be an utter failure and only hastened the coming of war between the British and the Boers. The details of the raid are well known.[9] In its aftermath Rhodes was toppled as the Cape Colony's prime minister, and Joseph Chamberlain, Lord Salisbury's colonial secretary, was implicated in an ever-widening political scandal. Although Chamberlain emerged largely unscathed, the affair had political ramifications outside of Britain, notably the dispatch of the German kaiser's sympathetic telegram to Kruger, which disrupted Salisbury's foreign policy. The conflict between the British and Transvaal governments heated up considerably afterward.

The success of Rhodes's plan had hinged on the dissatisfaction of the large immigrant population in Johannesburg, the Uitlanders, and their willingness to participate in an armed insurrection. The Uitlanders, the majority of whom were British or had come from British colonies to work in the mines or serve the needs of the mining community, proved far from enthusiastic. This did not, however, stop the London government and, in particular, its newly appointed representative at the Cape, Sir Alfred Milner, high commissioner of South Africa and governor of Cape Colony, from seeing the path to success in South Africa through them.

Uitlander grievances against the Boers were numerous, and indeed some were legitimate, but Rhodes and his allies deliberately exaggerated their plight. Winning civil liberties and solving the franchise question were at the forefront of Milner's attack. He believed that since the Uitlander population had come to make up a majority of the Transvaal's population by 1899, a "big concession of the franchise question would be such a score that we could afford to let other concessions drop quietly into the background or settle them by compromise."[10] The rationale behind this claim was Milner's expectation that an enfranchised population loyal to the British Empire could dictate the Transvaal's future. Thus, the British government could gain dominion over the Boers without resorting to armed conflict.

Milner, Chamberlain, and Salisbury were astute politicians. They recognized that the British voting public, recently extended by the Third Reform Act, might not be convinced by economic or legalistic arguments but would be sympathetic to the plight of fellow Britons who did not enjoy the same rights they did. Milner, therefore, with Salisbury's approval, pushed the franchise question, eventually forcing the Boers to the negotiation table in June 1899. Although Kruger was willing to make some concessions, Milner, believing that he had the stronger hand, increased British demands. Talks fell apart, and an angered Milner walked away. At this point he may have decided that force was the only option left to safeguard British interests, but the London government was still unwilling to accept the inevitability of war. Chamberlain informed the high commissioner that the cabinet was doing all it could to reach a "satisfactory settlement," but those were idle words.[11]

As the events of the next four months demonstrated, if the British government was going to insist on maintaining suzerainty over the Boer republics, then it had run out of options. But Milner's strategy had paid modest dividends. Although playing the "franchise card" may have failed in South Africa, it succeeded in Great Britain. Sections of the public, particularly the industrial working class, remained disinterested, but the government's manipulation of the Uitlander grievances highlighted by Milner's dramatic "Helot Dispatch," in which the high commissioner compared the state of the Uitlanders to the oppression and servitude of the ancient Spartan serfs, won over the middle class, and this later proved essential to Volunteer enrollment.

The government and the press, by using the Uitlanders, put a human face on the brewing conflict.[12] So too did Percy Fitzpatrick, whose *The Transvaal Within* became a major bestseller in 1899.[13] The hard-working, English-speaking Uitlander man, as *The Daily Mail* put it, was "fighting for freedom of his people, for the right to speak his own language, to have his say in the ruling of his own affairs, to carry a weapon if he chooses, to protect his women from insult, to hold himself at least the equal of any man in any country in which he lives."[14] In this way interested parties equated the rights of the Uitlander with the rights of the Briton and paved the way for a moral justification of the war: the defense of liberty.

The press, in particular, played an essential part in returning South Africa to the front and center of British imperial concerns. The reconquest of the Sudan and the Tirah Campaign had focused public eyes elsewhere. Both had been successful missions, and great honors and accolades were bestowed upon the army and its officers.[15] The sense of failure that had surrounded the First Anglo-Boer War was all but forgotten. It was now time, or so *The Times* argued, to solve the South African problem, for if Great Britain shirked in its responsibilities, the repercussions would ripple throughout its empire. "The progress of events in South Africa," *The Times* commented, "is watched as keenly in Canada and in Australia as in this country, and it behooves Her Majesty's Government to justify the confidence everywhere displayed in their ability and determination to uphold in this emergency the rights and interests of the empire."[16] The press argued that British political and economic interests in South Africa were being subordinated to the greater interests of the British Empire. In this way too it gave the government the moral right to act with force.

Through August and September, Salisbury and his cabinet debated the merits of issuing the Transvaal government an ultimatum. But the prime minister was still unsure whether the British public would support a war.[17] What transpired was the delivery of what the *Pall Mall Gazette* cleverly labeled a "penultimatum," a list of demands to which the British government insisted the Transvaal comply. "The dispatch does not hold a cocked pistol at Mr. Kruger's obstinate head," the *Gazette* assured its readers. "Nor is there a watch hung up before his eyes, ticking away given minutes at the end of which, if nothing be said by him, the trigger will be pulled. A penultimatum is what it is, a last word delivered in friendly form."[18] The penultimatum debate, however, was simply a device created by the pro-war press to convince their middle-class readership that hostilities had just cause. More popular newspapers also followed this tactic. Yet most of the antiwar press, labeled as "pro-Boers" by their opponents, avoided reporting on the "compassionate" Britain offer and instead focused on the specifics of Chamberlain's September dispatch.

As it turned out, the Kruger government responded in a way that made it easy for the British to continue to claim the moral high ground, delivering a real ultimatum on 9 October. Military action could now be sold as a reaction to Boer aggression rather than as part of an active policy that simply wanted the Boers to address British concerns, a more difficult argument to make. On 12 October Britain declared war.

The breakdown in talks between the British and Transvaal governments back in June had led Kruger to take steps toward preparing the republic for hostilities, purchasing weapons, readying commandos, and hammering out a military pact with the Orange Free State. British military preparations, however, did not begin in earnest until September, a delay that proved costly. As a result, when the fighting began, maps were faulty, supplies were insufficient for a lengthy campaign, and even the defenses of the Cape Colony and Natal were severely lacking. Although Gen. Sir Redvers Buller had already been selected to lead British operations, Lansdowne kept him in the dark until late August and did not approve his war plan until the end of September.[19] In addition, Britain did not have the manpower in place to defend its holdings, much less to take the war to the Boer states. Nor were soldiers marching back and forth across Salisbury Plain, drilling and awaiting orders to set sail for South Africa. The government hesitated. There were still those who hoped that war could be averted. Wolseley had first suggested an early mobilization back in June, yet it was not until the end of September, a little over a week before war was declared, that the First Army Corps, forty thousand men in all, was finally mobilized.[20] This long delay assured that the Boers could determine strategy in the opening the months of the war.

And they did. Shrewdly identifying the northwest region of Natal as a weak spot in British defenses and an area favorable to their advance, the Boers struck early at Dundee, jeopardizing the security of the entire colony. Although this drive was halted at Elandslaagte, the British could not follow up on their success and unwisely withdrew to Ladysmith. The Boers followed in pursuit, though not quickly enough, allowing the British the chance to entrench and build up the defenses of the town.[21] A lengthy siege followed (commencing 30 October), temporarily eliminating the largest British force in southern Africa. Buller would have to wait for the arrival of the First Army Corps before he could go on the offensive and, thereafter, was burdened by the political necessity of relieving Ladysmith as quickly as possible. Further tying his hands were successful Boer strikes into the Cape Colony that led to the sieges of Mafeking and Kimberley (commencing 14 and 15 October, respectively), the latter of which was particularly sensitive because of its importance to the diamond industry and because its leading figure, Cecil Rhodes, chose to remain in the city. Buller was forced to attempt to lift the siege and free Rhodes. The British government had erred in its military planning and was paying the price.

Despite the setbacks of the opening weeks of the war, London remained calm. There was no reason to panic. The government and the British people were confident that once the Regular Army arrived on the scene, the affair would be rapidly resolved. Most of the opposition also remained quiet. Certainly, all believed that a "bunch of farmers," as they disparagingly referred to the Boer forces, was no match for their battle-tested army. In November the First Army Corps finally landed in South Africa, but despite his better judgment, Buller divided it up for the purposes of relieving the three beleaguered garrisons. The British took the offensive with drives in the northern Natal and in the western and northern Cape Colony. Although there were growing signs of trouble, notably Lord Methuen's difficulty in forcing entrenched Boers from the banks of the Modder River (28 November), the British government, public, and officers remained certain that their troops would be celebrating in Bloemfontein and Pretoria by Christmas.[22]

That confidence was shattered during the second week of December. On the ninth Lt. Gen. Sir William Gatacre's force of three thousand men, advancing in the northern Cape Colony, attempted to seize Stormberg, the site of an important railway junction. A night march using poor maps and unreliable information left the tired and hungry force confused and demoralized. After a brief skirmish with Gen. J. H. Olivier's commandos, Gatacre attempted to get his men out of the way of further harm. But in his hasty retreat, the British commander forgot to transmit orders to nearly a third of his force. These men, numbering more than six hundred, stayed in place. The next morning, abandoned by their officers, they surrendered without a struggle. After Stormberg, British attention quickly shifted to the western Cape Colony, where Methuen and his First Division continued their advance toward Kimberley following the pyrrhic victory at Modder River. Like Gatacre, Methuen attempted a night march to get his men safely into firing range of a large Boer force entrenched at Magersfontein. At first light on the eleventh, Gen. Piet Cronjé's men discovered British soldiers only a few hundred yards away and still in close formation. The result was disastrous for Methuen. The First Division suffered nearly a thousand casualties, and the attempt to relieve Kimberley was halted until further reinforcement could be found. Then on 15 December, Black Week came to its climax. Intent on relieving Ladysmith and hoping to restore morale after these two setbacks, Buller, personally commanding the drive in the northern Natal, ordered an attack on the enemy's position at Colenso. The Boers, strongly entrenched, easily stopped the British. Although Buller still had a sizeable force and options available, he withdrew his men without launching a second assault.[23] British operations in South Africa ground to a demoralizing halt for the remainder of the year.

There seemed to be good reason in October to believe that the Regular Army possessed the necessary tools to accomplish the task set out for them. After all, they had been victorious along India's northwest frontier and in the Sudan. But even more impressive to its leaders and the public was the nation's record of success during its thirty years of empire building and consolidation leading up to the South African War. This helped create a national mindset that seldom doubted British superiority. Byron Farwell, in his exhilarating episodic narrative *Queen Victoria's Little Wars,* lists more than ninety campaigns, expeditions, and actions in which British soldiers took part during this era of small wars.[24] Setbacks, seldom encountered, were almost always purged from the historical memory by ultimate success in the campaigns. The British army in South Africa, of course, had a checkered past, with defeats at the hands of the Zulu at Isandhlwana (1879) and the Boers at Majuba Hill. But these had been suffered nearly twenty years earlier. And besides, the military could still cite numerous victories in South Africa going back to the Royal Navy's successful landing in 1795. It is no surprise that the heroic defense at Rorke's Drift (1879), following so rapidly on the heels of Isandhlwana, took on the mythical stature that it did, for it was victory, not defeat, that the British wanted to remember. And to a generation of young Britons, imperial defeat was virtually unknown.

Most Britons had a firm belief in the moral and physical superiority of their troops. Despite the emerging reports that industrial life was taking a heavy toll on the bodies of its people and that the nature of military life and its poor pay ensured recruitment from the lowest economic stratum of society, or "the hand to mouth class," few doubted the physical abilities of Tommy Atkins.[25] He was expected to endure the hardships of imperial campaigns, whether they were fought in the mountains, desert, or forest, in torrential rains or 100-degree temperatures. Other races, for example the Sikhs and the Gurkhas, may have been considered by late Victorian Eugenicists and other so-called race experts to be better suited biologically for war, but few questioned that British soldiers led by British officers could overcome all opponents.[26] British officers, they argued, possessed the intelligence and proper upbringing to lead and the values of respectability to succeed.[27] Their motive was loyalty to Queen and Country, not individual glory or personal greed. Those latter traits were thrust upon their Asian and African opponents.

Like other Europeans in the late nineteenth century, the British were fascinated by technology and believed in the blessings that it bestowed. Advancements in military technology were to be embraced and not feared. (Doomsayers like Ivan Bloch, who predicted that modern innovations would lead to utter physical destruction and the erosion of all social organization, were viewed as crackpots.)[28] And the British possessed significant technological advantages in their imperial conflicts. At times these advantages, whether they were in communication, transportation, or firepower, proved insurmountable. Against the Boers, the British had good reasons to trust in their own capabilities. True, as mentioned above, the Boers had access to overseas markets, and European arms manufacturers were both sympathetic to their plight and eager to turn a profit. British naval supremacy, however, could ensure that those markets would be closed to the enemy once the war had begun. Then, once their stockpiles ran out, the Boers would be unable to keep up with British production. The industrial base of the Boer republics was nascent, and what existed was built around mineral production. Many Britons doubted that an irregularly constituted force with virtually no training could properly employ modern weaponry on the battlefield.

The British also possessed technology that the Boers lacked altogether. Balloons and radio, which were experimented with during the war, gave the British advantages in signaling and reconnaissance. Lyddite, a newly developed explosive for artillery shells, was expected to drive an entrenched force from its positions with ease.[29]

In addition, the British had a highly trained corps of engineers and the Royal Army Medical Corps. The Boers would have to rely on the specialized expertise of foreign volunteers, of which doctors (and their medical supplies), in particular, were in short supply throughout the conflict.

There was yet another reason for British confidence. Although their poor planning predicated Boer numerical superiority at the onset of the war, British numbers could grow to a strength the enemy could never hope to match. The government calculated that the two republics combined could field a maximum force of around 54,000 men.[30] No one, however, expected a force that size to ever assemble, for many burghers, it was correctly assumed, would choose not to fight. The actual number planners anticipated was around 40,000 men, roughly the size of the British force mobilized on Salisbury Plain in late September. This estimate, though a bit high, did not fall far from the mark.[31] As for the British, in addition to their garrison of close to 10,000 men already in South Africa, another 12,000 had been dispatched from Great Britain and India prior to the start of the war. Most of these had arrived prior to the declaration of hostilities.[32] The size of the (effective) Regular Army in 1899 was 234,963 men. These ranks could be supplemented (and were, in part), by 24,128 reservists, 105,122 militiamen, 10,114 yeomanry, and 230,785 volunteers, not to mention the Indian army and colonial contingents.[33] Great Britain, therefore, had an enormous pool of uniformed men from which it could draw and, in an emergency, many more who were out of or not yet in uniform.

The Militia and Volunteer numbers were quite impressive on paper. But the quality of these forces (and the Yeomanry too) remained questionable. The radical imperialist Sir Charles Dilke, in his 1888 exposé of the military, recognized the deficiency of the auxiliary forces as the major weakness in the British army.[34] Militia and Volunteer officers he found particularly lacking in leadership abilities and thought that "they would not know how to handle their troops skillfully" if needed in an emergency.[35] But Dilke saw great potential in these men. He believed that if they were properly reformed, they could be turned into a reliable force and used not just at home, but, if the regulations were changed, abroad as well. Above all, he had confidence in the Volunteers, which he argued represented the best in middle-class spirit and intelligence. But it was a prescient remark about the Yeomanry that showed Dilke's astute knowledge of military reform. "With a little encouragement," he wrote, "the Yeomanry might be developed into just such a body as the Boers, who gave our troops under General [George Pomeroy] Colley a lesson in the power of irregulars when the partisans are bold riders and good shots."[36] Buller shared Dilke's view in 1899, asking Lansdowne for more troops the day after his defeat at Colenso. "Would it be possible," he telegraphed, "for you to raise 8,000 irregulars in England, organized not in regiments but in companies of 100 each? They should be equipped as mounted infantry, be able to shoot as well as possible and ride decently."[37] The Imperial Yeomanry, born in the crisis of December 1899, was the realization of that request.

"In short, the whole organization of the Auxiliary Forces of the Crown [on the eve of the South African War] was in a highly confused situation," wrote Col. John Dunlop in his history of the British army.[38] Dunlop's assessment was right on target. It is easier to see the link between the auxiliaries and the rise of cultural forces like militarism and patriotism than it is to see what material role they played in home defense.[39] This disjunction was largely the result of economics. Everyone agreed that if Great Britain were to rely upon the auxiliary forces for home defense, the Militia, Yeomanry, and Volunteers would have to undergo significant reform. But this would come at a high financial cost, and not everyone agreed that it was worth paying. As director of military intelligence from 1886 to 1891, Maj. Gen. Henry Brackenbury refocused Britain's attention on home defense. Naturally, discussion ensued regarding the auxiliary forces. Brackenbury, Wolseley, and their allies in Parliament, however, had a very difficult time convincing others that Britain was in danger from a "Bolt from the Blue." The "Blue Water" school remained preeminent, and with its emphasis on naval defense, it remained opposed to any unnecessary army-related expenditures. Without any immediate threat, discussions eventually shifted away from home defense to other matters, and the role of the auxiliaries was never fully fleshed out.

During the early 1890s, as interest waned, enrollment in the auxiliary forces began to decline even as the population of Great Britain grew. The Yeomanry, in particular, was hard hit.[40] Of the auxiliary forces, its health was obviously most subject to the effects of industrialization. With urbanization and the agricultural depression, the rural base from which the Yeomanry could be culled was gradually reduced. And with the modernization of the police force, their raison d'être came into question. Each trooper was required to provide his own mount, and thus cost presented yet another deterrent to enrollment. Rumors spread about the imminent elimination of entire troops. Although none seem to have been cut entirely, permanent staff were significantly reduced. The status of the Yeomanry plummeted. New regulations came into effect in 1893 and brought about some mild reforms, but heading into the war, the Yeomanry was well below strength, and since members were still drilled as cavalry and not as mounted infantry, they would need to undergo major retraining before they could be an effective force in South Africa. In 1901 the Militia and Yeomanry Act subject the Yeomanry to military law, leading Col. H. Le Roy-Lewis, deputy assistant adjutant general, to write, "the Yeomanry . . . have now been practically made Militia."[41]

Although much larger and better trained than the Yeomanry, the Militia remained too small and disorganized to play a major role in home defense. It was a collection of battalions and not an army organized to defend against invasion. Like the Yeomanry, establishments were dropping.[42] And even though it was in the best interest of the government to keep numbers high, it was a very difficult task to win over recruits. The prospect of missing up to twenty-eight days of work was not very appealing to employers. And even when the Militia was able to lure young men to the recruiting offices, there was no guarantee that they would meet the minimum requirements to enroll. As the South African War revealed, the health of Britain's urban poor, the natural recruiting pool for the Militia, was in an alarming state. In 1897 one-third of the more than 77,000 applicants were rejected by medical officers. Another one-sixth were scared off by the examination process. The pool was further reduced by non-health-related rejections and desertions. In the end, fewer than 34,000 men were admitted into the Militia.[43] To make matters worse, the best of these left at the earliest opportunity for positions in the Regular Army; the worst deserted or were discharged before their time was up. On average, only about 20 percent of recruits completed their six-year obligation and entered the Militia Reserve.[44] Despite some effort to shape its men in a way that they could complement the Regular Army, like their inclusion in the 1898 autumn maneuvers, the Militia remained largely unreformed and of little apparent value. Wolseley, for one, thought very little of the service.[45]

The Volunteers had problems too. Despite a sizeable presence of officers in Parliament, little public money flowed to the force. In 1899 it remained short of equipment and supporting services, its training was deficient, and the number of officers was inadequate. Although there was more initiative among the Volunteers than in the other auxiliary forces—displayed in their experimentation with bicycles, railroads, and balloons; their encouragement of marksmanship; and their adaptation of "sensible" uniforms—as a fighting force, there was much room for improvement.[46]

As far as the future of the Volunteers was concerned, two disturbing trends arose in the 1890s. First, the ranks were shrinking. Although numbers rose every year during the first half of the decade, they fell continuously after 1896. The outbreak of the South African War and the scare of Black Week led to a resurgence in its strength.[47] Second, the social makeup of the force was in flux. The Volunteers had originated in the 1859 invasion panic and a middle-class commitment to playing a role in the defense of the state. It was this historical association of the Volunteers and the middle class that led many to believe that this was the only auxiliary force with potential for improvement. Critics spoke of the character, intelligence, and adaptability of the Volunteers, but these were mere code words for middle-class virtues. Yet middle-class participation was becoming a thing of the past as the working class came to dominate the service. Military critics questioned whether working-class volunteers would possess the same intelligence and initiative their middle-class predecessors had displayed. The ranks of the Militia and the Yeomanry, not to mention the Regular Army, were already filled with workers and the underemployed. The disappearance of any uniformed middle-class presence raised some concerns about the auxiliaries' commitment to state and imperial defense. These concerns, however, proved to be unwarranted.

Another problem facing the Volunteers and how they could be employed was eliminated in 1895 by the Volunteer (Military Service) Act. The Volunteer force could only be used under certain emergency circumstances. Unlike the Militia or Yeomanry, these units could only be called upon if a danger to Great Britain was considered actual, though not, for example, imminent. The threat had to constitute a genuine national emergency. This rule limited their function as an instrument of defense. But the 1895 act allowed for Volunteer mobilization in the event that the Militia was embodied and still could not meet the needs of home defense. Although they still could not be used overseas, the extension of these service regulations encouraged the force's defenders.

As war loomed in the summer of 1899, it was those advocates, chief among them Col. Sir Howard Vincent, who pressed for the inclusion of the Volunteers in the impending conflict. In August Col. Eustace Balfour of the London Scottish Rifle Volunteers offered to raise one thousand men for active service. Vincent, a veteran Volunteer officer with more than twenty years of experience, followed with a similar offer to raise one thousand sharpshooters. Although primarily motivated by patriotism, he also saw that "an excellent opportunity had risen of showing that the Volunteers must be taken seriously."[48] Despite the Volunteer MPs being a reliable Conservative voting block since 1895, they could not get Salisbury's government to accept their offers.[49] Indeed, the only response Vincent received from the War Office was the brief notification that his proposal was delivered "through the wrong channel."[50]

Not surprisingly, all such offers were rejected at this early stage of the crisis. Salisbury and Lansdowne were not overly concerned with the Boer challenge. After all, they were doing little to prepare the Regular Army for the conflict. Certainly, the use of auxiliary forces would have seemed unnecessary. The outbreak of actual hostilities did not change the government's attitude, and Vincent was rebuffed a second time. An offer by the Middlesex Yeomanry to raise a detachment for overseas service likewise was rejected, as were those made by Lord Lucas, Captain Campbell of the Glasgow Yeomanry, and Lord Lonsdale.[51] Lonsdale had gone as far as to mobilize and equip five hundred men of the Westmoreland and Cumberland Yeomanry and prepared their sea transport only to be informed by the adjutant general, H. E. Wood, that his move was premature and unsanctioned.[52]

Even if Salisbury's cabinet was not yet prepared to accept offers from the Yeomanry and Volunteers, it gladly accepted offers from Canada, Australia, New Zealand, and its South African colonies. It also asked for the assistance of the St. John Ambulance Brigade to provide trained medical orderlies.[53] Lastly, the government did not forget about the Militia. On 26 October the Queen proclaimed that the "state of affairs in South Africa does in Our opinion constitute a great emergency" and authorized its embodiment.[54] A week later it called up twenty-four battalions, and three weeks after that, it called up eight more.[55] Although there was still no plan to send Militia battalions to South Africa, these decisions show that Salisbury and Lansdowne were losing confidence in the ability of the Regular Army to get the job done alone.

The British government entered into a war in 1899 largely of its own doing. Yet it was surprisingly unprepared. Salisbury's Unionist coalition enjoyed both a majority in the Commons and in the Lords. The Queen offered no impediments to his rule. His "men on the spot," notably Milner, provided the prime minister with the "right" information.[56] The majority of Britain's newspapers also offered their support for the impending conflict. Although large sections of the public remained either unconvinced or in opposition, Salisbury had a large base of support to which he could appeal. And yet when war erupted in October 1899, British military personnel and planning were inadequate.

The auxiliary forces were also unprepared to play any major role in the war. Government neglect through the 1890s had left them without a clear purpose. Full integration with the Regular Army had never been achieved. Legal obstructions continued to hamper their flexibility. Their numbers were down, morale was low, and training was inadequate: the forces were incapable of either playing a major role in the defense of the nation or in aiding the Regular Army overseas.

And yet even before the war began, Militia battalions, Volunteer corps, and Yeomanry companies were showing their support for and their eagerness to play some role in the coming conflict. When the government balked, patrons of the auxiliary forces continued to apply pressure. No doubt some thought that this was the perfect opportunity to demonstrate the importance of the auxiliaries and, in a sense, save them from a diminished future. The War Office, however, remained hopeful that the Regular Army could win the struggle on its own. Black Week shattered these illusions, and in its aftermath the auxiliary forces were finally given their chance to prove their worth.

3

Recruitment

Few who were in England at the time will forget the gloom of that black week in December, when the news of Magersfontein, Stormberg and Colenso followed hard upon each other till the triangle of misfortune was complete. The thing became intolerable; it was impossible to go on doing the ordinary things of life; something had to be done; new men and measures must be devised. So among many other measures, the Imperial Yeomanry was devised, and in six or seven weeks many a man, who had never had any idea of bearing arms, found himself sailing on a troopship to the Cape, clad in khaki, equipped as a mounted infantryman with many things both necessary and unnecessary.[1]

In December 1899 British military forces in South Africa suffered three substantial reverses.[2] On the ninth Lt. Gen. William Gatacre's small force was stopped near Stormberg. In the confusion that followed his abortive attack, Gatacre failed to send orders to the Second Battalion Northumberland Fusiliers. Abandoned and left to their own devices, more than six hundred of them surrendered the next morning, bringing the total number of British casualties at

Stormberg to close to seven hundred. On the eleventh Lt. Gen. Lord Methuen attempted to force the Boers from their well-defended position at Magersfontein in order to open up the road to Kimberley. The attempt failed, and the British force suffered nearly a thousand casualties. Many in the Highland Brigade, demoralized by the loss of so many of their comrades and the death of their commander, Maj. Gen. Andrew Wauchope, pledged to never again serve under Methuen. And on 15 December General Buller ordered an attack on the Boers at Colenso to relieve pressure on the besieged garrison at Ladysmith. He had no more success than Methuen and Gatacre. The British foolishly pushed their guns to within a thousand yards of the enemy and into the zone of fire. All of the gunners were shot down, and every attempt to save the artillery failed. British casualties numbered more than eleven hundred, and the Boers maintained their position along the Tugela River. Black Week was a complete disaster.[3]

The news of these defeats shocked everyone in Great Britain. Few anticipated that "the flower of the British army [could be] outmaneuvered and repulsed three times in one week by undisciplined Boer farmers."[4] The pangs of defeat were felt keenly throughout the British Empire, though no place more strongly than at home, where they created an atmosphere of forlornness and desperation. "The upset and discomfiture in most London circles at the close of that week, as the news of the blow after blow came through," one critic remembered, "were more poignant, more depressed, than similar feelings aroused at any given moment during the Great European War."[5] Something decisive had to be done. The tide of the war had to be turned and the spirit of the nation lifted. A new face, untainted by defeat and accusations of defeatism, had to go to South Africa to breathe life back into the campaign and restore morale at home. As the year drew to its close, Lord Salisbury's cabinet selected its hero. General Lord Roberts, accompanied by Maj. Gen. Lord Kitchener as his chief of staff, was sent to take over Buller's command.[6]

Under tremendous pressure to turn the tide in South Africa, the War Office also opted to change the composition of British forces there. The Sixth Division was mobilized and a seventh division was readied in reserve. General Lord Wolseley, the commander in chief of the British army, issued orders to call up the Army Reserve and to raise a force of mounted infantry. And to solve additional manpower problems and provide a much-needed mobile force in the field, the government gave its consent to allow volunteers raised at home to serve overseas.[7] By war's end, the Militia, the Volunteers, and the Imperial Yeomanry furnished the British army in South Africa with more than 100,000 men.[8]

The Militia provided more than 45,000 officers and men for the war effort. In addition, another 75,000 transferred directly from the Militia into the Regular Army. Nearly 20,000 Britons went to South Africa as members of either Volunteer Service Companies or the City of London Imperial Volunteers (CIV), the only Volunteer regiment to serve in the war. Moreover, smaller numbers of volunteers served as engineers, medics, and cyclists. During the course of the war, 35,000 men served in the Imperial Yeomanry, which went out to South Africa in three waves. The first contingent was raised early in 1900; a second about a year later; and a third in the winter of 1901–1902. Imperial Yeomanry companies (later called squadrons) were typically raised through the existing apparatus of Yeomanry regiments, though only a portion of the recruits were themselves experienced yeomen. Volunteers and civilians filled out the ranks.

The government's decision to use auxiliary forces overseas was not made lightly, but it was reached fairly quickly after Black Week. In part, it was one born out of mounting pressure, though also a way to harness the public's restless energy. And it was a decision overwhelmingly supported by the press and public.[9] There were some newspaper editors who questioned the government's reaction to the crisis and its motives in calling for volunteers, but even they were carried along with the charged tide of public opinion. The nation had spoken. The editors of *The Leeds Mercury,* for example, which had opposed the war from its onset, challenged the government for taking an "alarmist view," acting in panic, and taking advantage of the sympathies of volunteers. But by 21 December, the overwhelming response by the citizens in and around Leeds to the call for able-bodied men silenced the editors' opposition.[10] For the rest of the war, even when the conflict seemed to drag on aimlessly, the Militia, Volunteer, and Imperial Yeomanry units remained rallying points for local and regional nationalisms and ensured at least a modest amount of continuing support for government policy.

In the wake of Black Week, offers from Militia, Volunteer, and Yeomanry notables, as well as from civilian elites, flooded the War

Office. Lord Lovat sought permission to raise "150 stalkers and ghillies" in Scotland.[11] The Middlesex Yeomanry made their second pitch to raise a detachment of men. And most famously, the lord mayor of London, Sir Alfred Newton, offered to raise, equip, and transport a regiment of Volunteers to the front, a force that became the City of London Imperial Volunteers.[12]

Following the battle of Colenso, Buller begged for mobile reinforcement. The British cavalry in the field was too small and ill trained for reconnaissance and chasing after the Boers. Some even challenged the rationale for its continued existence, seeing it as a branch that changes in military technology had rendered obsolete. Buller sought troops more akin to mounted infantry: eager young men who could ride and shoot. On 18 December 1899 Lords Lonsdale and Chesham met at the War Office to discuss the scheme they had proffered back in November to raise a large force of Yeomanry at their own expense. Later that day the Army Board for Mobilization Purposes met to discuss that offer and some other business. The proceedings (marked secret) reports: "The Board considers that [Chesham and Lonsdale's] patriotic proposal should be accepted. They recommend that this force should be regarded as distinctively the contribution of the Yeomanry of the Kingdom to the present war, preference being given to members of the Yeomanry to enlist in it."[13] This meeting resulted in the creation of the Imperial Yeomanry.[14] Buller would get the force he wanted.

The next day the War Office issued its call to arms.[15] Recruiting-office doors were thrown open throughout Great Britain. The response was overpowering—men came streaming in. To cite just one example, within twenty-four hours, the Nottinghamshire contingent had already signed up more than enough men to fill a company.[16] Overwhelmed by the popular outburst, the War Office felt compelled to make further allowances. Although the original plan was to raise only three thousand men, the first contingent of Imperial Yeomanry eventually numbered more than ten thousand. By war's end, 177 companies of Imperial Yeomanry served in South Africa.[17]

The Imperial Yeomanry Committee had no experience in steering such a large force, and many of the decisions it made in the winter of 1899–1900 would be second-guessed. Members did not have time to consider all unforeseen events and evaluate all the repercussions that might be caused by their decisions. They had to get the troops together, offer them a modicum of training, and transport them to South Africa as quickly as possible. Percy Fitzpatrick's warning to a colleague in South Africa was appropriate. The Imperial Yeomanry, he wrote, "is an emergency force gathered together very hurriedly. There is a considerable deal of confusion about the management and organization of it and you must not expect the force to be first-class riders or shots, but undoubtedly there will be a good deal of absolutely first-class material in it and all that we can do now is to give those who are not first-class every opportunity of becoming so."[18] Indeed, when Maj. Gen. J. P. Brabazon, the commander of the Imperial Yeomanry in South Africa in 1900, made his report on the force's service during the war, he prefaced it with a brief discussion about the conditions surrounding its initial organization. "One can only marvel," he wrote, "at what was accomplished in the time and under the circumstances."[19]

Despite the drawbacks associated with their chaotic organization and mobilization process, Brabazon believed, as did many of his contemporaries, that the recruits possessed a potential that Regular Army recruits did not. And this potential, he argued, allowed them to overcome, in the long run, any initial shortcomings.

> The personnel of the men, I consider, leave absolutely nothing to be desired. There is a very large leavening of men well born and well educated. The yeoman class is largely represented: to my knowledge a large percentage gave up remunerative situations and comfortable homes to come out here. In the ranks you found, in addition to the blood, bone and sinews, the intelligence of the English nation represented.
>
> It must be remembered that the great majority of the men were ignorant of discipline and had practically no military experience to start with, but they soon fell into the ways of both, for they wanted to do what was right and were anxious to learn.[20]

Although Brabazon may have exaggerated the participation of the yeoman class and the "well born and well educated," there is no doubt that, in comparison to the Regular Army, the Imperial Yeomanry enjoyed recruitment from among a wider spectrum of Britons who better represented the nation as a whole.

Organization of the Volunteers was quite different than that of the Imperial Yeomanry. The commander in chief's committee to consider questions relating to operations in South Africa recommended on 16 December that a company be formed from the existing Volunteer battalions linked to each English, Welsh, and Scottish battalion currently on service in South Africa. A second company would also be raised just in case.[21] Enthusiasm for the Volunteers was as great as it was for the Imperial Yeomanry. The response to the government's call was greater than anyone could have expected. George Wyndham, the undersecretary for war, wrote with some awe to his brother: "The spirit in this country is magnificent. Practically everyone has volunteered!"[22] Volunteer service companies and the CIV had many more offers than they could possibly accept. Nearly all of the battalions raised active service companies by New Year's Day to join their linked line battalions already in the field. Despite this enthusiasm, the government was reluctant to significantly raise the quotas for enlistment. It would have been a costly venture, and at the time it did not seem necessary.

According to the chronicler of the South Wales Borderers, every man of the Third Volunteer Battalion offered to go to South Africa. Fewer than twenty, however, were permitted into the First Volunteer Company.[23] Likewise, all of Birmingham's 959 volunteers were ready to go to the front or else serve in garrisons at home or abroad. Only about 100 were allowed to go.[24] And in a matter of days, the Fourth Volunteer Battalion of the King's Own Scottish Borderers had produced two companies, one for active service in South Africa and a second to be held in reserve. "Strapping, well-built fellows they were," one reporter wrote, "absolutely sound in wind and limb, and every man a skilled marksman. At their country's call these men had left behind them their civil occupations, their house comforts, and the society of all who were near and dear to them."[25]

The apparatus to mobilize the Militia was in place before the war began. Once a royal proclamation was procured, the Militia could be readied for action. Indeed, thirty-two battalions had already been embodied prior to Black Week.[26]

The major obstacle that remained in place afterward was the voluntary nature of overseas service, for militiamen were not required to serve outside of Great Britain even in the event of an emergency. But as with the Yeomanry and the Volunteers, there was great enthusiasm and excitement for the war within Militia battalions. The men overwhelmingly elected to serve overseas. "In no case," H. W. Wilson writes, "did any Militia battalion when invited to give its services show the smallest reluctance."[27] Wilson may have exaggerated a bit. Still, all but four battalions agreed to serve.[28]

Why did these men leave their homes, their families, and their jobs to sail halfway around the world and potentially put their lives in grave danger? For most contemporaries, the answer seemed simple. "Who does not remember with pride the great outburst of patriotism which, like a volcanic eruption, swept every obstacle before it," a yeoman wrote, looking back in 1901.[29] Men were willing to make the "ultimate imperial sacrifice" out of their strong sense of patriotism—their love of country, respect for British institutions, and support for the continuance of the empire. Bernard Porter writes that "whether or not the South African War really was a 'popular' war in Britain, it was widely assumed to be so at the time, even by those who opposed it."[30] But the war was popular. In a speech delivered in Norfolk to honor the Forty-third Company Imperial Yeomanry, Alfred Haldinstein stated what so many others in the room felt. "There was a feeling everywhere that [the Imperial Yeomanry] were doing the duty of every Englishman in maintaining the honour and pre-eminence of their great Empire. They were going to fight on behalf of that civilisation which was found wherever the flag of England floated, and every man among them would have the opportunity of making his special mark. They were all born heroes."[31]

Even those who opposed the war had difficulty speaking against it after Black Week. Robert Blatchford, one of the founders of the important Socialist voice *The Clarion,* wrote: "I am a Socialist, and a lover of peace but I am also an Englishman. I love my fellow men of all nations . . . but I love England more than any other country. I am not a jingo, I am opposed to war. I do not approve of this present war. But . . . my whole heart is with the British troops."[32] Blatchford was not alone in his sympathies. As an Irishman, the Fabian writer and famous playwright George Bernard Shaw might not have felt the same way toward Great Britain's immediate mission, but he did recognize that most Englishmen did. After the war he complained bitterly about English attitudes toward the conflict: "All classes in proportion to their lack of travel and familiarity with foreign literature are bellicose, prejudiced against foreigners, fond of fighting as a cruel sport—in short, dog-like in their notions of foreign policy."[33] Both Blatchford and Shaw believed that the South African War was extremely popular among all walks of life in Great Britain, even among pacifists too, for many Quakers got caught up in volunteering.[34]

Certainly, the way Britons treated their volunteers in late 1899 and early 1900 supports the notion that the war became very popular. The first letter a new recruit sent home after starting his journey inevitably described his send off amid rousing choruses of "God Save the Queen,"[35] "Rule Britannia," and "Soldiers of the Queen." Patriotism indeed filled the air. "Half a million people watched and cheered when the 1st Army Corps sailed from Southampton," wrote one.[36] Similar, albeit smaller, scenes were enacted daily in late January and early February 1900 as companies of Imperial Yeomanry marched past town halls to train stations and docks. Trooper A. S. Orr remembered that "the citizens of Glasgow turned out by the thousand, and their numbers were swelled by friends of the other companies from Lanark, Edinburgh and Ayr. It was a scene that we can never forget, and was a final proof that we carried with us the kindly thought and good wishes of those who had already done so much for our comfort and success by showering upon us everything that could possibly be of use in our future campaigning."[37] In London, Colour Sgt. Guy Scott, City Imperial Volunteers Mounted Infantry, witnessed high-spirited crowds packed so close to one another that his regiment's march from St. Paul's Cathedral to Nine Elms Station, a mere five or six miles, took four hours to complete.[38] Bernard Moeller, who enlisted in the same regiment, remarked: "I shall never forget that march! The streets were packed the whole way twenty deep, and we simply had to fight our way through."[39] And Trooper Frank Charge, departing from Worcester, wrote to his father, "Mothers kissed sons, sisters kissed brothers, lovers kissed sweethearts—and, on the spur of the moment, somebody else's sweetheart too."[40]

This image of the exuberant farewell and the boisterous town-hall meeting, and even the call to arms made by the archbishop of Canterbury, however, do not tell the whole story.[41] Beginning in the late 1960s, some historians began to reject this paradigm, claiming that not everyone in Great Britain supported the war unconditionally and not all the volunteers were as eager to go fight for their Queen and country as it appeared. Henry Pelling and Eric Hobsbawm argued that these scenes were representative of the middle class's commitment to imperialism but did not reflect the true expressions of the working class.[42] The latter did not support the South African War, they argued, and if some of its members fought under the Union Jack in this conflict, they were motivated to do so solely out of economic need. Hobsbawm writes: "Patriotism compensated for social inferiority. Thus in Britain, where there was no compulsory service, the curve of volunteer recruitment of working-class soldiers in the imperialist South African War simply reflect[ed] the economic situation. It rose and fell with unemployment. But the curve of recruitment for lower-middle-class and white-collar youths clearly reflected the appeals of patriotic propaganda."[43] In other words, when the working class signed up for military service, they did so out of economic desperation, untouched by the strong imperial forces emanating from the press, music halls, pulpits, and primary and secondary schools. For Hobsbawm, the members of the middle class, however, swept up by those same forces, did what they were compelled to do—show their support for the empire.

Richard Price, in his groundbreaking work *An Imperial War and the British Working Class,* advanced the most thoughtful argument to date for working-class indifference or sometimes even outright hostility to the war. He recognized that an "orgy of patriotism" permeated society, "the like of which had never been seen before."[44] Yet working-class institutions were rarely affected and notably absent from discussions in support of the conflict. Price found that the majority of their newspapers, trade councils, and social clubs and colleges were at least sympathetic to the antiwar movement. He argues persuasively that the Khaki election of 1900 was not the "litmus test" for patriotism that Colonial Secretary Joseph Chamberlain made it out to be. Far from being a landslide victory for the governing Unionist alliance, Price claims that "the overwhelming feature of the election was voter apathy."[45] He also effectively combats the "myth" that the sometimes violent demonstrations that took place on 18 May 1900, following the relief of Mafeking, were an expression of working-class jingoism and its support of the war. These crowds, he states, were led by and consisted of mostly young middle-class men.[46]

As far as recruitment goes, Price follows Pelling and the others. Workers, he claims, only joined for the money. Unemployment rose in Great Britain at the end of the century, and the war did little to alleviate the immediate economic concerns of laborers. As the middle-class volunteers and Imperial Yeomanry began to worry about their careers and businesses, and as their image of war as a "Sunday-afternoon hunting party" began to fade, they returned home in droves.[47] Workers, lured by the competitive wage offered by the government for military service, filled the vacuum.[48] Price notes that working-class enlistment peaked, not with the sudden outburst of patriotism generated by Black Week, but instead with the problems of seasonal unemployment in the winter of 1901–1902.[49]

This argument, driven by economic reductionism, is very unsatisfying for a number of reasons. For one thing, it does nothing to dispute the claim that the war was popular among the upper class, the middle class, and the "clerks," a group that Price argues was materially working class but consciously middle class. In fact, in his attempt, as with Hobsbawm's, to demonstrate working-class apathy toward the conflict, middle-class support is basically conceded. Patriotism, therefore, was a major impulse at least in driving some men into uniform.

But the popularity of the war did extend to all classes. As Andrew Thompson reminds us, "the Boer War deeply touched British people in a way most now forget."[50] Jon Lawrence's work on Wolverhampton, for example, has shown that working-class patriotism did exist and was particularly strong during the war.[51] The town's workers turned out for pro-war speeches, celebrated en masse on Mafeking Night, and donated generously to relief funds for soldiers' dependents. Wolverhampton's working class was not an exception.[52]

Secondly, as Price himself acknowledges, recruitment figures and volunteering figures are not the same thing. Many more men volunteered to serve than were accepted into the ranks. In 1899, 33 percent of those men medically inspected were rejected as unfit; in 1900, 28 percent; and in 1901, 29 percent.[53] After the war the Inter-Departmental Committee on Physical Deterioration appropriately linked determinations of medical unfitness to urban poverty. Thus, most of those rejected for service were members of the industrial working class. It follows that a thorough study of working-class volunteers for the war must include both those who were accepted for duty and those who were not. Unemployment can certainly explain why some men went to war, but a historian would be hard pressed to fit such large numbers into their model considering the healthy economic situation of 1899–1902.

Thirdly, this sort of reductionist argument, by denying other motivating factors for military service, obscures the fact that the unemployed had other options. Although there were individual cases of outright coercion, and certainly peer pressure pushed more than one man into signing up, recruitment was ultimately a voluntary action. No one was obliged to serve. Large numbers of full-time and seasonally employed workers volunteered for service.[54] Even the unemployed had choices. They could hold out in the hope of finding work, could turn to charitable relief or familial support, could go abroad, or could even turn to crime. The alternatives may not have been attractive, but indeed they were alternatives. In her work on the forging of the British nation in the eighteenth century, Linda Colley looked at British motivations for volunteering for military service during the Revolutionary and Napoleonic Wars. The reasons she gives are applicable here: "The role of ordinary human courage, of aggression and excitement of a natural desire to protect one's own hearth should not be downplayed just because those who experienced these emotions happened in the main to be poor. All the evidence suggests that volunteers who were working men, like volunteers who were not, could be swayed by a variety of different motives, not just by direct incentives or because of pressure from above, but also by instinct, by idealism, by a desperate concern for their homeland and by their youth."[55] The evidence presented a hundred years later supports the same conclusion. Men were motivated by a number of factors to volunteer for service against the Boers.

Contradicting Price, Edward Spiers argues convincingly in *The Army and Society* that there is no substantial evidence to suggest that unemployment was the main motivator for voluntary enlistment during the war. Many of the unemployed were too old, too young, or too unfit to join. Looking at late Victorian patterns of recruitment in general, he writes, "the vast majority of the unemployed preferred the condition of unemployment to enlistment."[56] The army was never a popular career path for Britons. Challenging what would seem to be a logical assumption, his research suggests that when unemployment decreased, enlistment in the army actually increased.[57] Spiers concentrated on Regular Army recruitment, and while it is true that terms of enlistment in the auxiliary forces during the war were more favorable, the conclusions he draws can be applied to the auxiliaries as well.[58] Money was not enough to convince most men to risk their lives in South Africa.

During and after the war, soldiers commented on the eclectic makeup of the Volunteer force. In time, with the growth of regimental esprit de corps, differences based on religion, age, or accent often became inconsequential, though when the men were first brought together such dissimilarities made quite an impression. Age restrictions for the ranks varied within the auxiliary forces, with lower limits set at twenty years old for the Imperial Yeomanry and Volunteers and eighteen for the Militia; upper limits were set at thirty-five and forty years of age, respectively. Both younger and older men managed, without much difficulty, to elude the red tape of the War Office and the examination of the medical inspector. Typically, enlistees hovered close to the lower age limit, were unmarried, and were in good health.[59] Samples of the Imperial Yeomanry attestation forms reveal average ages of 24.8, 25.3, 24.5, 26.3, and 24.4 among the first contingent of Nottingham, Wrexham, Bath, Leicester and Lanark recruits, respectively.[60]

Many were particularly mindful of class and social backgrounds and often drew their correspondents' attention to the wide variety of occupations held by their comrades prior to enrollment. "The ranks were filled by all sorts and conditions of men," H. G. McKenzie Rew wrote, "gentlemen of independent means, old soldiers, sailors, clerks, mechanics, farmers—in fact, there was hardly a trade or profession which was not represented."[61] Similarly, Harold Josling, who served in the First Norfolk Volunteer Active Service Company, listed more than a dozen trades and professions in his unit: artists, agricultural laborers, auctioneers, boiler-makers, bricklayers, bakers, bank clerks, chemists, carpenters, engineers, farmers, grocers, merchants, postmen, and surveyors.[62]

Some volunteers, especially those writing shortly after the war, overemphasized that volunteerism in the South African War transcended class. They therefore highlighted these differences. Yet most soldiers did feel as though they were part of a diverse body of men brought together by a singular cause and were genuinely proud of their unit's composition. As single young men, many were just launching their careers or not yet fully employed. Recruitment patterns changed during the course of the war and fluctuated due to seasonal conditions.[63] The Volunteer Service Corps and the CIV had a more urban content: lower middle class, artisans, and laborers. The CIV in particular overly represented the professions—clerks, engineers—rather than the trades.[64] As Harold Hardy wrote in the chorus to his song "The British Volunteer":

> A something in the City—a shopman or a clerk,
> A fellow with a pen behind his ear,
> A journalist, a lawyer, or an idler in the Park,
> Is the ready-when-he's-wanted Volunteer.[65]

The officers and men of the CIV, for example, represented over 125 various professions and trades. While there was a great preponderance of clerks in its ranks, there were also dozens of laborers, engineers, carpenters, builders, printers, and barristers.[66]

Muster rolls and attestation records reveal some heterogeneity within Imperial Yeomanry companies as well, though they were drawn primarily from the middle class and typical Yeomanry sources, that is, farmers and agricultural laborers. The roll of the Twenty-first Company (Earl of Chester's) Imperial Yeomanry, for example, indicates a high number of farmers, grooms, and rural tradesmen as well as a significant number of clerks.[67] Similarly, of a sample of 55 Imperial Yeomen raised in Trowbridge in December 1899, 24 listed farming as their primary occupation and 7 others indicated a rural trade.[68] A sampling of more than 525 Imperial Yeomen taken from eighteen different companies raised in the winter of 1899–1900, in which men identified themselves from more than one hundred different professions and trades, supports this conclusion.[69]

Although the government accepted a sizeable proportion of its Imperial Yeomanry from the "country" as it had hoped, these numbers indicate that the majority were not of "yeoman stock" and did necessarily have experience with horses and firearms.

The composition of individually raised corps, such as the Duke of Cambridge's Own, which recruited the sons of aristocrats and gentry, and Paget's Horse, which recruited heavily at gentlemen's clubs, varied considerably.[70] Militiamen came from the working class. But overall, volunteer recruits joined from a wide range of professions and trades, and many memoirists of the war were proud of that diversity.[71]

Fifteen Most Common Trades and Professions of Imperial Yeomen Raised in January 1900

farmers	25%
trades associated with horses	13%
clerks	8%
engineers	5%
butchers	4%
gentlemen	3%
merchants and traders	3%
blacksmiths and metal trades	3%
building trades	2%
grocers	2%
salesmen	2%
laborers	2%
students	2%
land agents	2%
servants	2%
none	5%

Regional patterns of Volunteer recruitment reflected the patterns of Regular Army recruitment. This meant, disappointingly to many in the War Office, that the shift continued to favor the large urban centers of England, while Irish numbers continued to decrease (though a large number joined Imperial Yeomanry battalions) and Scottish volunteers remained steady but below the desired level.[72] London's most publicized achievement was the establishment and outfitting of the CIV, but its citizens also joined the ranks of the more than twenty Imperial Yeomanry companies of Rough Riders and Sharpshooters.

So why did more than 100,000 Britons choose to fight in the South African War as auxiliary troops?[73] Again, powerful social forces were at work in late Victorian society, shaping men's attitudes toward war, their country, empire, and duty. The British took great pride in their civil society, often comparing it favorably to the martial society of their Prussian neighbors on the Continent. But they also were steadfast in their historical conviction that Britain never backed down from a fight. Although politicians firmly held the reins of the military, expressions of militarism permeated late Victorian society.

The popularity of the army was growing considerably in this age of heightened imperial conquest as formal rule increasingly replaced informal empire. New, aggressive racial ideas associated with Social Darwinism replaced more benign and paternalistic, albeit insidious, attitudes toward "the other." A stronger vision of nationalism, with a xenophobic dimension, supported the imperial mission and was inculcated in adults and schoolchildren alike.

The purveyors of formal education and popular literature in late-nineteenth-century Great Britain worked not only to shape beliefs about the empire and the military. They helped define the meaning of patriotism for a generation. In contemporary juvenile literature, the empire provided the settings and soldiers provided the protagonists. Value was placed in the active engagement of satisfying imperial needs. Heroic self-sacrifice was a necessary component of this action. Juvenile serials such as *The Boy's Own Paper, Chums,* and *Boys of our Empire* helped define values for these recruits.

Shortly after the conclusion of the South African War, G. A. Henty, one of the leading figures in boys' literature, wrote, "I know that very many boys have joined the cadets and afterwards gone into the Army through reading my stories, and at many meetings at which I have spoken, officers of the Army and Volunteers have assured me that my books have been effectual in bringing young fellows into the Army."[74] He was not making an idle boast.[75] By creating a literary world set in the adventure-story genre, with heroes "devoted to notions of duty, power and responsibility" and emphasis placed on their actions of honor, bravery, and self-sacrifice, Henty, Rudyard Kipling, and their contemporaries helped mold the values of a generation.[76] Boys' clubs and contemporary literature helped disseminate militarism and patriotism to all classes. Schools, with their increasingly nationalistic textbooks and martial drill, played a role as well. Cadet corps at universities and public schools proved to be some of the best recruiting grounds for future volunteers. In 1899 this generation was "at duty's call."[77]

Whether it happened through the vehicles of literature, the music hall, the sermon, or the political speech, late Victorian society was inundated with highly volatile images and ideas of militarism.[78] The once-despised Tommy Atkins became a national hero, and his likeness could be found on board games, cookie tins, and cigarette cards. Cults sprang up around such military "heroes" as Garnet

Wolseley, Frederick Roberts, and Charles Gordon. Loyalty, duty, self-help, and patriotism were ideals attached to the military and the empire and were ideals to which all graduating teens, working and middle class alike, had been thoroughly exposed.

But as Hugh Cunningham has shown, it was the Volunteer Movement that did more than anything to legitimize militarism and bridge the gap between the military and the civilians. The Volunteers became a point of community interest and civic pride, an aid to military authorities, and an outlet for entertainment. "Popular recruitment was enhanced and the scene was set for the dramatic waves of volunteering for the armed services in the Boer War."[79] The success of the Volunteer Movement, at least in terms of overall numbers, cannot be questioned. By war's end, in addition to those overseas, there were close to 350,000 volunteers at home.

Not all recruits volunteered without hesitation. Some were pressured to join by family and peers. Edward Manisty had considered the military but opted for a different career. After Black Week, in consultation with his father, he made the decision to go to war.[80] His firm gave him permission to leave, and Manisty obtained a commission in the CIV Mounted Infantry.[81] In a letter to his wife, Col. H. E. Belfield wrote that a trooper in the CIV had told him that the only reason he came out is that all the "women kept asking him why he hadn't gone yet."[82] Some men signed up because they had family problems and sought a temporary escape. Others saw the war as an opportunity to start a new life overseas. And some volunteers indeed joined out of economic need. But all of these recruits were brought up in a society in which tremendous value was placed on patriotism, the empire, and the military; these concepts, real or imagined, were embraced largely by all classes.

Most Volunteer recruits could not adequately express in words why they joined, but they nevertheless felt compelled to go to war. C. S. Jarvis was a trooper in the Twelfth Middlesex Volunteers in December 1899. Only nineteen years old and without political connections, he knew that he had no chance of getting into the locally recruited CIV. In order to see service, he traveled to Wales, lied about his age, and signed up with the Montgomeryshire Imperial Yeomanry. In his autobiography, *Half a Life,* Jarvis recalls how he was swept up in the patriotic fervor of the moment. His most vivid memory of the war, oddly enough, did not come during his service in

South Africa, but rather at home a week before the war erupted. Jarvis claims to have attended a play in which the great London stage actor William Terriss, joined by a half dozen other actors dressed as British soldiers, valiantly resisted an enemy attack.[83] Swept up in the drama and cognizant of current events, someone in the crowd yelled out: "That's the way Englishmen can die. To hell with the Boers." The play was then interrupted with rousing renditions of "Rule Britannia" and "God Save the Queen." The ebullient crowd swarmed the Strand and marched to Trafalgar Square. For Jarvis, this was the "first patriotic war crowd suffering from war fever" of which he had ever seen or been part. When it was time to volunteer, the same feelings overtook him. "I felt that queer, cold, invigorating shudder run down my spine and I imagine that all the yelling young men around me in the crowd felt the same."[84]

Harold Josling chose to tell the tale of his company's adventures through the eyes of his great coat. For Josling (and his coat), the motivation to volunteer was clear: "To uphold the prestige of the Motherland, to give equal liberty to all white men, to check corruption, and set up a just and God-fearing—not God-degrading—government; and once more to demonstrate to the world that the race had not deteriorated, and that the flower of English manhood will now as ever come forward to defend and give their lives for the greatest Empire the world has ever seen."[85]

A. S. Orr joined the Eighteenth (Queen's Own Glasgow) Company Imperial Yeomanry as a trooper. The Eighteenth was one of four companies raised as part of the Scottish battalion. Like Jarvis, Orr vividly recollected that "dark and anxious Christmas of 1899." In his memoir Orr writes that he too acted first and thought about the repercussions later: "We were very much carried away by the novelty and excitement of the moment. . . . It was a time of enthusiasm, excitement, and restless expectation. Each man could hardly believe his luck in being among the chosen, and caught his breath at the thought that some condition might still be imposed which he could not fulfill."[86]

Of the six Galston men who joined the Seventeenth (Ayr and Lanark) Company Imperial Yeomanry, Trooper John Paterson was one of four with Yeomanry experience. He offered his services immediately when the call to arms went out. His stated reasons were simple. It was his duty to answer his country's call. At a public meeting held in Ayr to honor the company, Paterson declared: "I think far too much has been made of our volunteering. I don't think we have done anything but what we ought to have done in the circumstances, and I think every young man with the necessary qualifications, in a crisis such as this, when the country is in danger, ought to rally round the old flag, and show the whole world that the ancient military spirit of Britain is not dead."[87]

Col. William Lamont, the honorary colonel of the First (Renfrewshire) Volunteer Battalion, Princess Louise's Argyll and Sutherland Highlanders, was overwhelmed by the "wild enthusiasm" of the people of Greenock in response to the government's call to arms. More than one hundred men in his battalion vied for the fifteen slots allotted to them in the locally raised active-service company. Many of those who could not get in opted to enlist in the Imperial Yeomanry. Others showed their support by joining the First Battalion and serving at home. Pressured by intense demand, the government later gave the unit permission to increase its size. The civilian response to the crisis was equally demonstrative. The corporation and individual sponsors provided great financial support, the clergy offered moral justification, and the townspeople provided a sendoff that few would forget.[88] "The enthusiasm was unparalleled in our modern history," wrote Lamont.[89] Public works stopped, children were let out of school to watch, and Union Jacks, regimental flags, and other colors lined the streets from the town hall to the railway station. All of these, Lamont insisted, were expressions of patriotism.

J. P. Sturrock, a trooper in the Twentieth (Fife and Forfar) Company Imperial Yeomanry, would have concurred with his fellow countryman. He wrote: "The Fife folk were determined to show themselves worthy citizens in this hour of crisis in the country's history. Patriotism beamed on every face and found a place in every heart."[90] Although only a few of the Fife and Forfar Light Horse offered their services, hundreds of civilians—farmers, doctors, lawyers, cabdrivers, and blacksmiths—were ready to volunteer. And when it was time to depart, despite the rain and the cold of February 1900, the city of Cupar honored the yeomen with a fireworks display and a fond farewell. The *Dundee Advertiser* reported, "In the Crossgate, shopkeepers and householders vied with each other in their demonstrations of loyalty and patriotism, and in their desire to wish the Yeomanry God-speed."[91] The yeomen were carried by the crowds through the streets to the railway station, and such was the enthusiasm of the civilians that the police had to struggle to keep them from delaying the departing train.[92]

Scotland was not the only scene of wild outbursts of patriotism. In Chester one journalist reported:

> The ancient streets, rows and walls of Chester have in their time witnessed many a stirring scene. But never, we believe, one to equal in depth of patriotic fervour the spectacle presented yesterday morning, when the Cheshire contingent of the Imperial Yeomanry left for South Africa. The citizens and inhabitants of the neighboring counties turned out in their thousands before the early hour, packed the Town Hall Square, and lined the route to the General Railway Station, in order to get a last glimpse of, and give a parting cheer to, the noble fellows who are making the supreme sacrifice of citizenship in volunteering to fight, and if need be, to die for their fatherland.[93]

The British press eagerly detailed the daily musters, parades, and sendoffs of the auxiliaries. Regardless of their political leanings, newspaper editors were united in their promotion of the Volunteer force. Alongside columns devoted to the "Stop the War" movement, for example, *The Manchester Guardian* described the departure of Volunteers and the well-wishing, enthusiastic crowds at Blackburn, Ramsbottom, and Burnley. In Oldham "thousands of people assembled" to say goodbye to just sixteen new Imperial Yeomanry recruits.[94] When thirty-seven volunteers of the Leeds Rifles left for South Africa in early February 1900, *The Leeds Mercury* described Leeds as "a provincial city gone mad." It continued: "The scene in and around the railway station was one to be remembered. . . . The arrival of the Volunteers was the signal for an outburst of abnormal enthusiasm. The majority of people took part in what might have been mistaken for a shouting match. Caps, hats, and even bonnets were waved, and amidst it all one or more bands were observed—they were hardly heard—to be playing. There were the usual hearty handshakes, the usual good wishes exchanged, the usual tearful faces, and the latter became the more bedewed as, amidst the strains of 'Rule Britannia,' the train steamed out of the station for York."[95]

But no scene in Scotland, Wales, or a "provincial city" received as much attention in the press as the sendoff of London's CIV. Although this was obviously significant news, most newspapers used several columns and even several pages to unabashedly praise the patriotism of the recruits and glorify the joyous response of the London crowds. This coverage went on for several days from middle to late January 1900. The *Daily Mail* remarked that the farewell service at St. Paul's on 12 January was one of the most impressive sights the city had ever witnessed.[96] *The Times* and other newspapers concurred.[97] As the farewell continued through the streets of London and beyond, thousands greeted the volunteers at the docks at Southampton with cheers and choruses of "Auld Lang Syne" and "God Save the Queen." At the close of one article, the *Daily Mail*'s correspondent reminded readers of Lord Denbigh's lunchtime words: "I believe that this is only the beginning of what the word 'Imperialism' really means."[98]

In P. T. Ross's often satirical recollection of his service in the South African War, *A Yeoman's Letters*, he lists the forty reasons why he joined the Yeomanry.[99] Although one ("to escape my creditors") reflects economic concerns, and a few (such as "Because I am Irish and wanted to fight" and "Poetry") defy categorization, the majority stem from a patriotic impulse produced by both long-term societal influences and immediate events. For example, Ross's list includes, "I considered it was the right thing for an Englishman to do; Because I thought it was my duty; I did it during the Patriotic Mania, 1899–1900; and, Sudden splash of patriotism upon visiting a Music Hall."[100] Nearly half of the reasons he provides can be directly linked to his sense of patriotism, obligation, and duty to his country.

It is easy to dismiss these pronouncements of patriotism as self-promotion. Certainly in published memoirs and autobiographies, and to a lesser extent in unpublished letters and diaries, it is the exception to the rule when a writer speaks of his motivations in terms of self-interest. Ross was much more reflective than most. Notwithstanding this claim, few volunteers expressed their patriotism overtly in the written word. The examples above are typical. What they were expressing was the patriotism of their family, community, and nation and how they were moved by and responded to it. Ultimately, most acknowledged that this was one of the most powerful forces shaping late Victorian society.

Patriotism not only drove men to take action but also defined what types of action were acceptable. Although late Victorian society saw a rise in the standard of living and the emergence of commodified leisure, life for many men was routine. The war offered an opportunity to step off the farm, get out of the factory, and emerge from behind the desk. Enlistment in the Volunteers or Imperial Yeomanry was more attractive and less disruptive than joining the Regular Army, for it promised a limited stint of service, a shorter period of training, and the recruits hoped, a less demanding form of discipline. Service in South Africa liberated men from the routine of domesticated Victorian society while providing the opportunity to fulfill their responsibility to home and hearth.

In reading the memoirs, diaries, and letters of auxiliary servicemen, one is overwhelmed by the recruits' desire, perhaps even need, to experience something new. Through the vehicle of patriotism, these men found an acceptable outlet through imperial service. Thomas Dewar, a trooper in the Fife and Forfar Imperial Yeomanry, assessed his comrades' motivations for volunteering in his memoir of the war, *With the Scottish Yeomanry.* He writes that a few of them entered to take on a new profession and to earn a livelihood as, for example, a saddler, a smith, or a groom. The majority, though, went in to engage in an action that rewarded them with a sense of psychological fulfillment. Dewar identifies over 250 men who enlisted out of "patriotism, ambition and love of adventure."[101] But what he did not adequately express is that for late Victorian society, ambition and love of adventure were inherently linked to patriotism.

Frederick Barnado, a medical student, joined the Fife and Forfar Imperial Yeomanry because the war seemed more exciting than pursuing a career in medicine. He was motivated by a "call to adventure."[102] Rennie Stevenson, who joined a London-raised company of the Imperial Yeomanry, wrote that he and his comrades all had a "desire to see the pomp and circumstance of war on the veldt."[103] And indeed, his memoir reads like an adventure tale. In addition to "Love of War" and "For Sport," P. T. Ross added that he joined the Imperial Yeomanry "for the sake of a little excitement, which I can't get at home."[104] For all these men, the thirst for adventure could only be satisfied when it was coupled with their sense of patriotism.

As C. S. Jarvis writes, "Life in England was very humdrum, Victorian and prosaic in the 'eighties and 'nineties; it was so entirely uneventful and supremely commonplace that one could with safety make plans for one's holiday five years ahead and feel complacently secure that nothing whatsoever would arise in the interim to upset these plans. Abroad, however, in our Colonies and Dependencies there were opportunities for a young man of spirit and enterprise to lead the sort of life of which every youth dreams—or should."[105] In South Africa these men could experience something new and different. They could meet new challenges and see a new world. They could fulfill their dreams and become something they could never be at home: heroes.

For many who lived through both the South African War and the First World War, it was surprisingly the former that aroused greater feelings of despair. Britain's military might had suffered very few setbacks in the second half of the nineteenth century, and the government, the military, and the people had grown complacent. Fighting in South Africa against the Boers was supposed to be an easy task. But it was not. Black Week brought an end to the nation's overconfidence. The government was forced to take action to provide assistance to the Regular Army in the field. In addition to using regular British and imperial troops raised overseas, it authorized the domestic recruitment of volunteers. The response to the government's call to arms was loud and enthusiastic. Yeomanry offices and Volunteer headquarters were flooded with recruits. In a short time the Imperial Yeomanry, the Militia, the CIV, and a number of Volunteer Service Companies joined the Regular Army in South Africa.

Patriotism was a powerful force that shaped late Victorian Britain. All classes to some extent embraced it. Those who were not influenced by the manufactured patriotism of the daily paper, school, musical hall, or brass band were subject nevertheless to its spontaneous outburst created by the disasters of Black Week. The subsequent call to arms gave rise to the ultimate manifestation of this force. Every man who volunteered did so in this atmosphere. Although there were a variety of economic and social factors influencing one's course of action, the most widespread reason for enlistment in the Volunteers and Imperial Yeomanry during the South African War was the need for psychological fulfillment found in the expression of patriotism. Ultimately it was this need, and not an economic one, that the majority of recruits wanted to meet.

4

The Journey to South Africa

. . . And to Bisley we went down,
Some five hours there we stayed;
While we remained, I trow there was
A murd'rous fusillade.

Then at Knightsbridge and at Chelsea
Six weeks we rode and drilled,
Till with all martial knowledge
We were completely filled. . . .

E'en so it proved with us,
For lo! behold, at last,
We embark aboard the "Tagus,"
and England's shores fade fast.

Then as she leaves Southampton,
And for Cape Town shapes her course,
She has aboard two thousand men
Including Paget's Horse. . . .

. . . Our voyage was uneventful
(At least so I should say),
Though some wished they had stayed at home
Before they'd crossed "the Bay."

At last we came to Table Bay,
And much to our delight
The war was not yet over,
And we'd still a chance to fight.

From "The Story of the Piccadilly Heroes,"
author unknown[1]

The British people were traumatized by the events of December 1899. "The nation," Leo Amery, the editor of *The Times,* wrote, "was more deeply stirred, more profoundly alarmed, than at any period since the eve of Trafalgar." Depression and uncertainty, however, gave way quickly to anger and action. The government, which had hemmed and hawed since the summer, now acted decisively. Fresh leadership, untainted by defeat, and Regular Army reinforcement were hastily dispatched to South Africa. The War Office heeded the demands of the men on the spot and prepared a force of mounted infantry. And most importantly, for the first time since the days of Trafalgar, the government called for and raised a large body of volunteers for active overseas service. By taking these steps, the defeats at Stormberg, Magersfontein, and Colenso could be cast as temporary setbacks, with Britain now heading, once again, down the road to ultimate victory. Through volunteer recruitment, the spirit of the nation was renewed.

Most of the men who answered the government's call to arms had never been out of the country before; indeed, few had traveled any length of distance from their homes. For those who returned home afterward, the war was an experience they would never forget. In their letters, diaries, and stories, they left behind vivid impressions of combat, camaraderie, and the landscape of a war-torn South Africa. But often overlooked by readers of these accounts are the first and often most dramatic experiences: their assemblage, the journey to the dockyards, and their voyage. It was through these events that the men were introduced to military discipline, drill, and of course, each other.[2] And it was during this process, long before they saw the enemy for the first time, that these citizen-soldiers were first subjected to one of the greatest hardships of war, that of being away from home and family.

As noted earlier, the response to the government's call for assistance could not have been more enthusiastic. Recruiting offices of the Imperial Yeomanry, Militia, and Volunteers were flooded with eager young men willing to make the ultimate sacrifice for their country.[3] Age and health restrictions stopped many would-be volunteers, and still more were denied by the quantitative enrollment limit set by the War Office. Although the numbers began to fall off as the war dragged along into its second and third years, few were disappointed with this initial response. One would-be poet put it best (or worst):

> We joined the British Army when we heard our country's
> call,
> To fight our nation's battles—do our best, however
> small.
> Don't think that we are funking—We don't want to do
> it all.
> We did'nt [*sic*] join the regulars, our physique was
> not the best;
> We couldn't swear sufficient, and we couldn't "chuck a
> chest."
> But we "chucked" our situations, and sailed forth with
> glee,
> We knew the way to ride and shoot, so joined the
> Yeomanry.[4]

In many ways, volunteering was as much a response to local identity as it was to nationalism. This was felt most strongly in the English countryside, the Scottish Highlands, and in Wales, areas traditionally ripe for Regular Army recruitment but which had dropped late in the century.[5] In those areas paternalistic methods were influential in driving recruitment. Local dignitaries played important roles in raising, administering, and financing auxiliary units. But private influence and money were used throughout the land to organize Volunteers. There were independent special corps like the Duke of Cambridge's Own raised by the Earl of Donoughmore in

London's West End and Imperial Yeomanry outfits like the Twenty-first and Twenty-second Companies, raised by the Earl of Harrington in Cheshire.[6] And in the case of the First Volunteer Battalion, Royal Warwickshire Regiment, the *Birmingham Daily Post* acted both as an agent of recruitment and as a fundraiser to organize and finance the unit.[7]

Diarists and memoirists peppered their writings with regional boasts to the government's call to arms rather than national ones. William Home, a lance sergeant in the Berwickshire section of the First Volunteer Service Company, King's Own Scottish Borderers, recollected: "Towards the end of 1899 . . . when the outlook was gloomy, and the issue of the war seemed uncertain, Britain called upon her 'citizen' soldiers to lend a hand in driving back the hordes of the enemy who had invaded her dominions in Cape Colony and Natal, and she called not in vain. Tens of thousands of young men, eager to strike a blow for their country's cause, answered the call, and asked to be led against the foe, and nowhere was this patriotic spirit more apparent than in the Borderland."[8] Not to be outdone, Godfrey Smith recalled: "I suppose that in no town in the British Isles did the volunteer movement reach such dimensions as in the old town of 'Glesca.' Every drill-hall was inundated with names of willing aspirants for the army. . . . I suppose that more willing or enthusiastic recruits never were enlisted for her Majesty's army."[9]

Local men filled the ranks of locally raised companies and squadrons. Many had strong connections to the prewar auxiliary services. More than half of the Imperial Yeomanry raised after Black Week in Warwick, Nottingham, and Newcastle, for example, had previous experience in the Yeomanry. One-third of the Sixth (Staffordshire) Company Imperial Yeomanry had served with the Yeomanry or Volunteers. And in a small sample of attestation forms given by the recruits of the Seventeenth (Earl of Carrick's Own) Company Imperial Yeomanry, all but one of the twenty-five men had served in the Yeomanry in Ayrshire.[10]

Communities throughout Britain embraced the volunteers, and these locally raised units became focal points of civic pride. Urban and rural folk alike financially contributed to the well-being of "their" volunteers. Subscriptions were established to help supply the men with uniforms, rapid-firing guns, and chocolate. The Holy Trinity Church in Dorchester donated Bibles and writing cases.[11]

One woman supplied field glasses for all of the NCOs of the first contingent of Rough Riders; a man did the same for the Seventh (Dorset) Company Imperial Yeomanry.[12] A group of Cupar women presented gaiters and hats to the men of the Twentieth (Fife and Forfar) Company Imperial Yeomanry (and nosebags to their horses).[13] The Eighth (Derbyshire) Company Imperial Yeomanry received so many gifts that one of its lieutenants complained in his diary that he would not be able to "carry all the useless things they have given us."[14] Not only was each man of the Twenty-first and Twenty-second (Chester) Companies Imperial Yeomanry given a set of binoculars and a compass, he was also given one pound sterling as pocket money.[15] In addition to material items, subscriptions raised relief funds to assist wives and children while their husbands and fathers served overseas. Life insurance policies were often donated as well.[16] And at St. Andrew's Hall in Glasgow, each man of the Second Scottish Rifle Volunteer Service Company was given a burgess ticket "entitling him to the freedom of the city."[17]

Individuals contributed in all sorts of ways. Shopkeepers decorated their windows with placards and flags, and local dignitaries feted the men at churches and town halls. "That our Yeomanry and Volunteers are all over the country stepping forward with offers to proceed to the front in South Africa," one journalist reported, "is, in a country which has a wholesome fear of conscription and regards it as an evil to be kept as far distant as possible, a thing which calls for liveliest gratitude, and makes everyone feel that the hearty send-offs which are being given our citizen soldiers everywhere are but the least communities can do to show they appreciate truly the heroic spirit which is being expended on their behalf."[18]

Of course, volunteer life in early 1900 was not simply a series of celebrations. There was also a difficult period of drill, physical displacement, and mental anxiety. The time between enlistment and setting sail for South Africa could last two months or more. Just waiting around for muster could take a month or more. Frank Fox of the Royal Gloucestershire Hussars Yeomanry enrolled in late December 1899. Within a week he had passed his medical inspection and his riding and riflery examinations. Two months later he was aboard the *Cymric* with the Third (Gloucestershire) Company Imperial Yeomanry and heading for Cape Town.[19] A. G. Garrish volunteered and was enrolled in the East Surrey Volunteer Service Corps in late

December 1899. On 22 January the people of Kingston enthusiastically sent off his troop. After a brief stop at Hounslow to pick up the Middlesex Volunteer Service Corps, Garrish, aboard the SS *Tintagel Castle,* set sail for Durban.[20]

H. S. Gaskell had a more difficult time getting to the dockyards. After spying a flier at the University of Edinburgh, Gaskell managed to be selected from among the many men of the Queen's Royal Volunteer Battalion for active service. He then failed his medical inspection. Undeterred, the next week he traveled to Buckingham, where he successfully joined the Thirty-seventh (Royal Bucks Hussars) Company Imperial Yeomanry. After five weeks of drill at Wycombe, he set sail aboard the *Norman* from Southampton amid rousing choruses of "Auld Lang Syne" and "Home, Sweet Home."[21]

For some, the wait seemed like an eternity. A. S. Orr, a trooper in the Eighteenth (Queen's Own Royal Glasgow) Company Imperial Yeomanry, remembered: "It was a time of enthusiasm, excitement, and restless expectation. Each man could hardly believe his luck in being among the chosen, and caught his breath at the thought that some condition might still be imposed which he could not fulfill."[22] The press corroborated the stories told by Fox, Garrish, Gaskell, Orr, and others. The government, wisely, did not rush the volunteers to South Africa.[23] Organization and training took time. Delays were frequent. Soldiers and civilians were anxious through the early months of 1900, and all were quite relieved when the day of departure dawned.

Waiting was only one of the hurdles that volunteers had to clear. Like many of the men who joined the auxiliary forces after Black Week, Maurice Fitzgibbon had no military experience.[24] He was studying classics at university in Dublin when he read an announcement on 26 December in the *Irish Times* that a company of Imperial Yeomanry was being raised in Newbridge. Fitzgibbon's experience was similar to that of other volunteers. Swept up by the outburst of patriotism and excited by the opportunity to travel and see Africa, he applied and duly reported to the commanding officer, Thomas Pakenham, the Earl of Longford. After filling out an attestation form and submitting himself to the poking and prodding of a medical officer, he left to await the results. Fitzgibbon received a positive notification and returned to the barracks, this time with his horse to take a riding test. He had to demonstrate his horsemanship in and out of a ring;

walking, galloping, and trotting; and mounting, dismounting, and jumping. Having passed, he headed to the rifle range to take the first of two shooting tests. He passed these as well. Fitzgibbon and the other vetted volunteers became the Forty-fifth (Dublin) Company.[25]

From 13 January to 17 February, Fitzgibbon's unit remained at barracks. Reveille commenced at 0630, fall in at 0700, breakfast at 0800, muster at 0900, dinner at 1300, parade at 1400, tea at 1700, last post and lights out at 2200. A typical day involved drill, rifle and horse instruction, and fatigues such as cleaning, cooking, and gathering coal. The day was long but not exhausting. Finally, after a concert, dinner, and inspection by the Duke of Connaught, the Forty-fifth Company left for the Curragh during a driving snow. Once arrived, they were quartered and received further drill and instruction. In the early morning of 12 March, after fighting their way through thick crowds, they embarked for Cape Town to the sound of four brass bands.

Most men wrote little about their drill and fatigues. Since the units were raised locally and the instruction took place at the local regimental barracks, the volunteers were still in contact with their friends and loved ones. Most letters detailing this episode of their experience were written by the few men who did not join the local troop. Also, in the diaries and memoirs published after the war, most men did not feel compelled to leave behind a written record of what they considered a commonplace activity. Drill was more or less ordinary to late Victorians. They did it at school; they did it after school with the Boys' Brigades and Cadet Corps; and they watched others perform it on weekends in town squares and at parade grounds. Although the focus was now on them, the spectacle itself was not new.

Nevertheless, drill was a very important tool in building primary-group cohesion. Many of the men may not have known each other prior to the war. Class, religion, politics, and age may have separated them. Commonality of purpose would have to be stronger than social discord within the company for it to operate effectively in South Africa. Drill was important to building horizontal bonds and vital to forming new vertical bonds. Deference to class had to be replaced by deference to rank. The hierarchical relationship of the recruit to his commanding officer and his NCOs was forged during training. The uniform went a long way in stripping a man of his past, but drill was vital to the company's future and would shape the serviceman's actions both on and off the battlefield.

Drill was difficult for some. Mick Gallagher, a self-described "patriotic Liverpool-Irishman" and volunteer in the King's Liverpool Regiment, had a hard time with the training he received at Oxford Barracks in Warrington. It was "pretty stiff, making some of us think we were being born again."[26] J. P. Sturrock, Twentieth (Fife and Forfar Light Horse) Company Imperial Yeomanry, remembered foot and bayonet drill as well as a number of mounting and dismounting exercises that he had to perform daily, sometimes with a rifle in hand.[27] John Paterson, a farmer's son from Galston who enlisted in the Seventeenth (Ayrshire) Company Imperial Yeomanry, recalled six weeks of drill at Ayr. When the tide was out, the men were drilled on the sands. He wrote, "Our fingers used to get numb and powerless holding the reins and rifle in the bitter cold weather we had."[28]

The rigor of drill was not enough. It had to be practical. Volunteers who wasted their time on the parade ground would be quick to lay blame when something did not go as planned on the battlefield. This adversely affected morale. John Paterson's biggest regret was not the difficulty of his training, but its impracticality. For example, he was never taught how to pitch a tent, something he had to do immediately after landing in South Africa. Sidney Peel, who joined the Fortieth (Oxfordshire) Company Imperial Yeomanry, also emphasized what he and his company were not drilled in. In his memoir he complained bitterly that there was little training in horsemanship and no training at all in marksmanship. According to Peel, the men were provided with no instruction in outpost work, flanking patrol, or advance-guard duty. "The one piece of drill which we thoroughly mastered," he wrote, "was standing at ease and standing easy."[29]

Even as they drilled, the decision to volunteer for South African service had yet to make a full realization on most of the recruits. Their daily routines may have changed, but they were home and their activities were familiar. The war was distant. They were still more or less civilians in soldiers' clothing. This began to change when they were ordered to proceed with their company or regiment to a port city such as Southampton or Liverpool for embarkation. It was suddenly time to say goodbye and head for the war.

In "The Old 50th to the New," an unknown poet and trooper of the Fiftieth (Hampshire) Imperial Yeomanry versed:

We'd thirteen weeks in Barracks, and they worked us
very hard,
When we couldn't groom our horses we were sweeping out
the yard.
But when evening came and work was done, we went out
on the spree,
A liveliest lot of characters I never wish to see:
If a man chanced homeward *sober*—he got 14 days C.B.

At last, our larking ended, we were ordered out to
fight,
We were shipped away like convicts in the middle of
the night,
For a month aboard our lugger we were bounding o'er
the main,
We cut some sorry figures, and experienced awful pain,
But in spite of that, we all agree *we'll risk it home
again.*[30]

Although it is true that a few companies of men were whisked away in the "middle of the night," even they were hardly treated like "convicts."[31] The Sixty-third (Wiltshire) Imperial Yeomanry, for example, was met by hundreds of torchbearers who lit their way to the Trowbridge station.[32] More often than not, the men were met with an exuberant, almost carnival-like, atmosphere as well-wishers from across the county descended on the train station to bid them farewell. The first diary entry or letter sent home by a volunteer, usually in a thankful and enthusiastic tone, invariably included a reference to the sendoff.[33] Most commented on the size of the crowds. J. W. Milne, First Volunteer Service Company Gordon Highlanders, wrote in his diary: "We left Aberdeen at two o'clock amid the cheers of the people, a scene which I will never forget. . . . We were gradually being crushed into single file till at last we dropped into the Station one by one and into the carriages."[34] *The Worcestershire Echo* reported that the crowds were so dense in Worcester to see off their volunteers that the "Yeomanry could only be distinguished by their khaki-coloured helmets."[35] Lt. H. L. Birkin of the Twelfth (South Notts) Imperial Yeomanry was amazed by the size of the Nottingham crowd that accompanied his men to the station as they entrained for Liverpool. It was "a wonderful sight," he wrote, as the band played and the people sang "Auld Lang Syne."[36]

One Chester newspaper described the sendoff of the Twenty-first (Cheshire) and Twenty-second (Cheshire) Companies Imperial Yeomanry: "People were here, there and everywhere—some clinging to the train, others standing on boxes, trucks and even on the roof of an adjoining train. In fact, whichever way the eye turned there was a sea of faces. What a send off! There were thousands of men, women and children, all bent upon raising a parting cheer . . . As the warning whistle sounded . . . hats and handkerchiefs in their thousands were waved frantically and the parting cheers echoed against the roof. Thus departed the Cheshire Yeomanry to fight for Queen and country."[37]

When one of its hometown battalions departed, *The Manchester Guardian,* which had been critical of the government's policies and opposed the war, could not help but get caught up in the enthusiasm: "The hitherto restrained enthusiasm of the people then found vent, and there was a great sound of cheers. Chester Road . . . was filled with men and women, and the soldiers . . . began to struggle through a crowd which as they passed slowly along came together more closely and became more earnest in the heartiness of their farewells. By the time the station was reached one saw nothing but moving masses of men, through which, guided by a strong body of police, the soldiers in single file made a straggling way."[38]

The sendoff that attracted the largest crowds and received the most press coverage was that of the City of London Imperial Volunteers. For days the men paraded from one event to the next, and the national and metropolitan press covered the story in full. On the day of the departure of the first troops, 13 January 1900, hundreds of thousands of men and women lined the route from Bunhill-row to Nine Elms. Although other departures followed, none witnessed scenes like the one the *Times* reported: "On no occasion in recent years, except the Jubilee, have such immense crowds been seen in the streets. Certainly, only at the Jubilee has there been so extraordinary an outburst of popular feeling, so varied a display of patriotism, loyalty, and affection, as was evoked by the march through the metropolis of these gallant young fellows who have voluntarily left their avocations in civil life to endure hardships and perils and face death in defence of the Empire."[39]

Even most antiwar newspapers carried the event in a proud and sympathetic manner, though *The Leeds Mercury* managed to paint a darker portrait of the sendoff:

> Perhaps never in the long history of the City of London has the martial spirit of its citizens had more to feed upon than during the past week, culminating, as it did on Saturday, in scenes of excitement which have probably never been paralleled in this or any other country. For some of the Imperial Volunteers, the . . . memory of those scenes will long remain as a not too pleasant experience, for although nothing but joy and admiration appeared to move their fellow citizens, the very violence of the mob's caresses was fraught with immense discomfort, and even danger. Almost from the very start the intended military procession was burst in upon by the surging crowds, choking up every yard of the three miles of route, and defying the efforts of the police, the Imperial Volunteers, and hundreds of their comrades from various metropolitan regiments, who struggled through the crowd and tried to force a passage for their departing friends, and to preserve some semblance of order. . . . The police seemed helpless in the hands of the mob.[40]

At last came the moment in which the reality of the situation was driven home: the final farewell to kith and kin. It was not reading about Black Week, signing the attestation form, or drilling a few miles from home that brought the first genuine assessment of the future; this came as the images on the shoreline slowly receded and the silence of the open water began to overtake the distant shouts of their countrymen. The men were now left to their own thoughts and to privately assess the decisions they made. Off Southampton, Trooper Frank Charge and sixteen hundred imperial yeomen aboard the SS *Canada* "left sight of the Needles in the beautiful moonlight. The next lights we saw were the lights of Bournemouth. After that we commenced to steer south west and gradually lost sight of the shores of England."[41] Some regarded the sea voyage "as the most gruesome episode of their lives."[42] But it was not just the heat, seasickness, and drill that made it so. It was the coming to terms with the idea that they might never return home.

The silence of the voyage would not last long. There was much work to be done, and work, at least in the short term, could boost morale and help a man shake off any regrets. One of the first tasks was to prepare sleeping accommodations. But as with tents, drill instructors had neglected to teach the men how to set up their hammocks. "A hammock is a very simple looking arrangement when it is securely fixed," one imperial yeoman wrote, "but to pick it up in a tangle from the floor and sling it in its proper position is, to a tyro, as exasperating as a Chinese puzzle. . . . Loud was the laughter, and many were the execrations before those 450 hammocks with their occupants were finally swinging in space, and even then an occasional bump and a loud 'D—' would proclaim that at least some of them had not been securely fastened."[43]

Other men were simply troubled by the accommodations to which they were confined. Lionel Curtis, who later served as Alfred Milner's private secretary in South Africa and became an influential member of the Round Table, volunteered as a cyclist and was attached to the CIV. Onboard the *Ariosto,* he wrote to his mother, "I never realized before how many men could be got into so small a space."[44] Frank Charge concurred: "The living is vile and the accommodation fearful. We are packed in a low place below decks like sardines, in fact, at night the hammocks cannot sway, we are packed so tight and the heat is terrific. There are a lot of fellows who would never have come if they had thought we were going to be treated so badly."[45] Claustrophobia was a serious concern.[46]

Many of the men had never before been aboard a ship, and the rough passage in early 1900 left many disarrayed and feeling lousy. The discomfort of seasickness affected nearly everyone, typically during the first few days of the three-to-four-week voyage before open waters were reached. Almost all of the accounts mention this.[47] Lionel Curtis estimated that 80 percent of the men aboard the *Ariosto* got ill, one so violently that he had to be put in chains.[48] William Home put it best when he wrote, "Somebody has said that during the first hour of sea-sickness a man fears that he is going to die, but during the weary hours which follow his only fear is that he is going to live; I think most of us after our experience that morning can vouch for the truth of this statement."[49] As John Paterson bluntly wrote, many a man "had to feed the sharks."[50] William Grant of the Seventeenth (Ayrshire) Company Imperial Yeomanry unhappily entered into his diary on 3 February 1901 that some of his shipboard mates did not successfully make it to the rails, and he was stuck swabbing the deck of the *Tagus*.[51] The rough seas were particularly hard on the SS *Cavour*, which transported a number of horses as well as men. "*Damnable* is only a *mild* word for it," Lt. W. S. Power, Eighth (Derbyshire) Company Imperial Yeomanry, wrote to his cousin. "After all the bad weather we have had, it's now worse than ever & here we are 'lying to' God knows where. It's been something awful, and if we hadn't stopped we shouldn't have had a live horse on board. They were being knocked about like peas in boiling water."[52]

Once the seas quieted down and the men acclimated to their new environment, the work began in earnest. As was the case on land, few chose to write about their daily duties at sea. Most made only passing references to drill, parade, lectures, and guard duty. For target practice, wooden crates were thrown overboard. Kit inspection was a "never ending harassment to the men."[53] Evidence indicates that shipboard responsibilities varied considerably, though they were greater on ships transporting horses. The animals required a great deal of attention: three feedings a day, regular exercise and grooming, and daily treatment and "mucking out" of the stables. Aboard the transport ship, some like Capt. R. S. Britten, Thirty-seventh (Buckinghamshire) Company Imperial Yeomanry, began to regret their decision to volunteer. "Fighting for one's country sounds fine until you start on the job," he recorded in his diary.[54]

For most, however, it was aboard ship that a real sense of camaraderie began to develop, and nothing was more important to primary-group cohesion than the time spent together in leisure away from drill and duty. Entertainment and sport were vital elements of the soldier's experience of war. These activities shaped his outlook on events and how he remembered the war. They sustained morale by keeping him content and his thoughts occupied. And they helped develop esprit de corps. Officers were well aware of these benefits of organized entertainment and sport and used this time in transit wisely.

Most volunteers preferred to write about shipboard entertainment rather than work. No doubt they thought their families, friends, and others would prefer to read about it as well. There were a variety of organized events available to them. Many of the sporting competitions pitted the men of one company against another. There were potato races, boxing matches, mounted wrestling, and tug-of-war and obstacle-course competitions.[55] In a letter to his uncle, Julius Bernstein, a surgeon who volunteered in late 1900, described a form of shipboard cricket in which the ball was tied to a lump of string to allow for its easy retrieval.[56] William Home recalled "tilting the bucket," a game in which one man, carrying a lance while atop a second man, attempted to knock over a full bucket of water. If the lancer missed, water was poured over both men's heads as they charged under it.[57]

Unlike the games, church services, smokers, concerts, and other regularly scheduled events—all relatively ordinary activities—"crossing the line" was a truly unique event. For centuries, veteran British sailors crossing the equator have subjected first-timers to an initiation ritual. During the South African War, volunteers, both officers and men, were forced to submit as well. Thomas Wetton left behind one of the better detailed accounts of volunteers "crossing the line."[58] Wetton first went to South Africa as a stretcher bearer with the Royal Army Medical Corps in 1900. When the third contingent of Imperial Yeomanry was raised two years later, he signed up with the 151st Company. Because of the poor performance of the second contingent, these men had to endure nearly five months of training at Aldershot before they embarked for the war. As a result, by the time Wetton and his battalion arrived in Natal, the war was over. In Wetton's *Reminiscences of the 34th Battalion Imperial Yeomanry*, he describes the ceremony aboard the *Assaye*.[59] After a fanfare of bugles, the men who had never made the crossing were "arrested" and dragged onto the deck. They were then cast at the feat of the ship's crew, who were dressed as King Neptune and his court. The men were forced to swallow cold soup, doused in flour, then a mixture of paste and tar was applied to their faces with brooms. Next they were ceremoniously shaved with wooden razors and dropped onto a canvas bath, where they were "ducked" and "hosepiped." Wetton's telling, which is similar to other accounts, suggests that the volunteers enjoyed the experience and were glad for the diversion.

Apart from organized entertainment, the men found a number of ways to keep themselves busy and to make the voyage seem a bit shorter. These included letter and diary writing, reading, and playing chess and quoits. H. R. Lister wrote home that the crew of the SS *Briton* had "rigged up a sail bath for us on the poop and I have been enjoying the sea water every morning."[60] Music and songs inevitably filled the evening air. One could hear bagpipes, flutes, bugles, and drums playing. On some transport ships, like the SS *Guelph,* there were pianos, and where there were not, the men improvised and played makeshift instruments such as covered combs and empty tin cans.[61] Aboard the *Manchester Merchant,* Charles Dixon Kimber, a lieutenant in the Forty-eighth (North Somerset) Company Imperial Yeomanry, organized a choir.[62] And on the *Ariosto,* J. Barclay Lloyd, Lionel Curtis, and other CIV troopers sang almost nightly, including one of Barclay Lloyd's favorite verses:

> Sons of the Empire marching on to war
> With our brave Colonials going on before
> CIV will conquer and break 'old Koojer's' [*sic*] jaw.[63]

Many others enjoyed playing cards while relaxing and listening to music. The men aboard the *Cymric* set up a daily sweepstakes on the run of the ship, a point of pride for J. P. Sturrock: "Thomas Atkins dearly loves a gamble, and the men of the I.Y. were no exception to this rule."[64] According to Lt. C. S. Awdry, First (Wiltshire) Company Imperial Yeomanry, there was also cockfighting aboard the *Cymric.*[65] Drinking and smoking were other ways to pass the time. Sturrock reported that three thousand bottles of beer were consumed daily aboard the *Cymric.*[66]

Food provided another welcome diversion. There were the standard rations that few wrote home about: porridge, meat hash, or salt ling, with bread, butter, and tea at breakfast; soup, meat, potatoes, apples, and oranges at dinner; and tea, bread, butter, and jam at tea.[67] But there were also treats. Along with field glasses and Bibles, individuals and local groups had donated food items such as cakes and chocolates. And then there was the food picked up along the way. William Grant wrote in his diary that he and the men aboard the *Tagus* were served red herring and curried rice for breakfast just after crossing the equator.[68]

Although the extended sea voyage, with its unchanging scenery could be monotonous, there were moments of excitement when the sea came alive. William Grant was awed by the sight of schools of sharks and flying fish.[69] From aboard the SS *Canada,* Frank Charge wrote to his father: "A school of porpoises were about and it was amusing to see them jump out of the sea just like steeple chasing and the pace they went at was about 17 miles an hour. Also we saw hawks wheeling around the ship all day. At night it was grand, the phosphorus in the sea, which commences about here, and which we see right through the tropics, was a brilliant sight, the sea being lit up with starry lights all round the ship, especially at the cut-water where it was nothing but a blaze of light."[70]

Transport ships bound for South Africa stopped for supplies at one of four islands: Madeira, St. Vincent (São Vicente), Grand Canary Island, and Tenerife. Except for the unlucky ones who stopped at St. Vincent, "a most wretched place," this brief respite from the journey was something to write home about.[71] For many volunteers, this was the first time they laid eyes on foreign soil.[72] Tenerife was described in splendor by many awestruck observers. As Stanley Pitt wrote to his mother, "I should not think there is such a pretty place in the world."[73] In a letter to his mother, H. R. Lister wrote, "I shall never forget seeing the sun rise that morning and its effect on the snow on the Peak."[74] And Lt. Bernard Moeller wrote in his diary: "At 6 o'clock . . . I saw one of the most beautiful spectacles I have ever witnessed in all my life. Fifteen miles away, on the port side, rose a magnificent mountain, 15,000 feet high, out of the water; the top was a rosy pink with the reflection of the rising sun; the sea beneath was deep blues. This was Teneriffe [*sic*]. I sat down and thought to myself what a beautiful world it all is!"[75]

From aboard the SS *Carthaginian,* John Paterson wrote of Grand Canary Island:

> This is the prettiest place I have yet seen. In the distance it just looked like the Isle of Arran on a large scale, but when we approached it we saw the difference. The islands look rather barren, the soil is a reddish brown with almost an entire absence of grass on it, but the trees are lovely. Every suitable patch seems to be cultivated and planted with date palms, oranges, bananas and other fruit trees. It seems to be a place of small holdings for all the hillsides are dotted all over with little gay coloured houses with flat roofs. The

> town itself [Las Palmas] looks beautiful from the sea. There is a fine bay and the town is filled all round it and rises in terraces on the hillsides. The houses are all painted in bright colours, and the gardens planted with trees, with deep glossy green foliage. The sky is a deep blue, and the bright sunshine on the sparkling waters of the bay, with the growing mountains for a background makes a picture once seen will not readily be forgotten.[76]

While going ashore was typically reserved for the officers, there was plenty to watch from the deck as "small fleet[s] of rowing boats laden with fruit . . . and cigars" swarmed the arriving ships.[77] Young, "nearly naked boys" dove for pennies and sold oranges and bananas at prices the men could not resist.[78] "I never tasted such good stuff before," wrote John Paterson to his brother.[79] Those men who were lucky enough to go ashore could explore the town, buy liquor, and obtain information on the course of the war or discover who was playing in the English Cup final. At Las Palmas an Oxfordshire yeoman obtained a monkey and gave it as a mascot to a Volunteer artillery battery attached to the CIV. The monkey managed to survive the war and was later donated to a zoo in London.[80]

If the brief stop at an island paradise was the high point of the journey to South Africa, the low point was the first casualty. Many units lost a man or two during these three short weeks, usually due to pneumonia, heart disease, or unidentified fevers. A few men drowned, and there was at least one reported stabbing.[81] Of course, many of the ships carried horses, and on these vessels, death was much more common. The large number of horse fatalities made some question the wisdom of the military authority. Loss of life was a harbinger of things to come, but it also strengthened the bonds of camaraderie among the survivors.

During the late 1890s, Dr. Almroth Wright, professor of pathology at the Army Medical School in Netley, developed an anti-typhoid immunization. Its first large-scale use was on soldiers bound for South Africa.[82] The inoculation was voluntary, and the doctors themselves did not wholeheartedly endorse it. "At present it is impossible to say what is the real value of this procedure," reported Maj. Charles Stonham, the commanding officer and chief surgeon of the Imperial Yeomanry Field Hospital.[83] When the principle medical officer aboard the *Canada* recommended against it, few men chose to be inoculated.[84] In February 1900 there was not enough vaccine to go around for all seven Volunteer Service Companies aboard the *Greek*. Those who missed out were promised the vaccine when they landed at Cape Town, but as it turned out, the men were ordered out of town before the vaccine arrived.[85] Frederick Barnado was a medical student when the war began. Attracted by the "call to adventure," he joined the Twentieth (Fife and Forfar) Company Imperial Yeomanry after Black Week. Aboard the *Cymric*, he assisted the medical officer in inoculating his company. Ironically, he forgot to inoculate himself and was later sent home with enteric (typhoid) fever.[86]

The inoculation, or "pig-sticking drill," was a painful experience: "Everyone survived but barely."[87] The vaccine was injected just below the belt, and cocaine was used to dull the pain.[88] Afterward the men were ordered to walk on the deck for an hour and then lie down and wait. Two or three hours later, high temperature, shivering, headache, and general fatigue usually set in. When Tom Fowler, First (Wiltshire) Company Imperial Yeomanry, managed to make it to breakfast the next morning, he surprised the doctor.[89] Most men needed several days to recuperate.

Even with the diversions, shipboard life was monotonous. Yet it was a very informative and important experience for the men. They got to spend time with one another out of the spotlight of the local media and away from their homes and families. They also got to laugh, drink, and even mourn for lost comrades with the officers who would soon lead them into battle. By the time they landed, accents, age, and social standing did not have the same meaning they once had. The men had come together and formed bonds that would prove vital on the battlefield and would sustain many throughout the long conflict.

As the volunteers approached their destination, the traffic in the shipping lanes increased.[90] News was passed from one ship to the next: some learned of Kimberley's relief, some of Gen. Piet Cronjé's surrender at Paardeberg, and some of a friend's death. The activity in Cape Town harbor and the chaos of the dock often meant a delay in disembarking of a day or more. The volunteers bound for Port Elizabeth and Durban could only watch the activities of others and ponder what was awaiting them.

Although the process of turning these civilians into soldiers had begun, it was not yet fully realized. The men had donned their uniforms, drilled and paraded, said farewell to their loved ones, and experienced camaraderie, hardship, and even loss in transit. But they had yet to face the enemy. For those debarking in Cape Town, that last look at the gangplank, before they touched land and joined the milling soldiers and African laborers, was an experience few would forget. All sorts of feelings raced through them. It was a moment of uncertainty and anxiety but also of pride and sense of purpose. As one volunteer put it, "I never felt better in my life than now but I should like a drink of ale—I would give a good bit for a pint."[91] The volunteers had arrived in South Africa.

5

The Experience of War

> The army whose movements the whole civilised world was watching, the army which represented Britain's might on land, which every true Briton trusted and prayed for, and before whose irresistible advance our foes were fleeing like chaff before the wind; men, weary and foot-sore, saw it, and in their pride and joy forgot their sufferings; when a man has lived to see a sight like that he has not lived in vain.
>
> William Home, observing Roberts's force outside of Kroonstadt, Orange Free State, March 1900.[1]

> It is a glorious experience, and if we only come through all right we shall one and all feel proud indeed that we have done our bit towards maintaining the integrity of our glorious empire.
>
> Lt. Meynell Hunt, Fifth (Warwickshire) Company Imperial Yeomanry, near Britstown, 16 March 1900.[2]

Just as large numbers of volunteers began arriving in the Cape Colony and Natal in early 1900, the conventional phase of the South African War was drawing to its close.[3] From February to May,

Lord Roberts's drive through the two Boer republics, the Orange Free State and the Transvaal, proved unstoppable. Bloemfontein fell in mid-March; Johannesburg, the last day of May. Boer morale was deeply affected by these losses. Many chose not to fight anymore. Six thousand Free Staters voluntarily handed in their weapons, and eight thousand Transvaalers did the same—in all, a quarter of the active Boer force.[4] For those who remained on commando, some tough decisions had to be made. What, if anything, could be done to stop the British? A new strategy had to be developed for dealing with Britain's growing and substantial advantage in numbers. In the end the Boers chose to abandon the strategy that had served them admirably through 1899, shifting away from maneuvering the British into fighting set-piece battles and toward engaging them in a protracted guerilla struggle. Although it took several months, the British reluctantly adjusted their military policy as well and embraced the tactics of counterinsurgency.

Thus by mid-1900, the nature of the South African War had changed dramatically. By the time most volunteers reached enemy territory, the war as they understood it and defined it was over. Much to their surprise and dismay, few of them ever faced the enemy on a conventional battlefield. Instead, they met them while guarding the lines of communication, manning isolated blockhouses, and accompanying convoys lumbering across the open veld. Although skirmishes with the rear guard of a Boer commando were common, British volunteers could go days and even weeks without ever hearing the sound of gunfire.

The South African War, of course, did not end with the fall of Bloemfontein and Pretoria, and over the next two years it became the largest overseas expedition in nineteenth-century British history, eclipsing the Napoleonic, Crimean, and Egyptian campaigns.[5] Few of the men who volunteered in the wake of Black Week could have anticipated that the war would have taken on an entirely different character. Indeed, despite the aggressive news coverage, even the volunteers of 1901 and 1902 envisioned war in the traditional sense, not as a protracted struggle against insurgents. They did not fully understand what awaited them in South Africa. As the enemy became harder to identity and the duties and responsibilities of these citizen-soldiers changed, their attitudes toward the war changed as well. The men had a difficult time making sense of their role and struggled to find meaning and purpose in it. Many began to question their original motives for volunteering. Increasingly, they grew tired, confused, and disillusioned. As despair set in, they longed for home. Although the realities of any war consistently defy the imaginations of inexperienced recruits, it was the underutilization of these men and the lack of clear purpose and direction in the war that promoted this rapid decline in morale.

While still at home in Great Britain, the new Imperial Yeomanry and Volunteer recruits, as well as the militiamen, had many distractions, and despite daily news reports, the war seemed distant. With the exception of a few newspapers like the *Manchester Guardian,* the press presented a unified front in its support for government policy during the winter of 1899–1900. And when it came to support for the volunteer effort, even opposition papers jumped on the bandwagon. Coverage of the local troop, from mobilization to disembarkment, saturated the pages of all London and regional newspapers, nearly always with the volunteers presented in the most positive light. Challenges were sometime made to administrative decisions, but no one ever doubted the hearts and minds of the men and what they were capable of achieving in uniform. If any of the recruits questioned the wisdom of volunteering for overseas service, they did not have to look far for affirmation. The press, the government, and their communities voiced their support vociferously.

The new servicemen were also distracted by their responsibilities. Drill, inspection, parade, and the like kept them busy, and since most units were raised locally, contact with family and friends was constant. Although some questioned the efficacy of individual training exercises, no one doubted that the process they were undertaking was necessary. Waiting one to two months, and sometimes even longer, could try one's patience, but the men could count on receiving satisfaction for their sacrifice once they arrived in South Africa.

But as they left the relative comfort of the regimental barracks, bid farewell to their loved ones, and headed to sea, anxiety grew, and so did their impatience. The sea voyage was a long one; it was hot, rough (particularly in the English Channel and off the coast of northern France), and rather dull. For several hours in a day, the restless volunteers might be left to their own devices. Cards, music, sport, and games could absorb some of that time, but boredom was inevitable. And boredom has deleterious effects on morale, leading men to question their actions and their purpose. Many began to gripe and complain.

Despite the reality of what lay close beyond, Table Mountain was thus a welcome sight to the volunteers. The familiar vista reinforced the righteousness of their decisions to enlist. Its physical beauty and majesty reminded many of mountains back home, places they loved and would fight to protect. The image reinforced the idea that they were fighting not to protect some vague notion of empire, but Britain itself. The busy harbor swarming with steamers, its docks dancing with movement, made a different impression—it awakened the sea-weary travelers. The stillness and quiet of the open ocean to which they had become accustomed those several weeks in transit was abruptly shattered: one adventure was coming to an end, and another was beginning.

Although a few volunteers wrote home to comment on Cape Town's architecture or the strange-looking seagulls unknown even to veteran British birdwatchers, the most memorable sight was that of the harried stevedores and porters unloading the cargoes of incoming ships. British travelers were often quick to pass judgment on the African laborers. "I never saw such wretched stevedores as the Kaffirs, or rather the Cape Boys," H .R. Lister, CIV, wrote in his diary. "They will stand chattering and slanging [*sic*] each other for ten minutes before they attempt unloading the crane basket."[6] Sgt. Harry Hopwood, Second Manchester Regiment Volunteer Service Company, only stopped in Cape Town long enough to board another transport ship bound for Durban, but in that short time his enthusiasm to risk his life in the defense of the empire was dampened by the sights and sounds of "begging Kaffirs."[7] And, as Thomas Wetton found out, similarly unsettling scenes awaited those men headed for Natal.[8]

But not all volunteers were put off by their first sight of black South Africans. Some were excited by this entirely different world. Frank Stephenson, Tenth (Sherwood Rangers) Company Imperial Yeomanry, watched from the deck of the *Dunottar Castle* in a state of wonderment. "About 50 or 60 Blacks came down to the docks this morning and amused us for an hour or two. I never saw such queer chaps in my life," he wrote.[9] Frank Charge, Sixteenth (Worcestershire) Company Imperial Yeomanry, could barely contain himself and desperately wanted to debark in order to get a closer look at the workers: "The Cape boys as they call the natives are the merriest fellows and hardest workers I ever saw. The amount of work they do is incredible but a great deal to with it is they never walk, all their work is done running and they can go the pace. There are a lot of Zulus running rickshaws in Cape Town now, they were almost obsolete here before the war, but since then they have come down from interior and there is no end down here now. They get themselves up in a most fantastic garb, wearing buffalo horns and ostrich feathers as a head-dress and a many coloured smock and breeches covering their body."[10]

Charge and the other volunteers got their wish, though sometimes it took a few days before the authorities had cleared enough room or, in at least one case, the seas had calmed down.[11] An outbreak of bubonic plague in 1901 delayed some transports for substantial periods of time and diverted others to East London.[12] After their long sea voyage, the men were finally able to touch solid ground again and walk through the busy streets of Cape Town. Loyal colonists and British soldiers and sailors were enthusiastic about the volunteers' arrival. One battalion of Imperial Yeomanry, the Fifth, was lucky enough to arrive during the spontaneous celebrations that erupted when the 118-day siege of Ladysmith was lifted on 28 February 1900. Much of the city's attention focused on these volunteers and saluted their anticipated contribution.

Except for those continuing on their shipboard journey to points farther east, the Volunteer camp at Green Point or the Imperial Yeomanry camp at Maitland was likely the first inland destination for drill and acclimatization. The march was short, just a few miles from Cape Town, but the logistical problems of moving thousands of men, horses, and supplies from the many ships in the harbor through the busy streets of the already overcrowded city were considerable. Most of the men, excited to disembark, were not troubled by the delays or the confusion in town.

The march to camp, however, was a sobering experience. The excitement of the harbor and the city was quickly replaced by the dullness of the road and the rigid order imposed by officers. Neither Green Point nor Maitland resembled anything that these men had seen before, even those who had some previous military experience, but they were hardly interesting places. While the scale of these camps was extraordinary, the conditions were not: they were abysmal.

The ground at Maitland Camp was "solid rock" in which tent pegs would not hold. That many of the men had not learned how to pitch a tent back in Britain made things even more difficult. Darkness and wind then contributed to the chaos. Once a tent was finally put up, thirteen men had to crowd into it and beat out the rats and snakes infesting the camp. All in all, it was "a pretty good squash."[13]

Once settled, the men got right to work. Many found themselves on sentry duty the very first night and realized that they were now at war and "not at an annual Volunteer camp."[14] The stay at camp was brief—four to ten days—but it significantly shaped volunteer attitudes.[15] The difficulty in pitching tents was symptomatic of a larger problem: the makeshift nature of the auxiliary forces. The camps were strapped for resources, poorly situated, and endured grave shortages of officers and manpower for maintenance. One yeoman recalled: "Maitland was principally noted for its sand-storms, which blew almost incessantly; its flies, which abounded in myriads and settled on everything, and its malodorous smells, which permeated all parts of the camp. As a result of these, dysentery and diarrhea were very prevalent, and broke out immediately amongst the Rough Riders."[16] He was right in this assessment. Disorganization led to sanitation problems and to the proliferation of rats and flies. The camps became breeding grounds for disease. Water was unfit for drinking, many had trouble finding food, and staying clean was next to impossible. Nearly everyone complained about the sand, dirt, and dust that pervaded everything. There was "sand in the soup and sand in the sugar."[17] "You ate it, drank it, and slept in it," Sidney Peel, Fortieth (Oxfordshire) Company Imperial Yeomanry, wrote.[18] Charles Dixon Kimber, Forty-seventh (Duke of Cambridge's Own) Company Imperial Yeomanry, concurred in a letter home. "Everything seems dirty."[19]

This same disorganization led to chaos, which hampered the allocation of resources and the transmission of orders. Although men were kept busy most of the time with drill and fatigues, there was still an abundance of down time, and many felt that they were just sitting around waiting for their officers to figure out what to do with them. Peel remembered with amusement "the immense number of yeomanry sentries who met you at every turn."[20] Certainly, an opportunity for further training was wasted. In particular, this would have been a valuable time to hone the green Imperial Yeomanry and the Volunteer mounted infantry's skills in horsemanship, two shortcomings that plagued British forces throughout the war.

The camps witnessed signs of what lay in store. The stampede of horses, knocking over men, tents, and equipment, was a nightly event.[21] Troopers continued to have a hard time saddling and keeping their horses under control. When it was time to depart the camp, inevitably a comical scene was reenacted in each company as saddles slipped and men went tumbling onto the ground. After witnessing his company parade in full marching order at Maitland Camp, Lt. W. S. Power, Eighth (Derbyshire) Company Imperial Yeomanry, wrote to his cousin: "Oh! What a time, these men are the greenest most useless devils on earth; why did they come out? You have to do everything for them, and they won't remember, but what can you expect when they have never put a saddle on before."[22] But an even more troubling sign than the inexperience of riders was detected by the few who knew horses well. The volunteers, especially the Imperial Yeomanry, overloaded their mounts with unnecessary and heavy equipment. The horses, overburdened and overworked, did not last long on the veld, creating delays during the war while yeomen awaited remounts.[23]

Despite the chaotic, difficult, and sometimes dangerous conditions, many left the camps with their convictions still intact. Some were even enhanced: "You have no idea of the power and might of Britain, till you see a place and scene like this," an Ayrshire yeoman wrote to his brother.[24] In his story of the Scottish Border Volunteer Service Companies, William Home wrote that he was overwhelmed by the numbers of soldiers and animals coming into and going from camp everyday and the sheer "vastness of Britain's resources."[25] The volunteers believed that they were making a difference in South Africa. They were willing to endure what they hoped were temporary, albeit unnecessary, hardships and turmoil. They believed in their officers and government. They believed that they would do what they had signed up to do—fight the enemy.

Morale was high as the men headed upcountry. The City of London Imperial Volunteers, or CIV, sometimes referred to colloquially as "Chamberlain's Innocent Victims" or "Covered In Vermin,"[26] arrived early enough in 1900 to participate in the British action at Paardeberg.[27] Most of the Imperial Yeomanry and Volunteer Service Companies arrived later and joined the CIV and the Militia battalions in the Orange Free State for Lord Roberts's advance on Bloemfontein. Others were diverted to Natal for the relief of Ladysmith and operations in the east. A few headed to more remote theaters like Rhodesia and the northern Cape Colony. The contribution of the Volunteers in terms of manpower was critical to British strategy in early 1900 and would become more significant as the war dragged on into 1901 and 1902.

The details of Lord Roberts's supersession of Gen. Sir Redvers Buller and the changes in British strategy in early 1900 are well known.[28] Roberts assumed the war would end once the capitals of the Orange Free State and the Transvaal fell. Therefore, the bulk of British forces in South Africa, including the auxiliary troops, were assigned to his sweeping advance on Bloemfontein. Boer strategy under Gen. C. R. de Wet and others, however, was already moving toward guerilla warfare prior to the fall of Bloemfontein, though traditional methods of combat were not totally abandoned until late May.[29] Roberts was either unaware that changes had to be made or unwilling to make them. But even without his direction, British tactics in the field evolved. Thus, well before Roberts headed back to London at the end of 1900 and Lord Kitchener took command of the British forces in South Africa and adapted a more systematic approach to dealing with the insurgents, British soldiers were actively engaged in a guerilla war.

Although Kitchener's response, including farm burning, the establishment of concentration camps, and (as Henry Campbell-Bannerman termed) other "methods of barbarism," may have been new even to regular soldiers, fighting a mobile force supported by a hostile population on largely unknown terrain was not.[30] Set-piece battles may have been pursued on the hilly Northwest Frontier of India, on the desert sands of the Sudan, or in the dense forests of the Gold Coast, but they were not always achieved. Veteran regulars were well accustomed to fighting "small wars." In contrast, volunteers, and perhaps more importantly their officers, were not.

This new strategy eventually dictated how the volunteers would be used in the war and fundamentally shaped their attitudes toward it. But during the first six months of 1900, while this strategy was still evolving, the volunteers were filled with the excitement of their decision to serve and their new surroundings. And even while the war was changing, they clung to the traditional image of war. It was a type of struggle these citizen-soldiers could understand. It was far easier to accept the loss of a comrade who fell while charging a position en masse, for example, than one who was killed on patrol by a bullet from an unseen sniper.

The reaction to one element of the wartime experience, however, did not change even while strategy did—that of being fired upon for the first time. To the volunteers it did not matter if their "baptism of fire" occurred in a battle outside of Kimberley or in a skirmish in a remote section of the Transvaal, the experience was invigorating and always memorable. There are few volunteers who do not mention it in their letters and diaries. By the end of their tour of duty in South Africa, being fired at had become routine, but that first action, no matter how dangerous, produced a rush that few could ever forget. In the excitement of the moment, it was also one of the few times in which the men were uncritical of their officers.

Godfrey Smith, Second Scottish Rifles Volunteer Service Corps, had been in Natal for only fourteen days when he was fired upon outside of Elandslaagte. "Most of us, I daresay, felt a trifle afraid," he wrote in his memoir after the war, "but that we did not appear so I'm certain."[31] Similarly, William Home stressed the coolness of the men under fire: "There was an entire absence of excitement in the company."[32] At Allandale on 13 April 1901, William Grant and the Seventeenth (Ayrshire) Company Imperial Yeomanry encountered two hundred Boers in the process of attacking a British outpost. The Imperial Yeomanry were ordered to advance. The Boers redirected their fire at them. With his pride still intact, Grant wrote in his diary after the engagement, "My first impression of being under fire, was that there was a hole in my stomach and I very much required a good tuck in, and my first thoughts were to crouch down on my horse's back as closely as I could, but on second thoughts I resolved to sit as I was not to show the white feather."[33] Regardless of when or why they wrote about this experience, soldiers were quick to admit fear but just as quick to stress their ability to come to terms with danger and their ultimate resolve.

Edward Day-Lewis, Eighty-fifth (Rough Riders) Company Imperial Yeomanry, had been in South Africa for nearly two months before he first experienced enemy fire. Outside of Winburg he came across a house with some armed Boers inside. "I felt awful when the shots began coming over my head," he wrote to his parents. "We were in a donga at the time, but after a while I got used to it and began firing myself, but you could not get any aim as none of us saw a Boer; you could only blaze away at the house."[34] Day-Lewis and his fellow Rough Riders remained in the donga with their heads down as their armed African scouts rushed the house with their bayonets. The Boers surrendered.[35]

The inability to see the enemy was very frustrating for the volunteers. Firing at unseen targets, they had no idea if they were hitting or missing. Sgt. P. C. Jonas, Forty-third (Suffolk) Company Imperial Yeomanry, arrived with the Twelfth Battalion Imperial Yeomanry in Cape Town in late February 1900. For almost two months he had done little more than drill, march, and ride the rails between Cape Town, Prieska, and De Aar. In late March his battalion was ordered to Dewetsdorp in the Orange Free State. Guerillas attacked them en route. Although the Boers never presented themselves as targets, Jonas dismounted and fired in their direction. The experience was both invigorating and horrifying. The noise of war made a lasting impression on the sergeant. "A pom pom is an excellent weapon when you are using it but it is a horrid thing when the other chap has got it. I really don't think it has ever done much harm on either side out here but the moral effect is great. It is a splendid thing."[36]

And then there were others like J. Barclay Lloyd, a cyclist in the CIV, who hid both their fear and frustration. Barclay Lloyd compared his first experience under fire to a great sporting event, describing it as "better than seeing Aston Villa's left forward score the winning goal."[37] At the end of his first encounter with the enemy, the British "got 'em," and the CIV were "amateurs no longer."[38]

As the guerrilla conflict took hold, battle became an increasingly smaller part of the overall volunteer experience. Yet many appreciated combat as the most exciting and rewarding occurrence in their tour. It was such experiences that they continued to share with their families and friends back home. Some of the reason for this is that the men assumed the details of their daily routine would bore their readers. After all, they themselves found it monotonous, and encountering it secondhand could only be more so. Additionally, to rationalize the positive nature of their contribution and to continue to find meaning in their service, they had to define the struggle in terms of combat. The conditions of fighting a low-intensity conflict were unknown to them and to their readers. The paradigm of war could not readily shift.

Most volunteers arrived too late to experience set-piece battles. The CIV did not. Some of its mounted infantry participated at Paardeberg in late February 1900. Also, on Roberts's left flank in his drive through the Transvaal, the infantry fought the Boers at Doornkop and Diamond Hill in late May and mid-June 1900, respectively.

The three defeats of Black Week had halted the British offensive in South Africa in December 1899. The War Office's decision to replace Buller with Roberts and build up a sizeable force to break the sieges of Kimberley, Ladysmith, and Mafeking necessitated a lengthy delay before resuming the attack. Although the British were not inactive during this period, their operations were limited in scope. In mid-February 1900 Roberts felt the time had come to renew the offensive and bring the war to the Boers in earnest. He ordered Lt. Gen. John French and his cavalry division to make a sweeping flank move on Kimberley. The strategy succeeded. With the city's relief and the Boer retreat that followed, Roberts commenced a major drive into the Orange Free State, its objective being Bloemfontein. Meanwhile in Natal, Buller made another attempt to free Ladysmith.

On 17 February the British trapped about forty-five hundred Boers under Gen. Piet Cronjé on the banks of the Modder River at Paardeberg. Rather than attempt to break through the still fluid British position, Cronjé ordered his force to dig in.[39] Lord Kitchener, temporarily in charge of the British infantry while Roberts recovered from a bout of fever in Jacobsdal, recklessly attempted to force the Boers from their entrenched position with a frontal assault.[40] In the end Kitchener succeeded, but the cost in lives was very high.

Most of the volunteers involved in the action at Paardeberg did not come under fire. Bernard Moeller, for example, was busy escorting Boer prisoners; likewise, Edward Manisty escorted naval guns. H. R. Lister, First Section, Second Company CIV, Mounted Infantry, spent most of his time on outpost duty. Bored and jealous of his Regular Army comrades, he longed for action: "Revenge is sweet and what revenge would be sweeter than to capture 4000 Boers and all their equipment on Majuba Day. I never before felt the lust of battle till I was told yesterday that to day would be Majuba Day and felt then that I would have given anything to have been up in the firing line with a rifle and a bandolier full of cartridges, and the Boers for a mark. I have anyhow realized the extreme desire of all us Volunteers, to be under fire, and I had *plenty* of it."[41]

As Lister states, he and his comrades would not have to wait long to experience battle. As the CIV continued to press on through the Orange Free State and into the Transvaal, they encountered increasing pressure from the enemy. Letters and diaries are filled with recollections about the actions at Zand River on 10 May, Doornkop on 29 May, and Diamond Hill on 11–12 June, where the CIV saw some of its "most desperate fighting." Maj. Gen. Henry Mackinnon, who commanded the CIV, saw special significance in Doornkop. "This is an interesting day for the English Volunteer Force," he wrote, "as it is the first occasion on which so many of them have been in any important action."[42] In the frontal attack on the Boer position there, the CIV were placed in the front line, a great honor, but one that exposed them to immense peril. The volunteers "stormed the steepest kopjes of the Rand," wisely advancing in short rushes and in extended order, thus avoiding the fate of the Gordon Highlanders, who simultaneously charged up the hill "Balaclava" style.[43] Barclay Lloyd proudly wrote that the battle of Doornkop proved "that the Volunteer Force of England was pure fighting metal to the core, and no mere electroplated imitation of the real article, for use on field days and garden parties only."[44]

In April, May, and June, the Imperial Yeomanry, Volunteer Service Corps, and the Militia experienced fighting for the first time as well. Their reactions to and observations of battle were similar to those of the CIV. Likewise, they emphasized the significance of their contributions as volunteers. But because these men were not held in as high esteem as the CIV, they were not always utilized to their fullest potential. When there was fighting to be done in the area, it was often carried out by regulars while the volunteers were left to man outposts and guard camps and prisoners. Experiencing combat, therefore, was not a common occurrence.

Several Imperial Yeomanry companies participated in the action at Boshof in early April as part of Roberts's drive through the Orange Free State. Lord Methuen, commanding the First Division, had seized the western Free State town of Boshof in mid-March. For the next four weeks, his troops operated in the triangle between Boshof, Kimberley, and Barkly West. On 5 April Methuen learned that a small Boer commando, led by "the Lafayette of South Africa," Comte de Villebois-Marueil, had passed through Tweefontein, just five miles to the south of Boshof.[45] Methuen ordered his Imperial Yeomanry to cut them off.

In his account of the war, H. S. Gaskell recalls the excitement of the moment: "The three squadrons of Yeomanry immediately turned out, and then ensued the most appalling 'rush' I ever had the misfortune to be in. All the horses were out grazing, over a mile away, and we had to run out for them. I couldn't find mine, so I seized another whose I don't know. We galloped them back to camp with only the halters, hurled the saddles on, flung the accoutrements on ourselves, and dashed on to parade in record time."[46] Although it took thirty-five minutes, Methuen did eventually manage to get the Imperial Yeomanry settled down and in order. At Boshof these volunteers met with "conspicuous success" in their first fight. "Not only did the Yeomanry show fine courage under fire, but they did their work throughout in exactly the same fashion that should be followed in all operations similar to that in which they found themselves engaged," a *Times* reporter wrote.[47] After the battle was over, one volunteer jotted down in his diary, "There is no great sport in fighting but we enjoyed that immensely."[48]

A. S. Orr, Eighteenth (Queens' Own Royal Glasgow) Company Imperial Yeomanry, was eager to see some action immediately upon his arrival in South Africa. At first, ten days of drill at Maitland Camp did little to distract him, but then his company seemed to fall into an endless pattern of drill and fatigue. They waited for horses, they waited for trains, and occasionally they waited while a few Boer prisoners were escorted past them. The only battle Orr experienced in April, however, was a "sham fight" involving some of the Imperial Yeomanry companies. In early May the Eighteenth Company loaded onto a train. Orr had no idea where he was going but expected more of the same monotony. To his surprise he learned that his company was heading to Warrenton to join in the relief of Mafeking. "Our delight knew no bounds," he wrote. "It had been drummed into us, both before we left home and after, that—oh! We would never see anything—that the Yeomanry were to be kept on the lines of communication—so that we could hardly believe our ears."[49] Within days Orr saw combat. "Certainly the first few times we were under fire we were far too much roused, excited, and interested to have any reasonable sense of the danger we were running."[50] But, Orr assured his readers, his company quickly adjusted and acquired the necessary discipline to make sound judgments in battle.

Harry Hopwood landed in Durban in mid-March to take part in Buller's operations in Natal, and four months later he was still waiting to be sent to the front. He was kept busy aiding in musketry instruction for Militia and Volunteer units, doing outpost duty, and "shifting camps every other day." In late June he wrote home, "As far as I can make out none of the volunteers in Buller's force have seen any fighting yet, but they say that our company has done more work than any other volunteer company that has come out here."[51] Hopwood, however, did not come to South Africa to dig trenches. He desperately wanted to see fighting. His letters are filled with despairing references to rumors that, if true, would have meant a quick end to the war and his unfulfilled ambition. The rumors, of course, proved false, and in late July he got his wish.

On 28 July, a bitterly cold day, Hopwood's brigade came under enemy fire near Zandspruit. In the third firing line, he extended ten paces, advanced in a short rush, fell to the ground, waited a few moments, and then got up and rushed again at the enemy position. He never saw a single Boer and never fired a shot. His letters indicate that this encounter, and a few others that followed, afforded him, rather than fulfillment, a better understanding of the reality of battle: it was loud, confusing, and men died without warning. "All this time," he wrote, referring to the advance, "we could see the puffs of dust in the ground where the bullets were hitting and hear the whiz, ping and pat all round, but for my life I could not see a single Boer and could not see whether they came from the right or left front."[52]

After his second encounter a week later, he wrote about the devastating effect the Boer 37-mm Maxim-Nordenfeldt, a belt-fed machine gun, had on British morale. "These pompoms are horrible things and although small they frighten you more than the big shells although perhaps this was because they fell closer than the others to us." Hopwood "expected that any moment might be [his] last."[53] By the end of August, he had had more than his fill of battle. In describing an encounter at Dalmanutha on the thirty-first, he wrote, "The bullets simply rained past and for about ten minutes after I got there I durst not raise my head." After finding cover behind a fourteen-inch ant heap, Hopwood fired his rifle, but "every time you fired one shot 15 or 20 fell round about you so you had to look handy and get your head down as quickly as possible after each shot." He commented sadly that even though the enemy was never seen, "people die nevertheless."[54]

Although the South African War posed great challenges to the British volunteers, and indeed great tragedies, battle was something the men could understand. Few had experienced it before, and no doubt many had glamorized it, but it was the activity for which they were prepared, mentally and physically. To them battle had purpose and meaning. There was a winner and a loser. They might not have been privy to the reasons behind the engagement or how it fit into the overall war, they may not have even expected a battle when it occurred, but they could understand the event, see their part in it, and feel that they were making a difference. Even when they had no visible target to fire at, their performance—how they behaved under fire, whether or not anyone ran—were actions they could judge and find meaning in. And importantly, they could share these experiences with their families and friends at home to justify their decision to serve.

War to these men meant battle, not sitting around waiting for a train, a remount, or a convoy; escorting prisoners; guarding a supply line; or digging a trench. Battle was the payoff for all the monotony, the drills, and the harsh conditions. As the war progressed and battles were fewer and further between, the volunteer lost sight of the connection between his actions and winning the war. Unfortunately for the morale of the men, officers did not often share with them knowledge about the war's changing conditions or help redefine their roles within it. Left to their own imaginations and rarely distracted from the monotony of life on the veld, the volunteers soon forgot about those early days in December 1899 and the reasons they had traveled to South Africa in the first place.

H.R.H. Prince of Wales shaking hands with officers of the Imperial Yeomanry before their departure to the front, 1900 (H. M. Paget)

"The City of London Imperial Volunteers for the Front: Passing the Mansion House, London" (*The Graphic*)

Officers of the City of London Imperial Volunteers standing before a ship's rail

Derbyshire Volunteers on the *Avondale Castle* en route to the Cape (Hudson & Kearns)

"The City of London Imperial Volunteers at Cape Town: Leaving for the Front" (*The Graphic*)

The Forty-eighth (North Somerset) Company Imperial Yeomanry

Officers of the Third Militia Battalion, King's Own Scottish Borderers

Field Marshal Lord Frederick Roberts, commander in chief of British forces in South Africa, 1900

Lord H. H. Kitchener, commander in chief of British forces in South Africa, 1901–1902

Lt. Gen. Lord Paul S. Methuen, commanding officer, First Division

Lord Chesham, Imperial Yeomanry

Maj. Gen. W. H. Mackinnon, commander of the City of London Imperial Volunteers

"The City of London Imperial Volunteers at Jacobsdal, February 1900" (Seppings-Wright)

"The Sixty-second (Middlesex) Company Imperial Yeomanry: Their First Fight, Twenty Miles from Kroonstad" (*The Graphic*)

<u>*NEW SONG*</u> <u>*JUST PUBLISHED*</u>

"The British Volunteer."

(READY WHEN HE'S WANTED.)

You thought we played at soldiers when we met upon parade,
You watched us shoot at Bisley with a sneer,
But the moment you are asking for a soldier ready-made
You find him in the British Volunteer.
It's easy to be fit and smart when fighting is your trade,
But we must do our drilling when we can;
In the busy rough and tumble the living must be made,
And that's the school that makkes the fighting man.

CHORUS:—

A something in the city—a shopman or a clerk,
A fellow with a pen behind his ear,
A journalist, a lawyer, or an idler in the Park,
Is the ready-when-he's-wanted Volunteer.

Our uniforms of grey and green you thought a sort of fad,
And Tommy dressed in scarlet made us small;
But now the British red-coat is a fellow khaki clad,
The grey-coat's not so dusty after all.
To-day you see us fighting with the Tommies side by side
In Freedom's cause and all we hold most dear;
We've shown you you can trust us, and we'll fill your hearts with pride,
And quit us like a British Volunteer.

CHORUS:—

A Something in the City—a shopman or a clerk, etc.

In spite of service red tape, the snubbings, and the sneers,
We're sharing in the work that's just begun;
It's the chance we'pve always wanted, we wanted it for years,
And now we've got the job until its done.
But what about the living now? If we should give our lives,
We'll ask the pals who b lessed us with a cheer,
Will you give a little something for the children and the wives,
And kindly help a British Volunteer?

CHORUS:—

A something in the city—a shopman or a clerk, etc.

WORDS BY
HAROLD HARDY.

MUSIC BY
STEPHEN RICHARDSON.

Published by WEEKES & CO., 14, Hanover Street, W.

"The British Volunteer," by Harold Hardy and Stephen Richardson

6

The Transition to Guerrilla War

Reveille 2.40 A.M. Marched 3.50. Halted 9 A.M. Trekked again 2 P.M. Nothing happened, just the usual plod on, and my feet are sore.

Pvt. Q.L., Sixteenth (Worcestershire) Company Imperial Yeomanry, near Frederickstad, 18 August 1900[1]

I was out foraging on Tuesday, I came to a house where there was a fine flock of geese, also at the house, a fine flock of daughters. I was after the geese!! But one fine pretty lassie persuaded me to have bread, milk and butter, so I went inside and had a talk with them. Quite a nice girl, I suggested that she marry me, and come with me to "my castle" in England; she seemed quite willing. The end of it was, I had to go somewhere else for my geese, for how could I rob defenseless women and children!!

Lt. W. S. Power, Eighth (Derbyshire) Company Imperial Yeomanry, between Senekal and Winburg, 6 June 1900.[2]

When we had the Roll Call, that seemed to have a sadness with it, when the questions are asked if anybody knows anything about so and so.

Cpl. Charles Stride, Second Dorsetshire Regiment Volunteer Service Company, Harmonds Nek, 12 June 1900.[3]

WANTED Immediately.—Several hundred able-bodied men to occupy trenches at salubrious farm. Must have some knowledge of firearms. Trenches have all the latest improvements, and there are also several alternate lines of defence, and seven Last Stands.

Cossack Post, 20 March 1901.[4]

With the fall of Bloemfontein and Johannesburg in May 1900, Lord Roberts felt confident that the war's end was in sight. The British army controlled the major population and industrial centers of the Boer republics, the disparity between British and Boer forces and equipment was growing, and significant numbers of burghers were laying down their arms. The Transvaal president, Paul Kruger, had fled for Portuguese East Africa following the battle of Doornkop, and much of his government had retired as well. (A few months later, safe in Europe, Kruger failed to convince the continental heads of state to fight on his republic's behalf. He died in exile a few years after the end of the war.) Although Pres. Marthinus Steyn stayed in South Africa and continued to urge resistance, the British annexed his republic as the Orange River Colony on 28 May. The situation looked desperate enough that several prominent Boer commanders, including Louis Botha, proposed surrender prior to a 2 June war council.[5]

Steyn's resolute position, however, carried the day at the meeting, and Christiaan de Wet and the younger Boer commanders were quick to return to the offensive. The British capture of Pretoria just a few days later on 5 June did not change their decision to continue the war. As a result, the winter of 1900 ushered in a new type of armed conflict in South Africa—guerrilla warfare. Accepting their inability to defeat the British in conventional battle, Boer strategy henceforth would be directed toward frustrating, delaying, and debilitating the occupying forces, which they hoped would cripple British morale, raise the cost of fighting, and force a negotiated settlement. To do this, they employed the tactics of low-intensity conflicts, such as cutting lines of communication and supply, attacking trains and isolated outposts, disrupting commerce, and when possible regaining territory temporarily occupied by the enemy.

Lord Roberts and his staff responded to these measures with caution and a great deal of uncertainty, unwilling to allow the Boers to dictate their strategy and unsure if a change was indeed prudent. As a result, without any clear direction, British officers in the field were left to their own devices. Roberts did initiate some counterinsurgency tactics like farm burning, but it was not until his departure and the elevation of Lord Kitchener to overall command in South Africa that a thorough strategy to deal with the Boer guerrillas was developed and implemented.

Regulars and volunteers alike were affected by these changes. Had the Victorian soldier been trained to be the "perfect killing machine," he would have had little to do in South Africa from July onward. But the Victorian soldier, and in particular the volunteer, had not been properly trained to fight a guerrilla war. He had drilled, paraded, and learned basic skills, but he was not an inveterate campaigner ready to stick it out on the veld. The citizen-soldier had enrolled at a time of crisis and was willing to fight while that crisis lasted. But with the political fall of the republics and the collapse of the Boer conventional effort, it was becoming more difficult for the volunteers to appreciate the true nature of the situation. As their responsibilities shifted from engaging the enemy in battle to implementing the "methods of barbarism," the auxiliaries saw themselves as policemen and not as soldiers, a shift that adversely affected morale.

Actual duties and responsibilities in the field usually fall far short of one's imagination and, for the most part, are anything but glamorous. The life of the "blooming ammychewer [*sic*]" was even more humdrum than that of the professional Tommy Atkins. This was mostly due to the fact that experienced officers preferred seasoned soldiers in battlefield situations. This became especially true after the disaster at Lindley in late May 1900, when unwarranted blame was assigned to four companies of Imperial Yeomanry who surrendered to Gen. Piet de Wet.[6] As a result, even before the capture of Pretoria, British volunteers in the field were feeling ignored and underutilized. "My work," a surgeon wrote to his uncle, "consists of tramping round the Enteric Wards and filling up diet sheets and then the Venereal Wards to do likewise."[7] Capt. H. B. Burnaby, First Battalion Wiltshire Imperial Yeomanry, bitterly complained to his parents, "We haven't seen any fighting as yet much to our disgust."[8] His men were kept occupied "bringing in Boer prisoners."[9] And Thomas Wetton, who served as a bearer in the Twenty-first (Brighton) Company and had arrived in South Africa only in April, proclaimed a month later, "One's enthusiasm for volunteering and the war by this time had sunk to zero."[10]

Indeed, keeping the men busy was not a difficult task, for there was so much to do. As Lt. W. S. Power quipped, "They can never say the Imperial Yeomanry are of no use, they use us for everything."[11] But few signed up to do wood fatigue, guard prisoners, or man an outpost. P. T. Ross sardonically noted that "drawing the fire of the enemy, had [become] the vocation of the Imperial Yeomanry."[12] John Paterson, Seventeenth (Ayr and Lanark) Company Imperial Yeomanry, wrote home with great disappointment: "I am afraid our job is to be guarding the lines of communications, a very needful job, but not exactly what we expected. It is a job you get plenty of work at and very little 'honour and glory.'"[13] And even Maj. Gen. Henry Mackinnon and his City of London Imperial Volunteers had little to look forward to by July 1900. The general felt that his regiment was being as neglected as the other Volunteer units. "Our principle duties," he wrote in his published account of the war, "were to put out of their misery the many dying animals left behind by the column, and to awaken all the exhausted men who had dropped asleep on the veldt."[14] It should be noted that only a month earlier, after witnessing the CIV in action at the battle of Diamond Hill, recently promoted Lt. Gen. Ian Hamilton borrowed Wellington's famous words, "With such troops, I could go anywhere and do anything."[15] By July, Mackinnon clearly believed the CIV were going nowhere and doing nothing.

The most routine jobs performed by the volunteers were line, camp, and picket details. Line-guard duties included checking horses and investigating anything or anyone that appeared suspicious. Camp guard involved moving from point to point around the perimeter of the camp and then, while sitting motionless, looking out for any unusual activity. Picket guard was the most difficult assignment. In a company, this involved a dozen or more men placed some five hundred to one thousand yards beyond the camp.

Typically, each man was placed on picket guard one in every three nights. This responsibility was the greatest, for an incompetent picket could allow for a devastating surprise attack in the middle of the night. It was also the hardest on the men. Picket guard was a "very lonely job," and every sound could rattle a man's nerves, play tricks on his imagination, and leave him tired and agitated throughout the next day.[16] "You never know when a Boer may pop up," John Paterson wrote to his brother.[17] L. A. Bethell, an officer in the Indian army who served during the South African War, reminded the readers of his *Outpost Duties as Learnt in South Africa* that picket duty was perhaps the most demanding job any soldier had to perform in wartime: "It must always be remembered that the force has probably marched on to its camping or bivouac ground late in the evening. Everybody is dead-tired, presumably hungry, and most certainly thirsty. The outposts have to be put up at once, and by the time they are in position it will be dark, or nearly so. Under these circumstances it is obvious that only a general idea of the ground to be occupied can be conveyed to company officers by even the most efficient staff officer."[18]

Even worse than the physical demand was the psychological challenge. In his account of the adventures of the Northumberland and Durham Imperial Yeomanry during the war, Karl Spurgin captured the essence of what many men felt while on picket duty: "It is wonderful what a terrible feeling of loneliness creeps over a fellow when on this kind of duty; he starts at every sound, wondering whatever can be the cause; the silence grows and grows until it feels intolerable; he tires to take his mind away from the present, and wonders what they all will be doing in dear old England—will they be picturing him alone on the open veldt, or will they imagine him snugly stowed away amongst his blankets; by Jove, how he longs to be there himself."[19]

During the day, when the men were not on the march, they were often occupied with fatigues. In general, fatigues did not require from the volunteers the same amount of physical or mental exertion as guard duty did. Yet the work could affect the company's well-being and how the men viewed their place in the war if it was perceived as unnecessary or overtaxing. Those writing in their diaries or corresponding to loved ones back home did not typically comment on these duties other than describing them in basic terms, such as when J. Stuart Hill, CIV, wrote, "they are not very heavy; the worst part is burying the dead which is a very unpleasant job."[20] Similarly, Hill's fellow CIV trooper, J. Barclay Lloyd, listed his various chores in a matter-of-fact way: loading trucks on railways, repairing lines, carting provisions, moving wounded to and fro, cleaning up after the horses, burying animals and humans, cleaning and sanitation, transporting items to outposts, and staying dry, the last of which was perhaps the most difficult.[21]

As one might expect in a war, even routine fatigues do not always proceed without incident. And when they did not, the men were more likely to comment on them. Cpl. P. T. Ross, Sixty-ninth (Sussex) Company Imperial Yeomanry, complained bitterly that he was sent on wood fatigue in areas where there was no wood.[22] This chore often turned into cow-dung fatigue, a "capital substitute."[23] William Grant, Seventeenth (Ayrshire) Company Imperial Yeomanry, was regularly assigned to watch sheep, or as he called it, "grazing guard." It often was not an unpleasant task. But on one occasion, Grant wrote in his diary, "the corporal in charge of the grazing guard had been so often on guard at this place that he became careless."[24] Of the ten men on duty, five were killed and three were wounded.

Digging trenches was another task that volunteers routinely carried out. Most men mention it, yet few ever go into any detail describing it. Yet when there was a problem, such as the time Sgt. Harry Hopwood, First Manchester Regiment Volunteer Service Company, had to dig for two hours in ground "so dry it was as hard as iron," the frustration comes through.[25]

Without the meaningful distraction that battle offered, the volunteers grew weary of their monotonous routine. There was no "payoff" when the trench was dug, the railway was repaired, or the water line declared safe and sound. The daily work seemed to become an end in itself and not a means to winning the war. Routine activity was soon perceived as inactivity.

With time on their hands, the men had to create their own distractions. P. T. Ross wrote about his daily ritual of searching for lice. "I have been told that the best way to get rid of these undesirable insects is to keep turning one's shirt inside out; by this means their hearts are eventually broken."[26] Drill and parade could also serve as temporary distractions, but these were not ones that the men were keen on. "Colonel Spragge, I am afraid is a failure," L. H. Elphinstone, Forty-seventh (Duke of Cambridge's Own) Company Imperial Yeomanry, wrote to his parents. "He has a marching order parade and makes everybody file past him, one by one while he . . . carps and turns you back after your kit because one buckle is an inch higher up the roll than the other. He is always fussing and worrying. He worries his officers who consequently worries his [NCOs] who worry the men."[27]

The men also engaged in sport. Lt. Brian Alt, CIV, wisely brought a football with him.[28] Lt. C. S. Awdry, First Battalion Imperial Yeomanry, and Harold Josling, First Norfolk Regiment Volunteer Service Company, wrote about playing cricket against locals and squads raised by other British companies.[29] The Seventeenth (Ayr and Lanark) Company Imperial Yeomanry had a rugby match with men from Wellington, and the Fourteenth (Northumberland) Company Imperial Yeomanry had a boxing match against some of the Tasmanian contingent.[30] Volunteers also played rounders, fished and swam, hunted, wrestled, and set up tug-of-war, running, obstacle, and sack-race competitions.[31] H. R. Lister, CIV, described playing "alarm," in which men would run to their horses, saddle up, and ride off to a designated point; Cholondeley, a type of relay race that involved riding and subsection volley fire; and the pipe-and-boot race, which involved finding one's boots, lighting one's pipe, and then running to a judge with one's tobacco still burning.[32] Other forms of entertainment included camp smokers, singing and storytelling, card and "house" playing, and reading mail and newspapers.[33] Letters, particularly those that offered any news of home, were a real treat, but because service was irregular, it could take anywhere from one to three months to receive mail sent from Great Britain. The other great treat was food—not rations, but fresh food, sweets, and drink, confiscated from Boers, purchased from merchants, or occasionally sent by the Queen or local communities back home. "It is worth undergoing what we have had lately," Harry Hopwood wrote, "just for the sake of enjoying a drink when you get one."[34]

Although much of the servicemen's time in South Africa was dedicated to activities in and around camp, they also spent weeks and even months at a time slogging across the veld. Volunteers were exceedingly proud of the number of miles they marched in pursuing the enemy, in escorting prisoners and supply wagons, and in relieving garrisons and blockhouses. Although they complained about their tired feet, their lack of sleep, and the often cold and wet conditions they encountered, they were also pleased by their accomplishments. The Scottish Rifles Volunteers marched in Maj. Gen. C. F. Clery's column in the northern Natal in April 1900. According to Godfrey Smith, they rarely saw the enemy, and many men got sick and had to leave the company. Yet Smith still showed great pride in the exercise. "I do not think that at any time during our long march did Clery's column seem more imposing; the deep tramp of thousands of feet, the hollow and menacing rumbling of the heavy guns, the jingling of harness, and the hoarse shrieks of the Kaffir drivers of the oxen-driven convoy making a very medley of sounds; the road, as far as eye could see, being covered with troops—artillery, cavalry, and infantry."[35] Granted, this trek occurred prior to the full onset of the guerrilla war, and so Smith's morale, no doubt, was high. Still, even in the last stage of the conflict, volunteers' accounts of their marches are full of boasts and a sense of accomplishment in their ability to endure and to cover so much ground on numerous treks.

During many marches, British soldiers confiscated cattle and property, burned houses and farms, and sometimes shot prisoners. Although some of the men questioned the morality and expediency of these actions, few hid what they were doing on the veld from their friends and families back home. Accounts published during and after the war likewise make no attempt to cover the brutality of these tactics. The seizure of stock, the destruction of property, and the forced removal of armed burghers to prisoner-of-war camps and civilians to concentration camps were perceived as a legitimate part of the British strategy to win the war in 1900 and 1901.

As mentioned above, Roberts's confidence that the war would end by Christmas 1900 led him to believe that the British should fight a typical small war. As Col. C. E. Callwell spells out in his seminal work, *Small Wars: Their Principles and Practice,* in a situation where a central authority exists, the objective in war is clear: the capital, or in the case of the Boer republics, capitals, should be seized. The successful capture of the city would force the enemy to fight a decisive battle that would hasten the end of the war. Fighting, according to Callwell, may continue afterward, but it would be of secondary importance.[36] Certain of victory on these terms, Roberts was reluctant to change his strategic direction of the war. Therefore, although he introduced some counterinsurgency measures, notably farm burning, his policies were not part of a well-conceived strategy designed to counter the developing Boer guerrilla tactics.[37]

Roberts's successor, Lord Kitchener, despite his many shortcomings, was aware that a change of strategy was in order. He attempted to rationalize the process and implement it uniformly. To break Boer resistance, the new commander employed two basic counterinsurgency techniques. One involved the erection of a series of blockhouses designed to pen in the mobile guerrillas.[38] The other was meant to strip the Boers of their resources and the noncombatants' ability to support the commandos in the field. In addition to farm burning and the confiscation of cattle and sheep, he established a network of concentration camps to remove noncombatants from the field and thus prevent the wives and children of armed burghers from providing aid.[39]

The volunteers played a key role in this strategy. They built and manned blockhouses, destroyed farms and confiscated property, and seized and transported noncombatant prisoners to concentration camps and armed combatants to the coast for removal to prisoner-of-war camps. William Home wrote of the "gentle art of commandeering," but it was often anything but gentle.[40] The men did not like it. Frank Stephenson, Tenth (Sherwood Rangers) Company Imperial Yeomanry, complained bitterly about having to search houses and "push around families."[41] Near Harrismith in June 1901, Lt. Gen. Sir Leslie Rundle ordered Captain Burnaby and the First Battalion Wiltshire Imperial Yeomanry to seize Boer herds and slaughter them. Burnaby wrote that killing thirty thousand sheep was the "most disgusting thing [I had] to do." He continued, with a sense of shame, "what brutes the Boers must think us."[42]

While some volunteers, like C. S. Awdry, were "very sick of it," others were more successful in emotionally detaching themselves from their actions and accepting that this strategy was a necessary component of the war.[43] But this was very hard to do. G. F. A. Reece, Forty-eighth (North Somerset) Company Imperial Yeomanry, spent most of 1901 clearing the countryside in the Transvaal between Krugersdorp and Klerksdorp. He and twenty-five, sometimes fifty, men would leave camp on patrol and seize cattle, sheep, goats, and mules; take prisoners in "everyday"; and after burning farms, look on while "the veldt was on fire." From Wolverdienst, he wrote in mid-May: "The farms and villages in this part of the Transvaal are something grand. I have never seen anything able to equal it at home. They grow fruit of all kinds but the only things in season now are oranges, quinces and figs. After we have passed through, you look back and then you can realize the horrors of war. The place that looked so peaceful before is nothing now but a heap of burning ruins. It seems a bit off but it is the only way to end the war. . . . Also we shoot every animal we can see."[44] Almost seven months later he still experienced mixed feelings toward what he was doing: "People at home would hardly believe but we are still bringing in Boer families and have been doing so for the last year and now they are not all in. We bring all the Kaffers [*sic*] along with us into locations alongside the line when we come to any crops they have to turn into it with hundreds of our niggers and reap them, then pile them in great heaps and then burn them. It seems a sin, don't it, but have burnt acres of wheat which our brother Boer relies on so."[45] Trekking a few days out from Dalmanutha, Harry Hopwood wrote: "I feel sorry for them [Boers] sometimes especially when we come across their burnt farms. Unless they are known to be loyal and not fighting, their farms are burnt down to the ground. Some of these farms are beautiful spots, always by the side of a stream and surrounded with fruit trees, which are nearly all in full bloom just now."[46]

British soldiers were ordered to search Boer farms for combatants and weapons and only seize the goods and animals and raze the homesteads of those families who were actively supporting the guerrilla effort. Perhaps it was inevitable that a certain amount of looting took place. Bernard Moeller, CIV Mounted Infantry, insisted that he paid for everything he took from the homes and shops he entered, but if rifles or ammunition were found on the premises, he "'naturally' loot[ed] the place."[47] But a few Imperial Yeomanry companies moved far beyond expectation and gained the notorious distinction of "looters." Col. H. E. Belfield, Lord Methuen's chief of staff, wrote to his wife: "The worst of them [Imperial Yeomanry] is that they are awful looters. They'll collar anything that comes in their way."[48]

Few volunteers, like Moeller, attempted to justify their actions in their letters; they simply described their activities. The companies that engaged in excessive looting were supplied no better or worse than other companies, nor were they active in a particular rural or urban setting. One must draw the conclusion that these units lacked the discipline of other companies. And it is clear that when officers and NCOs imposed discipline, looting stopped. For example, the Seventeenth (Earl of Carrick's Ayrshire) and Eighteenth (Queen's Own Royal Glasgow) Companies Imperial Yeomanry looted a village on their way to Florida in June 1900. The following month they did it again near Naawpoort Nek. This time, though, their new commander, Maj. Gen. Sir Hector MacDonald, vigorously condemned the action and threatened harsh disciplinary measures.[49] The looting stopped. In an anonymous record the author, Q.L., chronicled the activities of the Sixteenth (Worcestershire) Company Imperial Yeomanry:

> May 17—Looted two farms: had coffee in one.
>
> May 19—Some soldiers broke into a jeweller's [*sic*] shop. One sentenced to be shot.
>
> May 20—No more looting, all houses and farms out of bounds.[50]

Discipline, clearly, went a long way in solving the looting "problem."

A far graver matter than looting, but one that did not concern some senior British officers, was the execution of prisoners. Frank Stephenson wrote home, "There is an understanding out here among all our Soldiers that no prisoners are to be taken, if it can be possibly helped."[51] Very few volunteers were so candid. Indeed, few mention the subject in their letters home.[52] This reflects the fact that these incidents were very uncommon rather than that the volunteers were trying to cover up potential war crimes.[53] Indeed, some wished that they were at liberty to shoot Boer prisoners. H. R. Lister wrote in his diary: "Several of them ought to be shot, and I think our leniency does not act at all in our favor towards an enemy like the Boers. Take for example a lad of 16 who after his father has raised the white flag over his arm has been allowed all the privileges of neutrality, is found signaling from the roof to the enemy 5 miles away (of course on his father's instructions). They ought to have sent out half a section of [Mounted Infantry] and shot all the men found on the farm without satisfactory explanations instead of taking prisoners. We are too lenient toward our adversaries and I am sure they take it for weakness on our part."[54]

As mentioned earlier, in April 1900, in one of the first major engagements that involved the Imperial Yeomanry, Methuen's division defeated a small Boer commando at Boshof. The enemy force had been commanded by a French aristocrat, Comte de Villebois-Marueil, who was killed during the battle. To show his respect for his adversary, Methuen held a funeral and, out of his own pocket, paid for Villebois-Marueil's headstone. W. A. W. Lawson, later Third Baron Burnham, witnessed the burial. Although the Boers and foreign volunteers who served under Villebois-Marueil appreciated the noble gesture, Lawson was disgusted. "All the Froggies cried," he wrote, "and one made a speech at the funeral. Adieu, mon General, etc., and Methuen shook hands with him, God knows why, as they ought all to have been shot."[55]

W. S. Power did not write with the same anger and desire for retribution as Lister and Lawson, but he recognized that taking Boer prisoners posed a major problem. He wrote to his cousin en route to Bethlehem: "Not a word has been said yet, about not taking the man who had the rifle, prisoner. I don't want any prisoners, no good to me, only have to put a guard over them, and after you have turned them over to the [authorities] they are given a pass and told to go back to their farms."[56] The capture, transportation, release, and when it occurred, execution of prisoners took a heavy toll on the volunteers. These were not activities they envisioned doing when they signed up for service.

Volunteer attitudes toward the treatment of prisoners, of course, were shaped by their sense of morality. They were also affected by direct interactions on and off the battlefield with their adversaries. British volunteers had mixed feelings about the Boers, combatants and noncombatants alike. Stereotypes were hard to surrender even after names and faces were attached to the enemy. To volunteers like Frederick Barnado, Twentieth (Fife and Forfar) Company Imperial Yeomanry, the Boers remained "wily."[57] In his letters home, later edited and published, Sir John Gilmour of the same unit readily used the term "dirty" to describe them.[58] C. S. Awdry emphasized indolence as the trait he most detested in the Boers. "In the Free State," he wrote, "the only real drawback is the Dutchman's laziness, he only cultivates enough for himself though the great plains would grow corn beautifully."[59] Likewise, Frank Charge, Sixteenth (Worcestershire) Company Imperial Yeomanry, held on to some of the images of the Boers that he had embraced in Britain:

> The Boers are a peculiar race. He has very little ready money. He likes to deal by barter. He never milks his cows but lets the calves suckle and keeps on multiplying so that all his wealth lies in his stock. When his sons grow up and get married the father gives him so many oxen and the bride's father does the same, then they get a grant of land contiguous to the old man's piece and so the farm grows bigger and bigger and the old patriarch can say: "That farm there is my son's, that is my nephew's and that is my grandson's and so on," the whole extending for miles. They are mostly all one family. Incest is prevalent amongst them, that is why (them being so inbred) they are so currish and there are so many idiots and cripples amongst them.[60]

In one of the most vitriolic letters sent back to Britain during the entirety of the war, Charge expressed his hatred of the Boers: "The Cape Dutch and Boers are a dirty treacherous lot and as soon as the Transvaal is subdued and the beggars (those that survive) trek farther out of our way the better. We do hate them down here like poison. The rascally dirty varmints, they must be exterminated; the country swarms with them and their dirty compatriots the German Jew. The sight of them and their mean tricks is enough to make the mildest mannered man a demon. God pity the poor white or black under them when they have the power."[61]

Others' opinions of the Boers were radically shaped by a particular incident or encounter in the war. G. F. A. Reece, for example, witnessed a Boer execute three of his comrades after they had disarmed.[62] Sidney Peel, Fortieth (Oxfordshire) Company Imperial Yeomanry, was despondent when he learned of the Lindley disaster. As he rode past the dead yeomen, their helmets strewn about, he was filled with rage. But, ironically, his anger reached its peak a few months later when de Wet's commando, after capturing some

Derbyshire militiamen carrying British mail, burned all the letters. "We hated the Boers with a strong loathing," he wrote, "for such a useless act of wanton barbarity."[63]

There were also British volunteers who admired the courage and abilities of the armed burghers and sympathized with the plight of the Boer women and children. Lt. Charles Dixon Kimber, Forty-seventh (Duke of Cambridge's Own) Company Imperial Yeomanry, had been at Lindley with Spragge's force when the British surrendered. A few days later he wrote home: "The Boers treated us generously, both with their bullets and otherwise, and my opinion of them has risen. They are a brave, simple folk, and make a fighting force peculiarly adapted to this kind of country."[64] Lionel Curtis, CIV, wrote to his mother from Stydenburg: "The Dutch farmers are just the people you are used to in Herefordshire and Derbyshire talking another tongue. They are deeply religious, passionately attached to their spacious country life, and I should imagine constantly confronted with the difficulty of providing more square miles for their numerous families to live upon. The townee [*sic*] cannot understand these countrymen, nor they him."[65]

Volunteers' opinions of black South Africans were more uniform. They saw few cultural traits that they could identify as similar to their own and therefore, like most Britons of the late Victorian era, saw little of value in their customs, traditions, and lifestyles. For the most part, the servicemen treated them with disdain and contempt. Few made tribal, linguistic, or political distinctions —South African blacks were simply "Kaffirs."[66] Sidney Peel considered them lazy, dirty, and mere children.[67] Frank Stephenson compared black children to monkeys.[68] To H. S. Gaskell, Thirty-seventh (Buckinghamshire) Company Imperial Yeomanry, they were little more than "niggers."[69] Godfrey Smith referred to them as "semi-civilized blacks."[70] A. G. Garrish, East Surrey Volunteer Service Corps, clumsily attempted to praise the African scouts attached to his company by showing them to be different than "typical" Africans. The result revealed his deep-seated racism.

> The Kaffirs must not all be put down as mere savages. The common idea of them is, in the majority of cases, quite correct. The African native is a dull, ignorant, half-civilised animal, to whose mind kindness is a weakness or fear, and

> brutality strength. . . . Our men generally found brusque speech and a frowning brow sufficient to awe the blacks into servility.
>
> This type comprised by far the larger class, but amongst our coloured scouts we had men of intellect and education.[71]

Similarly, Sharrad Gilbert, Sixty-fifth (Leicestershire) Company Imperial Yeomanry, tried to describe the Zulu in terms more complimentary than other black South Africans but ultimately put them down as thieves.[72]

Although the British government did not advertise the role of black South Africans in the war effort, it was substantial. More than one hundred thousand participated as scouts, guards, or servants. By the end of the war, as many as thirty thousand blacks were armed and fighting on the British side.[73] Many volunteers such as Garrish and Edward Day-Lewis, Eighty-fifth (Rough Riders) Company Imperial Yeomanry, recognized this contribution.[74] Few, however, went as far as Sgt. P. C. Jonas in suggesting that black South Africans could play a far greater role: "[The Basutos] are a sturdy lot. It seems a pity that these people cannot be turned into a very good army. They are a fighting race, have never been beaten and they all ride splendidly. Why could not they and the Zulus be made into native troops like the natives in India?"[75] British command was not ready to accept Jonas's ideas and ratchet up the level of black participation. Had it, the course of the war and the process of reconciliation would have run quite differently. Kitchener and Milner were quite aware of this.

If British volunteers did not care for South Africans, the same could not be said of South Africa itself.[76] Many of them fell in love with the land; some even chose to stay after the fighting ended. Whether it was the magnificent orange groves outside of Johannesburg, the high kopjes behind Zeerust, the farms near Van Reenen's Pass, or the beautiful government gardens in the heart of Cape Town, volunteers trekked through a land they viewed as worth fighting for.[77] As his train, destined for the Orange Free State, crept at a speed of less than ten miles per hour through Natal, Thomas Wetton was struck by the beauty of the land. "Wonderful country," he wrote.

> Broad plains stretched away for miles—unbroken, uncultivated, and forsaken; at other times, huge mountainous

> ranges, conical, table shaped, and irregular, stretched away to the horizon. . . . Now we were passing through narrow gorges with half-dry spruits tracing their own paths amid the rocks; then up the steep sides of a gigantic mountain, winding with snakelike movements in and out, up and down, emerging finally triumphant in the sunlight and broad level veldt. Here and there ostrich farmsteads came into view and a most amusing sight it was to see the birds scampering off as we approached. On one occasion the view was obliterated by millions of locusts.[78]

A. G. Garrish was bewitched by the grasslands near Durban. "All around," he wrote, "nature is in her greenest robe; the sheep wander on the plain, the Kaffirs at work in the fields stop as we rush past to look at us, the only element of war in so peaceful and happy a scene."[79] Bernard Moeller and a detachment of CIV Mounted Infantry were already awake and riding toward Brandfort in the Free State when the sun rose on a late April morning. He wrote: "It was a lovely morning—clear, bright as crystal, and a magnificent sunrise. The whole veldt was covered with a white dew, and the tips of the distant hills were a rosy red. The life is unbeatable, and I am enjoying every moment of it. One lives day and night in the open fresh air, perhaps the freshest and best one can get in the world. One sees Nature in her best and truest colours, and the more one sees of her the more one loves her. The brooks and gullies are full of water, after the recent heavy rains, and the wide veldt has changed its old coast of a drab brown to a new one of fresh green."[80]

John Paterson thought he found the Garden of Eden when he entered Paarl, Cape Colony. A week later, however, he spied the Brede River. "It is the best land I have ever seen," he wrote, "and if I could get a farm in it I would never go home."[81] Frank Charge also used the phrase "Garden of Eden" to describe Marico, Orange Free State. But it was the sight of Johannesburg that stunned him. "Johannesburg . . . is a truly wonderful place. After oceans of veldt dotted remote distances apart by sleepy old-fashioned Dutch towns which are, at the best, no bigger than our villages, it was a startling marvel to see Johannesburg, this City of Gold. It is truly the jewel of South Africa. . . . Until, I saw it I wondered what we were fighting for."[82]

The beauty and the wonder of the South African landscape gave some meaning to those who searched for answers to why they were still fighting as they chased ghosts across the veld, arrested civilians, and burned farms. One of the psychological devices volunteers used to ease their concerns and to justify their actions was to draw parallels between scenes back home and the plains, coastline, mountains, and farms of South Africa. Familiarity reinforced imperial connection. One was not fighting a war on foreign soil but was temporarily transported back to the British Isles. Lionel Curtis, for example, saw a little bit of England when he stopped at a Dutch farmhouse in Hope Town for some fresh milk and ginger beer.[83] While guarding a bridge at D'Urban Road outside of Stellenbosch, John Paterson captured an image of "little thatched houses" teaming with "pigs, chickens and dogs" that put him "in the mind of Ireland."[84]

More so than England or Ireland, it was the familiar scenes of Scotland that several volunteers recollected. On 10 May 1900, J. W. Milne awoke to "the cold and clear frost air" of "a typical Scottish spring morning" along the banks of the Zand River.[85] To John Gilmour, Table Mountain looked like Buachaille Etive Mor, and a valley near Stellenbosch was "very like the view from Corries (in Fife) looking over to the Mount." The people living in the valley, Gilmour considered, were not unlike "what the Scottish farmer must have been a hundred years ago."[86] Not only did volunteers glimpse scenes of Scotland in the landscape of the Cape Colony, they also saw it in Natal and in the Transvaal. "The scenery of Natal," Godfrey Smith wrote, "it is no exaggeration to say, runs Scotland very close, hills and dales, covered on the lower slopes with beautiful foliage, being the main features in the landscape for the first fifty miles inland."[87] And as J. P. Sturrock, Twentieth (Fife and Forfar) Company Imperial Yeomanry, marched toward Pretoria, "the scenery was becoming every moment more Scottish in its character, the long valley through which the column had been wending became a rugged highland glen, and at every sharp turn in the road the wagons and water-carts were in danger of falling over the edges into the mountain stream which rushed amongst the rocks some fifty feet below."[88]

But other volunteers saw little in common between Great Britain and South Africa. The land and the people were too different to find any semblance of home in the valleys of the Cape Colony or in the mountains of the Free State. Instead of reinforcing their commitment to the war, these differences magnified their hardships and increased the drift toward indifference, and ultimately despair. They saw nothing worth fighting for. They did not like what they saw, and the more they saw of it, the more they wanted to go home.

It should come as no surprise that in an under-industrialized region like turn-of-the-century South Africa, few accounts emphasized urban conditions. De Aar was "a rotten little hole," Kroonstadt was a "foul and ill-smelling place," and Beira was little more than "a mammoth pleasure fair."[89] William Home spent five weeks in Pretoria and had very little to say about the architecture, commerce, or people. There was nothing there for him but lawlessness, confusion, and high prices. What he remembered most about the city was that because of enteric fever and dysentery, the "men died like flies."[90] Even Cape Town, which many volunteers described in positive terms as they passed through, dropped in stature once the initial euphoria of seeing the region for the first time passed. As Brian Alt wrote: "After leaving Cape Town, whose only redeeming feature is the mountain, I did not see an acre of ground worth fighting for. Nothing but stones, dust and thorn bush."[91] For many volunteers, once they left Britain behind, they left civilization behind.

The features that struck these men the most were, as Alt noted, the rocks, anthills, dust storms, heat, and heavy downpours which were not like "English rain."[92] C. S. Awdry wrote to his mother on his way to Bloemfontein from Norval's Point: "There was not a decent bit of country we passed through so far; all bare rocks with low heather scrub dotted about and no water, though there are many torrent beds and dried rivers. The stations mostly consist of a name board stuck on two poles and a siding sometimes or a crossing place."[93] This description was echoed time and time again in diaries, published accounts, and letters sent home. And these conditions affected the men's morale. Many shared the sentiment of W. S. Power, who opined, "I have not seen a blade of grass since we left Cape Town, and why anyone wants to fight for such a Godforsaken country, I can't imagine."[94]

When the news came that Pretoria had fallen, many volunteers were confident that the war's end was at hand and they would be sent home. Of course, this was not to be. J. Barclay Lloyd wrote that everyone was disappointed when they were given their marching orders.[95] While still in Britain, the men had accepted the necessity of drill and parade because they anticipated an eventual payoff. But few in the field, even officers, recognized the importance of their new role. They often judged their usefulness by the number of times they fired their weapons. H. B. Burnaby wrote home from the Leeuw River: "I can't tell you how we all long for the end of the war. The 1st Battalion have [*sic*] been treated very badly. We have seen no fighting and had much harder times and worse food than most of them."[96]

Having been sent to join the Rhodesian Field Force, Sharrad Gilbert questioned what he was doing standing pat outside of Beira, Portuguese East Africa, while most of his battalion contracted malaria and his camp became a "vast hospital."[97] Francis Appleton, First South Lancashire Regiment Volunteer Service Company, saw little value in digging trenches, escorting convoys, and confiscating Boer property. He craved a bath, a shave, and a fresh change of clothes.[98] William Corner, Thirty-fourth (Middlesex) Company Imperial Yeomanry, could not figure out what new role his superiors had created for the volunteers: "We frequently ask ourselves what our division is doing. . . . A motive is never offered us, we are unconscious of all except drudgery, and the necessity of obedience."[99]

The lack of information regarding not just orders and enemy movements but also how the auxiliaries served British strategy troubled many. No ordinary soldier is an unthinking automaton who coolly awaits his next order, and the volunteers were hardly ordinary soldiers. By most accounts, they lacked the discipline and the strict regimentation of the regulars. But they were also, especially the Imperial Yeomanry and Volunteers, better educated and more resourceful than regular soldiers. Onlookers praised their initiative and their ability to learn on the job. Volunteers wanted reassurance that they were doing something important for their country and demanded a purpose to provide themselves with a meaningful military identity. But by keeping them in the dark, Roberts, Kitchener, and British commanders only weakened morale in the field.

In an unusual outburst of frustration, Lionel Curtis wrote from the Vet River to his mother:

> When all is said and done, it appears you do not, as a rule, know whether you have won a glorious victory, or suffered humiliating defeat, until you are officially informed thereof.

> Standing on the spot we could do little more than conjecture, and then reflect how much you in England could have told us about what we should like to have known. But that is the oddest thing about a war. With the exception of actually manipulating the machine the nearer men are to the scene of action, the less they know what is going on. London knows more than Cape Town, Cape Town than Bloemfontein. The man who knows least is the man on the march.[100]

Likewise, Frank Charge wrote home, "You know more of the war in England than we do down here."[101] P. C. Jonas was not only frustrated by the lack of information given to his company but assumed that his officers knew little more than he did and were frustrated as well. He commented in his diary: "We very seldom knew much about the movements we were actually taking part in, it is astonishing how very little we did know. It was not until we got with Methuen that we even knew much of what had happened let alone what was going to. It seems to me that it would be much better if O.C. [officer in command] of Squadron or at any rate of [regiment] were told more about the operation. It would enable them to take a more intelligent interest in their movements."[102]

Jonas's assumption was correct. Even officers, who were privy to more information and were better positioned to see the big picture and the importance of their unit's contribution to the war effort, complained bitterly about the state of ignorance they were kept in by higher command. W. A. W. Lawson never knew where or when he and his men were going next. It was "always a big secret," he declared in a letter to home.[103] "You know," C. S. Awdry wrote to his father, "sitting idle here makes one think that it was a great pity to have come out at all, simply to do nothing."[104] Awdry remained frustrated for nearly a year, later complaining to his mother: "Altogether we have bungled this war worse than any other we have undertaken. I want to get clear of the whole thing."[105]

Not all volunteers harped on their futility, and some remained happily committed and optimistic throughout their tour, but few were content with their changing role in the war. Typically, letters, diaries, and even published accounts reveal a tipping point at which the author wanted to be anywhere other than South Africa. Sometimes these accounts repeat the word "transfer."[106] Officers, in particular, wrote about going to China.[107] H. B. Burnaby, for one, made enquiries about joining the Japanese army but was disappointed to learn that they did not employ foreigners.[108] Others began sharing with their readers the rumors that they heard about the war coming to an end or an impending decision by the government to recall the volunteers.

Some became increasingly critical of their officers. Harold Josling wrote in his account of the war that every time his company got near the enemy, someone ordered it away.[109] G. F. A. Reece placed the blame for his company's situation squarely on Roberts's shoulders. After participating in farm burning in the eastern Transvaal in May 1901, Reece wrote home, "If Roberts had done the same, the war would have been over [by] now."[110] After enduring six months of garrison duty in the eastern Free State, Lt. Sir Thomas Fowler, First (Wiltshire) Company Imperial Yeomanry, displayed his frustration with Roberts's lack of overall strategy in dealing with the insurgency as well. In his memoir he wrote: "We appear to continue our mistakes in tackling the enemy. According to accounts they are all over the country again. What the authorities have done with their mounted troops is a question that everyone is asking. There seem, however, none available to stop the Dutch from running all over the country. The effect of this will be far reaching and will delay the war as well as the final settlement some considerable time."[111]

Oddly, only some blamed the enemy for their predicament. Few cursed "Brother Boer" for starting the war and dragging them away from their homes and families to fight in some distant land. Indeed, as noted above, many men showed pity for the victims of the conflict, especially the displaced women and children, and were anxious about farm burning and the confiscation of property. While commandeering livestock outside Kroonstad in May 1900, Karl Spurgin, Fourteenth (Northumberland) Company Imperial Yeomanry, wrote that "even the hardest soldier turned away" from the tearful reaction of the Boer women and children.[112] Similarly, John Paterson felt great empathy for the desperate condition of the "poor women and children" in the western Transvaal and worried that their situation would deteriorate after his unit moved on and left them to fend for themselves against the "murdering Kaffirs."[113]

Those who did blame the Boers for their predicament, like W. S. Power, challenged the morality of the enemy tactics that, they believed, prevented a "fair" fight and therefore a quick end to the fighting. "I don't think this confounded war will ever be over," Power wrote to his cousin. "There is only one way to do them, drive all their cattle off, send all prisoners away to Cape Town, burn all farms where the owner is away on Commando, and shoot all rebels."[114] Likewise, Frank Stephenson did not trust the Boers and had heard rumors of an instance in which they had fired upon British troops after a white flag was raised. A volunteer in Strathcona's Horse told him that the Canadians were shooting every Boer they saw. Stephenson thought the policy a wise one.[115]

One clear pattern emerging during the war is that the conditions that plagued the volunteers and all soldiers throughout the campaign—the climate, terrain, disease, and poor supply—became more insufferable once the men had lost interest in the fighting and their purpose for being there became unclear. In other words, men's attentions only turned to the bleakness of their surroundings once they were looking for something to complain about. For example, Joseph Duncalf, Twenty-first (Cheshire) Company Imperial Yeomanry, was still willing to put up with the hot days and freezing nights around Bloemfontein but wrote: "All our men say they wish they were at home, they say they will never join the Yeomanry again and I am sure I shall not. I have had enough but we have to make the best of it now and we laugh about it and talk about what fools we have been to give comfortable homes up to come out here to be on sentry and sleep in tents on the hard ground instead of in a feather bed at home, but experience makes fools wise."[116] But two months of escorting convoys broke Duncalf's resolve. "I am fed up," he admitted, "with active service and so is everybody else, having to sleep on the open veldt on bitterly cold nights and then get up at 5.00 a.m. and keep in the saddle until dusk. You are ready to drop off as dead."[117]

Tempers ran hot and patience grew thin as the war dragged on. "The slow crawl of the trek-ox, the continuous stopping to close up, the monotonous shouting of the Kaffirs, cracking of whips, occasional halts to draw wagons out of heavy ground, and various other amusements of the same kind," Karl Spurgin wrote, "don't tend to improve the temper of Tommy Atkins."[118] Some grew impatient with the quality of their clothing and boots and the lack of mail, tobacco, and money.[119] Nearly every volunteer complained about rations. P. T. Ross joked, "We may be Imperial Yeomanry, but they don't give us Imperial Pints."[120] Others harped on the monotonous routine that they faced daily. Sidney Peel experienced three weeks of continuous marching around Prieska. The torrential rains, the cold, and the dreary habit of sleeping in pools of water took their toll on his unit, but what Peel objected to most was that after each march, he was ordered to polish his buttons. "There was very nearly a mutiny," he wrote in his published memoir.[121] The ritual may have seemed unnecessary and annoying back in barracks in Britain, but in South Africa it was absolutely objectionable.

One of the most disturbing features of the war was the sight and smell of dead horses and beasts of burden littering the veld: constant reminders of death. The volunteer force, and in particular the Imperial Yeomanry, was often criticized for their lack of horsemanship and horsemastery. As noted earlier, the British government had expected that the ranks of the Imperial Yeomanry, like its forerunner, would be recruited from mostly rural men who could shoot, ride, and take care of their mounts. This expectation went largely unfulfilled. Although there were riding tests, these were not rigorous, and many were able to enter the force without basic skills. Maj. (later Field Marshal) W. E. Birdwood, who served as Kitchener's deputy assistant adjutant general, recounted an anecdote, probably apocryphal, that he heard about the riding skills of the Imperial Yeomanry:

> [Lord Chesham] noticed a trooper leading his horse. He imagined that the horse's back had probably got touched by the saddle and that his rider was rightly saving him, so when, on the following day, he saw the same horse being led again by the same man, Lord Chesham rode up to him and congratulated him on the care he was taking of his animal. "He ain't touched 'is back, I've lost my left-hand stirrup-leather." Chesham, astonished, said, "Well, mount on the other side, then!"—to receive the incredulous cockney retort, "Get along with you! Why, if I did that I'd be facing the wrong way!"[122]

Even more crucial to the situation in South Africa was that most volunteers had little or no experience taking care of horses or pack animals, nor did they learn much during their few weeks of training back in Britain. Add this to the rigorous daily marches, insufficient foraging, and poorly acclimatized mounts, and the result was a significant death rate among mounts and animals used for transport. Horses were laden with so much equipment, it was "small wonder that many of these unfortunate animals died," H. G. Mckenzie Rew sarcastically wrote.[123] According to Sharrad Gilbert, horse carcasses were strewn about the Imperial Yeomanry camp outside Beira.[124] Harry Hopwood wrote in his diary: "Every 200 yards or so we passed dead oxen and mules, which stunk horribly. You were never out of sight of a carcass and sometimes two or three would be lying together."[125] Maj. Charles Stonham, the commanding officer and chief surgeon of the Imperial Yeomanry Field Hospital, found the rest camp at Bloemfontein in a horrible state in May 1900. Animal carcasses were everywhere and had attracted a "fly parade." The camp predictably became a breeding ground for typhoid and dysentery.[126] The British lost close to half a million horses, mules, and donkeys during the war.[127] The spectacle of dead animals on the South African landscape was one of the most memorable aspects of the war for returning volunteers.

"We saw a sickening sight on the station," Frank Charge wrote. "Row after row of soldiers down with enteric fever, in a dreadful state and of course no hope for them. When you are here you are nothing but a machine and you are treated like one."[128] Sanitation conditions at hospitals and base camps were wretched.[129] Medical staffs were short and supplies were lacking. Dysentery and enteric fever plagued all British forces throughout the war, and typhoid took many lives.

There are few personal accounts of the war that do not mention at least one visit to the hospital. Most men got sick, many were sent home, and some died. Thirteen thousand men, over two-thirds of all British military fatalities in the war, died from disease and illness.[130] The volunteers were witnesses to these deaths, and unlike battlefield casualties, they did not occur all at once nor was the attention of the unit distracted by combat. Like a sniper's bullet, fever could hit at any time and take anyone's life. And like a sniper's bullet, men felt helpless to prevent it from striking them down. Disease not only drained a unit of its strength but also demoralized the men.

Volunteer units were notoriously understrength.[131] Men were coming and going, frequently dispatched to guard prisoners, escort convoys, and garrison blockhouses. But those who got sick and those who died were not readily replaced. A. W. M. Atthill reported that on 9 May 1901, a parade day, only 35 of the 118 men of the Second Norfolk Volunteer Service Company were in attendance. Of the other 83 missing soldiers, 18 were in the hospital, 2 were at other stations, 1 was absent, 1 was "on pass," 8 were on fatigue, 12 were doing various services for the company, 1 was sick, 4 were coming off guard duty, 28 were on guard and picket duty, 3 had gone to the post office, 3 were acting as police, and 3 others were unaccounted by Atthill.[132] It was very difficult for such a reduced force to believe that it could make a difference in the war or that it would soon be employed in a more meaningful task.

Another factor that volunteers had trouble coping with was the perceived inequitable treatment they received from headquarters. Many thought that regular soldiers were better equipped, better fed, and of course, given more important responsibilities. P. T. Ross believed that whenever an Imperial Yeomanry company made a mistake, it made big news, but when the regulars did the same thing, the press ignored it.[133] The Imperial Yeomanry, Militia, and Volunteer Service Companies also had another issue—the CIV. Already jealous over their press coverage and Lord Roberts's attention, when rumors spread that the CIV would be going home early, all but the hopelessly optimistic, who believed they would join them, were furious. When the rumors proved to be true, there were few who were not terribly disappointed; most were livid.[134] John Gilmour wrote to this father that Roberts had offended the Imperial Yeomanry with this move.[135] And P. T. Ross expressed his displeasure in a poem:

> When you've said "the war is over" and "the end is now
>   in sight,"
> And you've welcomed home your valiant CIVs,
> There are other absent beggars in the everlasting fight,
> And not the least of these your Yeomen please.
> He's a casual sort of Johnnie and his casualties are
>   great,
> And on the veldt and kopjes you will find him,
> For he's still on active service, eating things without
>   a plate,
> And thinking of the things he's left behind him.[136]

The first contingent of Imperial Yeomanry had a long wait before they were finally sent home; indeed, some companies did not leave until July 1901. A few Volunteer Service Companies had to wait even longer. The men were disgruntled. In late December 1900 C. S. Awdry ran into the Fourth (Glamorganshire) Company Imperial Yeomanry near Winburg in the Free State. He had not seen them since their passage together aboard the S.S. *Cymric.* After four months of nonstop marching, they "were thoroughly worn out and disgusted."[137] Sir Thomas Fowler painted a similarly upsetting picture of his company. Their clothes were worn out, their station was "seedy," they could not buy any foodstuffs, and even though the garrison was safe, men were being shot down regularly while on patrol. "The men are getting tired of the campaign," he recorded in November 1900. "[It] never seems to come much nearer to its end."[138]

Some questioned whether the government had the right to keep them in South Africa. They had volunteered to fight in a war, and that war, many believed, had ended. After all, the Orange Free State and the Transvaal had been annexed as British colonies, and Lord Roberts had gone home a conquering hero at the end of 1900.[139] "What I do not understand," one critic wrote, "is why the Volunteers [and] Yeomanry . . . are not sent home. It is causing great discontent among the men. We volunteered in a crisis to help England, and that crisis is now over. True, we enlisted for one year or for such period as the War should last, but the War as such now is over, and the remaining fighting should be done by the Regulars and the police, whose job it is."[140] J. P. Sturrock agreed. After the fall of Pretoria, as far as he was concerned, Great Britain was safe. The work of the volunteers was over, the work of the police had begun, and it was time to go home.[141] Some tried to force the government's hand. According to William Corner, in January 1901 a few men in his company drafted a petition demanding that they be told when they would be sent home. With one exception, every man in the Eleventh Battalion Imperial Yeomanry signed it.[142]

W. A. W. Lawson did not challenge the legality of the government's decision but did question the wisdom of it: "Nothing much is ever done, as I fail to see how it can be; a few [damned] cattle and sheep captured, and a bit of nasty sniping; the most amazing and worst form of contest; good men hit, and nothing really tangible gained. The pleasure of command will soon cease if they keep our men out much longer. The worm will turn, and the Volunteer will not serve forever. [Lord] Chesham is at Johannesburg, but I fear has no power to help our men; many of them are, or will be, utterly ruined, all small farmers and tradesmen in country towns especially."[143] Many agreed with Lawson. Would men be as eager to sign up next time around if the public felt the government was dragging its heels in getting them returned home?

Lord Kitchener and Secretary of State for War William St. John Brodrick were certainly aware of the problem they had on their hands.[144] In a correspondence with the general on 15 December 1900, Brodrick related, "We realize the Yeomen are very discontented and can not be held indefinitely to their engagements."[145] Similarly, Roberts informed Kitchener the following month that he was pushing the cabinet to raise more Volunteer troops in order to relieve all the Militia and Volunteer Service Companies as well, believing that long delays in getting the men home could hurt volunteer recruitment in the future.[146] Kitchener felt things were moving as fast as they could. He wrote to Brodrick: "The volunteers are also being sent home as their relief arrives and I am getting them moved down country by degrees so that they may feel they are on their way home. I wish I could send them before their relief come and will do so when I can get these roving bands out of Cape Colony but while they last a number of small garrisons are necessary to prevent mischief being done."[147] But for men who longed for home, delays rarely seem necessary.

Enrollment in the auxiliary forces raised to serve in South Africa dropped off considerably after 1900.[148] In July 1901 *The Cossack Post,* a record of the comings and goings of B Squadron, Paget's Horse, reported that military and civilian officials were putting a lot of pressure on the men to reenlist. The effort had little influence. "Most of us will probably be content to rest on our laurels, and enjoy ourselves and have done 'Trooping.'"[149] In late 1901 Roberts was advised by the lord mayor of London not to call for any more volunteers for fear the response would be dreadful. His counterpart in Glasgow issued the same warning to Brodrick.[150]

The delay in getting the men home was only one factor for declining interest in volunteering. The groundswell of patriotism in Britain had died down as the sense of urgency in South Africa diminished. For many, the war was over. For others, it was dragging on without an end in sight, and they did not want to get involved. But no doubt the new role and responsibilities of volunteer troops were unappealing to many would-be recruits. Indeed, when Frank Charge learned that two of his friends had joined the second contingent of Imperial Yeomanry, which was sent hastily overseas in 1901, he assumed that they knew little of the situation in South Africa. "I am sure if they knew what was in store for them," he wrote his father, "they would infinitely prefer staying at home."[151] As to his own future, Charge was certain: "No more volunteering for this child."[152]

From 1901 through the war's end, the government continued to find men willing to serve overseas in the Imperial Yeomanry, Volunteers, and Militia. It was even able to convince some men in the field to "see it through" and extend their tour of duty. But the situation did not improve much for the volunteers. They continued to feel underutilized and, therefore, unappreciated. As a result, they succumbed much quicker to despair—not defeatism, for they remained convinced that the British would be victorious, but rather the feeling that they were running aimlessly around in circles, waiting around to catch a sniper's bullet or be stricken with dysentery. But when the end of the fighting finally arrived, it brought great joy and relief. The news meant that the volunteers could go home.

7

The Return of the Volunteers

It was our fault, and our very great fault, and *not* the
judgment of Heaven.
We made an Army in our own image, on an island nine by
seven,
Which faithfully mirrored its makers' ideals, equipment,
and mental attitude—
And so we got our lesson: and we ought to accept it with
gratitude.
We have spent two hundred million pounds to prove the fact
once more,
That horses are quicker than men afoot, since two and two
make four,
And horses have four legs, and men have two legs, and two
into four goes twice,
And nothing over except our lesson—and very cheap at the
price.

Rudyard Kipling, "The Lesson"[1]

To have been able to go at all was the most extraordinary piece of good luck that ever was. I would not have missed

> the months during which I wore her Majesty's uniform for anything in the world. When I think how many people have been drilling all their lives and could not go, while I, a mere civilian, with many others, went on active service without any of the bother of military education and peace training, I realise that we are much to be envied.
>
> Sidney Peel, Fortieth (Oxfordshire) Company Imperial Yeomanry, 1901.[2]

By 1902, most Britons had lost interest in the South African War. The conflict was now entering its fourth calendar year, and any progress made on the ground by British troops seemed inconsequential when compared to the growing costs. Much time had passed since the celebrations that followed the fall of the Boer capitals, Bloemfontein and Pretoria, and the triumphant returns of Lord Roberts and the City of London Imperial Volunteers. The British mission in South Africa was struggling to find meaning as the guerrilla campaign plodded on hopelessly without any end in sight. Newspapers reminded the public daily that thousands of miles from their homes, Britannia's most able-bodied sons continued to die. And in many ways, this fact was made worse by the nature of these losses. By the end of the war, the British had suffered nearly twenty-two thousand deaths among its soldiers, two-thirds of whom fell not to the enemy but instead to disease and illness. Although few made direct comparisons to the mismanagement of Britain's mid-century Crimean War, high casualties due to disease are always disturbing to a public that envisioned war in terms of battles and losses in terms of firepower. The British public grew war weary, and if the Conservative victory in the "Khaki election" of 1900 managed to shroud the full extent of that displeasure, by 1902 it was clear to most that the conflict had to be ended and the soldiers brought home.

Men who once had been eager to volunteer and risk their lives for their country and empire were now nervously counting the hours before they could return home. Fewer and fewer considered enlisting for a second tour of duty, and it was the extremely rare volunteer who chose to remain in South Africa for the stated purpose of "finishing what he had started." It was also harder for the War Office to find men in Britain to fill the departing volunteers' places. The lord mayors of major urban centers warned the War Office that it should look elsewhere for recruits. With so many men invalided, recovering in hospitals, or sent home, the size of companies and battalions in the field was often dangerously low. Sometimes, divisions were patched together with men from so many different units that group cohesion was impossible. Lord Methuen's Kimberley Column of thirteen hundred men, for example, came from fourteen different units. Since men did not know one another, officers had never worked together, and units had different levels of experience and different histories of drill, training, and recruitment, it became increasingly difficult to predict how the soldiers would act in battlefield situations. Officers seldom dared to take the offensive and were hard pressed in the event of a massed Boer attack.

Despite the shortages in the field, the War Office was under tremendous pressure to get the volunteers home as quickly as possible even before the Treaty of Vereeniging had been signed on 31 May and the last of more than twenty thousand Boers had surrendered on 10 July.[3] Large numbers of servicemen began arriving back in Southampton and Liverpool in late June and July. Yet the pomp and circumstance that accompanied the sendoff of these troops was seldom heard upon their return. British newspapers were much more interested in the coronation of H.R.H. The Prince of Wales and, later, Lord Salisbury's resignation than in the homecoming of soldiers, Lord Kitchener's arrival aboard the *Orotava* on 12 July being the one exception.

Kitchener was hailed, much as Lord Roberts had been, as a conquering hero, and as he walked down the gangway at Ocean Quay in Southampton, the First Hampshire Volunteer Artillery band welcomed him with Handel's appropriately titled "See the Conquering Hero Comes."[4] He was feted at nearby Hartley Hall, at Basingstoke, at Paddington Station, in Hyde Park, and at St. James Palace. The crowds "were dense and full of enthusiasm everywhere. . . . In the congested streets with their draperies of flags there was one incessant roar, and the air seemed to dance with waving handkerchiefs. Then the fact that a part of the route was through Hyde Park allowed an enormous concourse of people to assemble and applaud."[5] For *The Times*'s special correspondent, it was Kitchener's meeting with Roberts that provoked the greatest sense of awe and admiration (and hyperbole):

> The reception given to the patient and indomitable General was the most imposing celebration of its kind within the

> memory of living man. In every mind was the thought that not since Waterloo—I am not forgetting the Crimea, but remembering that the issues there were not really of equal gravity—had the Empire been engaged in a land war of equal importance. In every brain was the feeling that associated together before the eyes of many witnesses were two great and distinct heroes whom they might salute together as the accomplishers, each in his own way, of a great feat of arms. There was the Commander-in-Chief, who, by grand and bold strategy, had turned the tide of battle and broken up the enemy's armies, come to greet his successor in South Africa who had finished the work by dint of such an application of the policy of "thorough," in the best sense of the word, of tireless patience and perseverance through good and evil report, as the world had never seen.[6]

Lesser dignitaries received but short notices in the major newspapers when they returned from the war. Spottier still was the coverage reserved for the volunteers, who were lucky to get a line of print. Communities and local newspapers, for their part, continued to welcome home their soldiers with some enthusiasm throughout the summer months of 1902. For example, Honorary Col. T. W. Lemmon, Third (Militia) Battalion East Surrey Regiment, wrote fondly of the large crowds that received his men when they returned in July, and C. J. Hart wrote that the Birmingham crowds were as large to welcome home the Royal Warwickshire Regiment, Second Volunteer Service Company, in May 1902 as they were in 1901 when the First Company returned.[7] The 104 volunteers of the King's Liverpool Regiment, Second Volunteer Service Company, were greeted by 3,000 local volunteers and several thousand well-wishers when they arrived at the Central Station in Liverpool in early June. Likewise, Dumfries warmly received its Third (Militia) Battalion King's Own Scottish Borderers in late June after the regiment's two-and-a-half-year service. Five hundred men had gone out, and just over half were now returning. The Duke of Buccleuch presented each militiaman with a medal, and the regimental colors were restored to the city's officials.[8]

Still, the interest in the volunteers and their significance as a focal point of nationalism and local patriotism had died down considerably since Black Week. Perhaps it was inevitable that the return of these men would generate less enthusiasm than their sendoff. Or perhaps the ritual of recognition and commemoration had been observed repeatedly already in 1901 and early 1902, and the ceremonies were becoming tedious and burdensome. After two and a half years, many Britons were trying to forget about the war. They had buried their dead and were tending to their wounded. They cared little about the debates concerning the inadequacies of military leadership and technology and were ready to move into the twentieth century and tend to growing concerns of social welfare, taxation, and labor.

One additional explanation for the public's lack of enthusiasm may be the mixed perception of the Volunteer force's performance in South Africa. There were many officers and reporters who were very critical of the Militia, the Volunteers, and particularly the Imperial Yeomanry, and they did not mince words when writing home or speaking to an audience. The lack of training and discipline, critics argued, far outweighed any advantage intelligence and motivation may have given the volunteer soldier. For example, in October 1901 Maj. Edmund Allenby wrote to his father-in-law: "These Yeomen are useless. After being some months in the field, they learn a bit; but by the time they are any use, they have probably been captured two or three times, presenting the Boers on each occasion with a horse, rifle and 150 rounds of ammunition per man."[9] Another future field marshal, Maj. William Birdwood, also saw little value in the Imperial Yeomanry force as long as it continued to be sent to South Africa with inadequate training. There was no sense in sending them "till they can all ride really well and the men have become quite first class shots," he urged in a telegram. "Unless Yeomanry are thoroughly trained to ride I think we would get better value from them and lose fewer horses if their departure were deferred until they are passed . . . as competent horsemen and horsemasters."[10] And W. A. W. Lawson wrote: "I don't fancy the Yeomanry force now as much as I did; they mean well, but they never knew what they were going to do, and they are not as keen as they were. These chaps might be as good in a year, but the time is too short for the job." Lawson expressed this sentiment again a few weeks later. "Good chaps, but rare food for Boers, cannot ride, certainly not shoot, or look after their horses. They want 3 months training, or more, as they are not the same stamp at all as our old lot."[11] Remarks like these were commonplace.

Support from the public and from key figures like Lord Roberts meant that the CIV were beyond reproach. Volunteer Service Companies were well integrated into their battalions, and the Militia was largely ignored. The first contingent of Imperial Yeomanry had received mostly praise. It was the second contingent, however, that received most of the criticism.

The first contingent of Imperial Yeomanry had many advocates. Through 1900, the force performed admirably in South Africa. Yet in May, when Col. A. G. Lucas, the deputy adjutant general of Imperial Yeomanry, contacted the War Office offering to raise more drafts, he was kindly instructed that the services of such units would not be required in the future. No doubt the capture of Bloemfontein and the impending fall of Pretoria had buoyed the confidence of Lord Lansdowne and the War Office. Any future recruits, therefore, were to be raised within its own apparatus. In mid-December, though, the confidence of the new secretary of state for war, William St. John Brodrick, was badly shaken when Boer commandos led by J. B. Hertzog and P. H. Kritzinger invaded the Cape Colony.[12] Lucas renewed his offer to the War Office. After initially saying no, Brodrick reconsidered and reversed his decision in January 1901, giving Lucas permission to raise five thousand yeomen. By March, when recruiting was stopped, close to seventeen thousand had been enrolled in the Imperial Yeomanry.[13]

The organization and training of the second contingent was very different from that of the first. With the exception of a few battalions raised by special army orders, all recruits attested at local Yeomanry recruiting offices and then made their way immediately to either Aldershot or the Curragh. After a series of carelessly proctored medical, riding, and shooting exams, they received some insufficient training and then were shipped off to South Africa, often without their officers. Kitchener had felt strongly that it was more important to get the men to South Africa in a hurry with little or no training than it was to get them a few months later and better prepared. After all, he believed, they could get their training on the job. As a result, the men were hastily organized, did not know each other or their officers, and did not sail as battalions. There were few opportunities to develop any sense of esprit de corps in Britain or at sea. Another major problem was that many were deficient in skills or in health after they arrived in Cape Town. The weeding-out process was done on the job and not at home, where ill-fitted volunteers could have been discharged with little cost and readily replaced. Although many actually were sent home, a number of the new Imperial Yeomanry, both officers and men, continued to be employed when they should have been rejected.[14] All in all, the second contingent faced great obstacles.[15]

Many battalions could not overcome these issues in the field. Brodrick was apologetic to Kitchener by the summer. "I am sorry for what you say as to the new Yeomanry," he wrote. "I feared we had made a risk in training them so little before sending out. If you require drafts we must keep them two months at Aldershot first."[16] When the third contingent was raised beginning on 1 January 1902, the War Office did its best to rectify the preparation problems. More than seven thousand recruits underwent substantial examination, drill, and exercises, lasting at least two and often as long as three months, at training camps at Aldershot, Edinburgh, and the Curragh. Men got to fraternize with one another. Officers learned names. Undesirable men were weeded out. Roberts was quite impressed by his visit to Aldershot in January 1902 and wrote words of encouragement to Kitchener.[17] This force assuredly would have been better prepared to meet the Boers in battle had the war not ended before they had the opportunity.

A few disasters in the field greatly affected how the public viewed the Imperial Yeomanry.[18] Lindley was one such episode. Vlakfontein was another. On 29 May 1901 Brig. Gen. H. G. Dixon's rear guard was attacked in the western Transvaal by J. C. G. Kemp's commando. Many of the 150 men of the Seventh Battalion Imperial Yeomanry "fled in fear from the guns and left their officers or those who stood," wrote Julius Bernstein, a civil surgeon attached to the Scottish Horse, who witnessed the action. "And since then," he continued, "the I.Y. have likewise distinguished themselves as arrogant cowards."[19] Sixty of the 150 imperial yeomen became casualties of Kemp's attack. At Brakspruit, 60 more troopers were taken prisoner in what H. G. Howell, Cape Mounted Rifles, called a "damn bad piece of work."[20] And more seriously, on early Christmas morning 1901, Gen. Christiaan de Wet struck the Eleventh Battalion Imperial Yeomanry, guarding the eastern extent of the British blockhouse line in the northeastern Free State at Tweefontein (Groenkop). The British commander, Maj. F. A. Williams, had not prepared the camp's perimeter adequately. His men, of which the Thirty-fifth (Middlesex) Company was dangerously understrength, reacted poorly to the surprise assault. "The fact cannot be disguised that in the course of twenty minutes nearly a third of the force gave way to panic and fled, half-dressed and in many cases unarmed," Leo Amery wrote.[21] Although many of the men acted bravely, the action at Tweefontein reinforced what many had already concluded about the Imperial Yeomanry—they were careless and inefficient.[22] Kitchener reluctantly agreed: "But efficiency had often to yield to emergency, and captures of 'green' Yeomanry, with a valuable haul of rifles and ammunition, were not rare occurrences."[23]

The alarming sequence of Imperial Yeomanry defeats, often evaluated as disasters that could have been avoided, continued into the new year. Kitchener received word of several units "behaving badly" and found the news quite distressing.[24] He received little satisfaction from Brodrick that future Yeomanry units would be better prepared; he was dependent on the troops he already had in the field in early 1902 to win the war. Episodes like Gen. J. H. de la Rey's attack at Yzer Spruit in late February, which resulted in elements of the Fifth Battalion, under Lt. Col. William Campbell Anderson, "bolting," shook Kitchener's confidence in his ability to get the job done.[25] But it was the news of Methuen's defeat at Tweebosch that the British commander found the most upsetting.

Lord Methuen had been operating in the western Transvaal and northern Cape Colony for more than a year and a half. Once in command of the ten-thousand-strong First Division, which had moved on Kimberley at the end of 1899, he now rarely had more than three thousand men at his disposal. These men had to garrison dozens of blockhouses, guard supply lines, escort convoys, occupy a number of hostile towns, and carry out offensive operations against several Boer commandos operating in the region. To make matters worse, the thirteen hundred men he personally commanded and had available for larger operations came from a hodgepodge of British and imperial units. The Kimberley Column composed men from the First Northumberland Fusiliers; First Loyal North Lancashires; Fourth and Thirty-eighth Batteries, Royal Field Artillery; the Diamond Fields Horse; Cullinan's Horse; Forty-third (Suffolk) and Eighty-sixth (Rough Riders) Companies Imperial Yeomanry; Cape Police; British South Africa Police; Dennison's Scouts; Ashburner's Light Horse;

Cape Special Police; details from the Fifth Battalion Imperial Yeomanry; and some Khoi-San and "Coloureds."[26] Methuen had already complained about his troops. Other than his regulars, they could not be counted on. They lacked training, discipline, resources, and interest in the war. Many were sick; others were exhausted. Morale was low. In particular, Methuen identified the Imperial Yeomanry as a weak link. He had commanded Imperial Yeomanry units since they had first arrived in 1900. He was quite satisfied with the first contingent and had praised them on numerous occasions. But this contingent, he felt, lacked resolve and commitment. Few envied Methuen's command.

In early March 1902 Methuen headed out of Vryburg to conduct a retaliatory strike against Gen. de la Rey's commando. But he did not catch de la Rey, instead the Boer caught him. On 7 March at Tweebosch, in a most unconventional move, the Boers, dressed in khaki and resembling British troops, charged the unsuspecting column. Inexperienced, unprepared, and understrength, the Imperial Yeomanry and mounted colonial troops panicked and broke ranks. The rout was soon complete. Fifty-six British soldiers were killed and three hundred were wounded; 130 African drivers and support were also killed. Most of the remaining force surrendered, and the guns were captured along with them.[27] In addition, Methuen, one of Great Britain's most senior officers in the field, was severely wounded and taken prisoner by de la Rey. When informed of this disaster, Kitchener collapsed and did not leave his bed for a day and a half. The general ate nothing during this period, spending his days staring at his bedroom walls in a state of shock.[28] Tweebosch was, as Brodrick noted in a letter to Kitchener, "the worst business since Colenso."[29]

To what extent Tweebosch and these other British setbacks can be blamed on the Imperial Yeomanry is debatable. Brodrick, for example, held the colonial mounted troops responsible for the debacle.[30] But of course, he was not at Tweebosch. Frank Stephenson was not either, but he did put in a year's service with the Tenth (Sherwood Rangers) Company Imperial Yeomanry and was still on duty when the action occurred. Stephenson was convinced that the negative portrayal of the second contingent was deliberate, a result of a perceived inequity in pay: Unsure of whether the call to arms in 1901 would be met with the same enthusiasm as it had been in the wake of Black Week, the War Office decided to offer a higher pay rate to the second contingent of Imperial Yeomanry. This led to anger in some circles, especially in the Regular Army. Stephenson wrote, "I suppose from what we hear out here that us chaps have got an awfully bad name at home, the majority of yarns that are flying about are nothing but a pack of lies, started through prejudice because of the increase pay of the second contingent of Yeomanry."[31] He and others believed that the Imperial Yeomanry was being unfairly singled out.

Yet just as they had their critics, Britain's volunteers had numerous supporters, who also played a vital in role in shaping public sentiment. Even officers who commanded companies of the second contingent had positive things to say about them. Methuen, for one, remained convinced that the Imperial Yeomanry, and volunteer troops in general, were an asset to the British army, and if there were problems, they could be fixed through better governance, leadership, and training. "The Yeomanry," he testified before a royal commission after the war "gained in military knowledge to a surprising extent during the campaign. They bought their experience rather expensively at first, but I could place implicit reliance in them after a short time. The good result was due to their individual intelligence, and the confidence they, with justice, placed in . . . many of their officers."[32]

Lord Dundonald, who served in Buller's command in the Natal and, upon his return to Great Britain, was appointed by Brodrick to the Yeomanry Reorganization Committee in December 1900, remained a firm supporter of the auxiliary forces.[33] He felt that Roberts and Gen. Sir William Nicholson, director general of mobilization and military intelligence, greatly underestimated the "military capabilities of the British Citizen soldier."[34] In true Edwardian fashion, Dundonald argued that the auxiliaries just needed to be made more "efficient."

Lord Roberts was initially keen on volunteer service while he was in South Africa in 1900. In dispatches to Lansdowne, he praised the performance of the Imperial Yeomanry at Boshof in April and at Faber's Put in June.[35] As he watched the parade of British troops file past through the city streets of captured Pretoria, Roberts wrote to Lansdowne with great satisfaction: "The auxiliary troops are doing wonderfully well."[36] But he saved his highest accolades for his farewell to the CIV in October 1900: "I have always been a firm believer in the Volunteer movement, and have had strong convictions that some of the best material in the Army is to be found in our Volunteer force. . . . The admirable work now performed by the C.I.V., the Volunteers attached to the regular battalions serving in South Africa, and the Imperial Yeomanry, have, I rejoice to say, proved that I was right, and that England, relying as she does on the patriotic volunteer system for her defence, is resting on no broken reed."[37]

Roberts was not alone in his enthusiasm. Lord Chesham, who naturally had a close relationship with the Imperial Yeomanry and had a vested interest in their effectiveness, could not "speak in too complimentary terms" about their performance in 1900.[38] Lt. Gen. Sir Leslie Rundle wrote that he took great "pride in having such gallant and reliable horsemen under his command" as the Imperial Yeomanry.[39] Likewise, Lt. Gen. Archibald Hunter, who took command of the de Wet hunt in late June 1900 after Ian Hamilton was injured in a fall, spoke of the "excellent work done" by the Scottish Imperial Yeomanry. "The Yeomanry," Hunter wrote in a letter to Kitchener, "is daily gaining experience in actual warfare, which is all they ask for & all they require to make them rank with the best—This they now do."[40]

British officers remained dedicated to the volunteer force and continued to praise the auxiliaries throughout the guerrilla phase of the war. Capt. Richard Gubbins, Lt. W. S. Power, and Sgt. Harry Hopwood were all emphatic in defending the activities of the Thirty-fifth (Duke of Cambridge's Own) and Eighth (Derbyshire) Companies Imperial Yeomanry and the Second Volunteer Battalion, Manchester Regiment, respectively.[41] H. G. Howell applauded most of the Imperial Yeomanry companies he observed in 1901.[42] For every episode like Tweefontein and Tweebosch, there were a number of successes as well. On 18 December 1901, for example, Gen. de Wet attacked two regiments of the South African—raised Imperial Light Horse and the Eleventh Battalion Imperial Yeomanry. In the ensuing battle at Tygerkloof Spruit, in which the British were victorious, the Yeomanry, according to de Wet, "behaved very gallantly."[43] Two days later the Boer general Wessel Wessels attacked a small British force at Tafel Kop. In a ruse similar to the one later employed at Tweebosch, the Boers, dressed in khaki and mimicking the typical formations of the Imperial Yeomanry, casually approached the British and then charged at close range. Colonel Damant's Thirtieth (Pembrokeshire) and Thirty-first (Montgomeryshire) Companies

Imperial Yeomanry, responded brilliantly and, despite heavy losses, fought off the attacking commando.[44]

Historians must assess the overall Volunteer experience in the South African War in positive terms. In all but a few cases, the men did what they were trained to do and what was expected of them. When they failed, it was usually a fault of training, leadership, or administration in maintaining proper numbers and morale. The units after all were hastily organized, often consisting of men who perhaps should not have served in South Africa, and not properly trained for a lengthy conflict, guerrilla war or otherwise. If they did not meet the expectations of some, it is certain those expectations were set too high. The Gipps Committee, which examined the military efficiency and character of the second contingent, agreed. It believed that the "Imperial Yeomanry Staff in South Africa were inclined to expect and to exact a standard of efficiency higher than could reasonably be looked for from a force of comparatively untrained civilians."[45]

The volunteers proved to be more than capable soldiers on the South African veld. William Home elegantly voiced the feelings of most veterans in this regard: "We are glad that, as part of the army of 100,000 volunteers who served in the war, we have been able to show to those who have hitherto made it their business to sneer at our 'citizen' army as a 'paper' force, that, in the hour of national danger, the volunteer can take his place shoulder to shoulder with the soldier of the line, and that he can endure the same hardships, and face the same dangers, and die the same death, if need be, in his country's cause."[46]

That volunteers served when their country needed them was a substantial contribution in itself. But these men managed to do much more than just show up when they were needed. In the South African War, those same volunteers who had been mocked throughout the late nineteenth century showed their mettle and continued to perform admirably even after they had come to see the futility of the war.

Aftermath

Edwardian Reform

Then that little tin soldier he sobbed and
    sighed,
So I patted his little tin head,
"What vexes your little tin soul?" said I,
And this is what he said:
"I've been on this stall a very long time,
And I'm marked '1/3' as you see,
While just above my head he's marked '5 bob,'
Is a bloke in the Yeoman-ree.
Now he hasn't any service and he hasn't got no
    drill,
And I'm better far than he,
Then why mark us at fifteen pence,
And five bob the Yeoman-ree?"[1]

The debate over the readiness, efficiency, and reliability of the auxiliary forces continued for several years after the South African War. Interpretations of the volunteers' performance in that conflict were often guided by postwar rhetoric. Those, for example, who supported national service and wanted to see major reform in the British military naturally were more critical of the volunteer force. Those concerned about cost or who philosophically opposed conscription often took a different position. Even during the war it was apparent that the volunteers were already being "used" to push certain agendas. Sir Henry Campbell-Bannerman, a future Liberal prime minister and former secretary of state for war, no stranger himself to manipulating the political climate, wrote to Sir Ralph Knox, an undersecretary of state for war: "This howling against the Army system and administration will only result in prodigious waste of money and the expansion of the Army beyond our powers of maintenance. However on Saturday you will all be out, waving Union Jacks, and cheering the C.I.V.'s. Thank God I am in quiet country fields, where Union Jacks are unknown."[2]

The Edwardian army was in need of reform from top to bottom. There was little coordination of its services, the command structure was too top heavy in the person of the commander in chief, the reserve was small, training and education were suspect, overseas garrison duties were draining the strength of home-district Regular Army battalions, and the role of the auxiliary services in home defense was still unsettled. Brodrick and the next two secretaries of state for war, H. O. Arnold-Forster and R. B. Haldane, did their best to shape military reform and to solve these and other problems. All of their schemes, to some extent, involved the auxiliaries.

Of the three, Brodrick was probably the least interested in the volunteers. Eager to get started on his agenda, the secretary introduced his reforms before the war had even ended. The linchpin of his scheme hinged on the creation of a six-army-corps system in which three self-contained corps of Regular Army soldiers would be made readily available for use on the Continent as a striking force, while the other three, made up mostly of Volunteers and Militia, would be used for home defense. In order to carry out this plan, Brodrick needed to increase the size of the army. He planned on achieving this by making the military a more attractive career choice by raising pay, shortening the terms, and generally improving the conditions of service. In order to increase the efficiency of the force, he proposed additional training. As for the auxiliary services, Brodrick wanted to increase enrollment in the Militia, Yeomanry, and Volunteers; create a Militia reserve of fifty thousand men; improve pay and conditions; and increase the number of training days per year.

He also wanted to rearm the Yeomanry, turning it into a force that more closely resembled mounted infantry than cavalry.[3]

Although most in Parliament remained quiet and no serious challenges to Brodrick's scheme were posed while the war continued, once it ended, the opposition launched a fierce attack. The Liberals, led by Campbell-Bannerman, called his proposals excessively militaristic and too expensive. A large faction of Unionists, led by Winston Churchill, reunited with their former Liberal allies in their condemnation of the plan. They feared that resources spent on the army would naturally drain the navy of necessary funding. Supporters of the "Blue Water School" of national security continued to see home defense as primarily the responsibility of the Royal Navy and not ill-trained auxiliary forces. Militia colonels and Volunteer and Yeomanry elites protested over the regularization of their services. Others like Lord Roberts feared giving the auxiliary force too much responsibility. And still others like Sir Henry Rawlinson thought Brodrick was shortsighted for ignoring the need to create a general staff.[4] Eventually, the cabinet pulled its support from Brodrick, and his scheme died with his resignation.

In October 1903 Prime Minister Arthur Balfour appointed Hugh Oakley Arnold-Forster as Brodrick's successor. By winter, Arnold-Forster was ready to implement his own reforms. An adherent of the Blue Water School, the new secretary placed his confidence in the Royal Navy for the defense of Great Britain. The Regular Army, he believed, was also a valuable asset, an essential instrument necessary to man imperial garrisons and, when required, strike at an enemy overseas. To strengthen it he proposed creating two separate armies: one, a long-service army in which the enlistment commitment would be extended from three to nine years; and the other, a smaller short-service army whose obligation would be primarily domestic. As to maintaining the volunteer force, even an efficient one, Arnold-Forster believed the benefits were rather small and proposed drastic cuts to both the Militia and Volunteers. This part of his proposal proved to his ultimate undoing.[5]

Friends of the Militia and Volunteers launched an aggressive assault on the Arnold-Forster plan through the press. They secured a strong base of support in Parliament as well. Even in the cabinet Arnold-Forster found a hostile reception. The opposition objected to any reduction in numbers and rejected his belief that the Militia and

Volunteers could not be turned into efficient fighting forces. In an atmosphere in which national service was becoming a hotly contested issue, the Volunteers were able to position themselves as an alternative to conscription. Volunteer MPs were successfully able to obstruct the scheme long enough to see the fall of Balfour, Arnold-Forster, and the Conservatives.

Campbell-Bannerman's choice for secretary of state for war, R. B. Haldane, was not going to make the same mistakes as his predecessors. He did not dare initiate expensive military reforms, knowing that they would not be tolerated by his party or the public. He also knew not to dismiss the volunteer force as abruptly as Arnold-Forster had done. Although he believed volunteers could not go up against seasoned troops, he was quite certain that with ample training, the Militia, Volunteers, and Yeomanry could still play a key role in home defense and, if necessary, a supporting part in imperial and continental affairs. "I should like to see him used," he wrote, in a way that supplemented but did not imitate the function of the Regular Army.[6]

Haldane's eventual solution was the creation of the Expeditionary Force, the Special Reserve, and the Territorial Force. In a charged atmosphere of growing Anglo-German tensions, he refocused military responsibilities away from the defense of India and the empire and toward the Continent. A leaner, more efficient Regular Army was reorganized within a divisional framework and devised as a striking force. Haldane envisioned the Militia as an arm that could support the Expeditionary Force and provide drafts. Militia colonels were very reluctant to support any scheme that reduced their traditional control over their units and altered its terms to include foreign service. Without dismantling the Militia, Haldane thus proposed the creation of the Special Reserve, a semi-professional force whose better terms and conditions would attract militiamen. The plan worked. Within one month of its creation in January 1908, 60 percent of the Militia had transferred to the Special Reserve.[7] As for the Volunteers and Yeomanry, they were reorganized by the Territorial and Reserve Forces Act of 1907.[8] Although critics suggested that this force consisted of no more than the same old men wearing new uniforms, reforms were implemented to strengthen, reequip, and reorganize the Territorial Force for home defense. As with the Militia, Volunteer and Yeomanry leaders objected to the scheme.

Haldane, however, proved to be a much better politician than his predecessors. He carefully worked out the details of his plan with the cabinet, key reformers, and leading generals before presenting it to Parliament. He was much more willing to make concessions to the auxiliary force personages, such as excluding the Militia from the Territorial Force and giving greater control over the county associations to the Army Council. Winning the support of the King also proved vital for the bill's passage through the House of Lords. In the end Haldane was able to do what his two predecessors had not.[9]

The reform of the volunteer force in the Edwardian era was not principally shaped by the performance of the troops during the South African War. Rather, it was shaped largely by politics, personalities, and concerns of foreign policy. It was also influenced by a wider discussion of where Great Britain was heading in the future. One concern that was of particular relevance to the Volunteer debate was the issue of national efficiency.

The South African War stimulated and exaggerated feelings of insecurity among the British people. Some of these fears, such as the loss of global economic prominence and the weakening of imperial ties, were quite reasonable. Others, like the fear of invasion, a theme so pronounced in 1890s British literature, were not. Regardless, the difficulties in defeating the Boers dealt a very real blow to Britons' sense of national superiority.[10] If the state had such a difficult time tackling a foe with a weak industrial base and a small irregular army, what prospects lay ahead in a war with a European power? Although it was not yet time to panic, a degree of trepidation was probably healthy. In many circles the military was not held solely responsible. Instead, questions were raised about the quality of British national culture. "National efficiency" emerged as a term identified with social reform. Not only did it mean the rationalization of business and bureaucratic organization but also physical and racial reform.

British national physique became suspect to many at this time. As hostilities were ending in 1902, Frederick Maurice, future biographer of Lord Wolseley, Lord Rawlinson, and Confederate general Robert E. Lee, writing under the pseudonym "Miles" in the pages of the *Contemporary Review,* revealed to the public a shocking report about the alleged physical degeneration of Britain's army-aged male population.[11] The following year, using his own name this time, Maurice delivered a second bleak statement about the health of the nation. He claimed that 28 percent of all applicants were rejected for army service in 1900 and more than 29 percent were rejected in 1901.[12] An additional 15 percent of men initially accepted were discharged for health reasons within two years, shipped back from South Africa because of bad teeth, flat feet, heart weakness, "pneumatic troubles," and rheumatism. Maurice attributed these high numbers to poverty and urban decay. Children were not getting adequate nourishment, and the physical conditions of their upbringing—small houses, factory employment, and unhealthy mothers—stunted their development. By the time such kids reached maturity, they were unfit for military service. Although an Inter-Departmental Committee on Physical Deterioration concluded that physical degeneration among Britons was not as widespread as Maurice had indicated, it did call for the increased physical training of the nation's youth.[13]

Maurice approached the subject of physical degeneration from his interest in military affairs and home defense. Not only were large numbers of men turned away from the Regular Army but (as discussed in chapter 3) an alarming number of applicants were also rejected by the Imperial Yeomanry, Volunteers, and Militia. In the current climate Maurice feared that Britain would be hard pressed to defend itself from a continental attack. His solution was to raise health and welfare standards among the urban poor.

Others proposed a more radical solution, one to which Maurice himself did not prescribe. They focused away from the men rejected for service because of health issues and toward those who had opted to avoid military service in the first place. What these reformers called for was the implementation of national service. The conscription debate loomed large in Edwardian Britain (but will not be discussed in any detail here), and formed an important context for the implementation of military reforms.[14] What is important to note is that a real dichotomy existed between those who believed the volunteers, or at least a reformed volunteer force, assisted by the Royal Navy were capable of providing for home defense and those who thought Britain's manpower needs in the event of a European war could not be met voluntarily. The National Service League (NSL), formed during the closing months of the South African War, attempted to steer public and political sentiment toward supporting conscription. Lord Roberts, who initially did not favor compulsory service, came to embrace it and was later chosen president of the

NSL. He was joined in the organization by other South African War veterans such as Henry Wilson and Charles Repington. Although the NSL attracted many Conservatives to conscription, it failed to win over significant numbers of Liberals. Conscription was not a viable alternative open to Haldane. A solution that involved a voluntary force, therefore, had to be worked out to suit Britain's military needs and political reality.

Reform was also shaped by reports coming out of a number of royal and parliamentary committees established during and after the war, including the Dawkins Committee, the Gipps Committee, Lord Esher's Committee, Lord Ebrington's Committee, and War Office council meetings like the one that discussed the creation of an auxiliary forces advisory board.[15] The two most significant reports were delivered by the Elgin Commission, also known as the Royal Commission on the War in South Africa, and the Norfolk Commission, also known as the Royal Commission on the Militia and Volunteers.

The Elgin Commission entertained 114 witnesses between October and December 1902 and February and June 1903. It examined all aspects of the war, from military preparations to manpower, from arms and equipment to the organization of the War Office. It questioned officers about military behavior and efficiency in the field, including that of the auxiliary forces. But the commission steered clear of indicting any officers or men, believing that criticism of military operations would have been viewed as impolitic.[16]

Although the findings of the commission presented the Balfour government with some substantial challenges in explaining poor planning and deficiencies in manpower and equipment, they did not directly challenge the efficacy of employing the auxiliary forces overseas or their performance in the war. The commissioners did point to some weaknesses, like the second contingent of Imperial Yeomanry's "ignoran[ce] of the rudiments of soldiering," but culpability, they found, did not lay with the men but instead with the government in its planning for the war and in its preparations of its forces.[17]

The Norfolk Commission (see below) was appointed before the Elgin Commission finished its investigation. As a result, Lord Elgin and his commissioners felt no need to probe too deeply into the state of the Militia and Volunteers and purposely "decided not to take evidence which they had previously intended to take."[18] In regards to the Militia, the commission found a serious deficiency in the number of trained officers, and as a result many senior Regular Army officers were anxious about employing them in combat situations until the auxiliaries had gained enough experience. Until then, as Lord Roberts and others testified, militiamen were best suited to guard the lines of communication. The commission was more positive about the Volunteers' experience in the war. Its support for the City of London Imperial Volunteers, from its formation and organization through its homecoming, was unanimous.[19] The work of the Volunteer Service Corps was also applauded. Relying heavily on the testimony of Sir Howard Vincent, the force's most important advocate, it is not a surprise that the commission reached the conclusion it did. The one reform that it did support but did not mandate was the development of a centralized Volunteer staff within the auxiliary forces.

Since the Norfolk Commission's charge did not include the Imperial Yeomanry, the Elgin Commission examined its witnesses on the subject in greater detail. It was satisfied with the first contingent; organization, recruitment, training, leadership, and service were all appreciated. If there was one criticism, it was not with the force itself but with the government's decision to stop recruitment when so many men were willing to sign up for the right reason, the patriotic impulse following Black Week, and not the wrong reason, in their opinion, the five shillings a day offered later in the war.[20]

As to the second contingent, the commission was critical but kept their comments within the correct context of the discussion. Witnesses testified that these servicemen "knew nothing at all," they were "very bad," and they "could not ride at all."[21] Yet the commission ultimately deferred to the wisdom of the conclusions made by Lord Methuen, who had witnessed both contingents over long periods and in a variety of conditions. He testified:

> When the Second Contingent of Yeomanry came out their riding was hopelessly bad; they had no knowledge of a horse, or how to ride. . . . When I started my first trek when they were all new Yeomanry, I told Lord Kitchener that I did so knowing perfectly well the danger, and I pointed it out to him, and some of them suffered accordingly from not having any knowledge of shooting or riding. I wish to say of the Second Contingent (because there has been a good deal of adverse criticism against them), that they were not in a posi-

> tion either through capacity for riding, shooting, or discipline at first to render a satisfactory account of themselves, but by the time they had once got into a working order . . . [they] did their work intelligently, and I have not one single word to say against them. I am very glad you have given me the chance to say this much for them, because I have seen so many criticisms abusing the men for their want of pluck. It was not their fault, it was sending them out unprepared, and not giving them a chance when they got to the country of getting into order before they were in front of the enemy.[22]

Elgin and the others agreed. The second contingent, once it received some training, did well, despite the working-class backgrounds of its constituents, which many officers testified was an impediment, and their motivation, which those same officers concluded was a higher wage. The government's decision, largely shaped by Kitchener's wishes, to forego preliminary training at home and ship the recruits off to South Africa as fast as it could proved a very costly mistake. Therefore, future reform of the Imperial Yeomanry, the commission urged, needed to be largely organizational.

This commission sat during highly charged political times. When its report was eventually released, the Liberal Party pounced on it, using it to attack the government's credibility. The failure to conduct a war without major problems played a role in the 1906 Conservative Party defeat. The Elgin Commission's report, however, because it shied from criticism and urging major reform, was not overtly politicized despite attempts made by several witnesses to make it so. There were some members of the body who probably would have liked it to become political. Lord Esher was a major advocate of compulsion and thought that the volunteers were "a gigantic fraud."[23] Also, George Taubman-Goldie, along with Frederick Darley and John Edge, supported some form of mandatory military-training course. Taubman-Goldie later acted as president of the National Defence Association, a political lobby that attempted to co-opt men from both sides of the conscription debate into standing together for military reform, advocating for a more robust Cadet Corps, among other things.

The Norfolk Commission was subject to even stronger political forces since it dealt specifically with two groups that many felt very strongly about, the Militia and Volunteers. This investigation, charged with the task of examining the efficiency of the Militia and Volunteers (but not the Yeomanry), was no less extensive than Elgin's, examining 134 witnesses between May 1903 and February 1904 before submitting its report in late May 1904. The commission worked from the premise that the "Militia exist[ed] chiefly, and the Volunteers solely, for the purpose of resisting a possible invasion of the United Kingdom."[24] So although the investigation took place in the wake of a conflict that required these two forces to fight overseas, technically, the Norfolk's inquiry was only trying to establish the efficiency of these forces to provide for home defense in the event of an attack by "a first rate army." Indeed, the twelve-point "heads of evidence" memorandum delivered to many of the general officers who would testify before the commission did not include any topics related to Militia and Volunteer performance in the field.[25] Much of the evidence, however, was given by officers who witnessed the auxiliary forces in South Africa and drew conclusions about their efficiency based on those experiences.

Although a number of witnesses had positive things to say about these auxiliary forces, the report overall was damning. Drill and training were found to be insufficient. The report estimated that the average Militia battalion would require several months of continuous embodiment before it would be ready to take the field. Many Volunteer units lacked basic instructional equipment and accessible ranges, and they possessed considerable difficulties in obtaining time and space for training. In addition, due to the lack of training, officers failed to weed out an "appreciable" number of physically unfit Volunteer recruits. The commission also found both forces lacking proper organization, great disparities between battalion establishments and actual strengths, and field-artillery units with insufficient transport, equipment, and materiel.

Finally, and perhaps most upsetting to the commissioners, was the testimony they heard regarding the quality of the Militia and Volunteer officers. Militia officers, because of their poor training, were not ready to lead their men into battle, and many Volunteer officers were found to have "neither the theoretical knowledge nor the practical skill in the handling of troops which would make them competent instructors in peace or leaders in war."[26] As a result of these deficiencies, neither force, the report concluded, was prepared to meet the needs of home defense.

The Norfolk Commission was not prepared to recommend to Parliament that the auxiliary forces be scrapped altogether. Its members proposed measures to increase the efficiency of the forces and believed that they were capable of being reformed. These proposals included, for the Militia, an eight-year enlistment period, with a substantial increase of continuous training for new recruits and more incremental training for experienced militiamen, and the development of a permanent staff; and for the Volunteers, the reorganization of the force into brigades and divisions under a separate department managed by the War Office; an increase in the number of training camps per year; the provision of firing ranges, exercise grounds, transport, and equipment for mobilization; and the formation of tactical schools to better train officers. In addition, the commissioners wanted to somehow convince civil society that volunteers should not be discriminated against for time lost from work due to their military commitment. If these changes were made, the members believed, the auxiliary forces could act as an important supplement to the Regular Army in home defense. But they concluded that if the Regular Army or a large proportion of it was not available, even reformed auxiliaries could not prevent a successful invasion of the United Kingdom. Norfolk's Commission ultimately recommended that every capable "citizen of military age" be trained for and be ready to take part in home defense.[27]

The Report of the Royal Commission on the Militia and Volunteers was not drafted as a direct indictment of the performance of the auxiliary forces in South Africa. Few questions dealt directly with the war itself. Yet it seems impossible to read this document, produced only two years after the war's end, as anything but a strong condemnation of the auxiliary forces' performance. If the government's perception had been that these units did well, it is doubtful that Brodrick would have moved forward with any such inquest in the first place, and certainly, even if he had, the commission would not have called for such extensive reform. But with complete cabinet support, Arnold-Forster, who was in office when the commission delivered its report, simply ignored these findings and instead endorsed a different set of reforms.[28] Clearly, politics both influenced Norfolk's report and the government's response to it.

The conscription debate shaped many testimonies; answers to the commissioners' questions often had little to do with what they had observed in South Africa. Indeed, the NSL even submitted a lengthy report of its own that was included in the final report's appendix.[29] Similar politics permeated the makeup of the commission itself. With the notable exception of H. Spenser Wilkinson, many of its members supported conscription. It is hard to determine, however, to what extent their beliefs had been fashioned prior to their service on the commission or if the testimonies they heard pushed them in that direction.[30] Regardless, the debate over the efficiency of the auxiliary forces and their performance in the South African War was colored by the debate over conscription. And in the Edwardian era, it was impossible to separate politics from the issue of military reform. If there was a time during the war when military observers could have ever been viewed as objective, that time had long ended.

The aftermath of the South African War was none too kind to Great Britain's auxiliary forces. The volunteers left a hostile environment in Africa and returned to an indifferent one in Britain. Although local communities were glad to welcome back their citizen-soldiers, the national psyche was fixed on trying to detach itself from a three-year conflict fought on the other end of the world. There were enough mistakes, tales of cowardice and incompetence, and overblown and overconfident proclamations of easy victory over the Boers to make Britons want to forget about it all.

Of course, there were also fetes of excellence, tales of heroism, and successful strategies and innovations of tactics that should have been embraced by an interested public. Certainly there were some who wanted to make sure these stories, both good and bad, came out. The auxiliary forces were featured prominently in both retellings. What is particularly striking about the war's literature is how many firsthand accounts written by militiamen, volunteers, and imperial yeomen were published during and immediately after the war and how few came out during this highly contested period of reform. Obviously, publishers such as Edward Arnold; Longmans, Green, and Company; Methuen; and Simpkins, Marshall, Hamilton, Kent, and Company were most interested in selling copies and wanted to rush out their products before interest in the war subsided. Still, it is hard to believe that the market shrank so considerably in just a few years. More likely, these veteran volunteers feared that their accounts would be appropriated and their words twisted to fit a political agenda. It should therefore come as no surprise that the two most controversial titles, Leo Amery's *The Times History of the War in South Africa, 1899–1902* and J. F. Maurice's volumes of the *(Official) History of the War in South Africa, 1899–1902,* were released later in the decade, during the height of the debates over Haldane's reforms.[31]

Those who served in the Militia, Volunteer Service Companies, and Imperial Yeomanry were aware of their forces' deficiencies, and yet they were nearly unanimous in their praise for and their pride in the part they had played in the war effort. In a time of crisis, their country and their empire needed them, and they responded to the call to arms. Great Britain ultimately would not have been victorious without their contribution.

Back in early 1901, a volunteer in Paget's Horse had wondered "how many of [them would] return, of [their] own choice, to South Africa."[32] He did not have to ask how many of his comrades would volunteer if a similar crisis had occurred. He knew the answer. Despite the hardships of the war and the distasteful way the volunteers were used in the political debates that followed, Britons were ready to respond if needed. What that volunteer could not have known was how soon that crisis would come.

Notes

ABBREVIATIONS

GL	Guildhall Library, London
LHCMA	Liddell Hart Centre for Military Archives, King's College, University of London
NAM	National Army Museum, London (Chelsea)
TNA	The National Archives, Kew
WCM	Worcester City Museum, Worcester

INTRODUCTION

1. For a more detailed discussion on Methuen's operations in the western Transvaal, see Stephen M. Miller, *Lord Methuen and the British Army: Failure and Redemption in South Africa* (London: Frank Cass, 1999), 225–30.

2. Fransjohan Pretorius, *Life on Commando during the Anglo-Boer War, 1899–1902* (Cape Town: Human & Rousseau, 1999), 144–45.

3. Methuen wrote of that force, which included the Third, Fifth, and Tenth Battalions Imperial Yeomanry, "as for my Yeomen, I am quite in love with them, as they do their work splendidly." P. S. Methuen to his wife, 8 June 1900, Methuen Papers, Wiltshire Records Office, Trowbridge.

4. P. S. Methuen to I. Hamilton, 27 Feb. 1902, ibid.

5. L. S. Amery, ed., *The Times History of the War in South Africa 1899–1902,* 7 vols. (London: Sampson Low, Marston, 1900–1909), 5:503.

6. Ibid., 5:506.

7. This was not the case in Great Britain at the time. The battle of Tweebosch received much attention from politicians and the public as well.

8. For an excellent social history of the Boer forces in the war, see Pretorius, *Life on Commando.*

9. Neither the Militia, the Yeomanry, nor the Volunteers should be considered "irregular" since they were properly constituted, trained, and organized under the aegis of the state.

10. Richard Burdon Haldane served as the Liberal secretary of state for war from 1905 to 1912 and oversaw the overhaul of the auxiliary forces through the Territorial and Reserve Forces Act of 1907.

11. On the Regular Army, see, for example, Alan Ramsay Skelley, *The Victorian Army at Home: The Recruitment and Terms and Conditions of the British Regular, 1859–1899* (Montreal: McGill-Queen's University Press, 1977); and Edward M. Spiers, *The Late Victorian Army, 1868–1902* (London: St. Martin's, 1992). Will Bennett's entertaining account, *Absent-Minded Beggars: Volunteers in the Boer War* (London: Leo Cooper, 1999), is a notable exception to the scholarly neglect of Britain's auxiliary forces.

12. See, for example, Byron Farwell, *The Great Boer War* (New York: W. W. Norton, 1976); Thomas Pakenham, *The Boer War* (New York: Random House, 1979); Bill Nasson, *The South African War, 1899–1902* (New York: Oxford, 1999); and Denis Judd and Keith Surridge, *The Boer War* (New York: Palgrave Macmillan, 2003).

13. H. Cunningham, *The Volunteer Force: A Social and Political History, 1859–1908* (Hamden, Conn.: Archon Books, 1975); Ian F. W. Beckett, *Riflemen Form: A Study of the Rifle Volunteer Movement, 1859–1908* (Aldershot: Ogilby Trusts, 1982); and Beckett, *The Amateur Military Tradition* (Manchester: Manchester University Press, 1991).

14. See, for example, Greg Cuthbertson, Albert Grundlingh, and Mary-Lynn Suttie, eds., *Writing a Wider War: Rethinking Gender, Race, and Identity in the South African War, 1899–1902* (Athens: Ohio University Press, 2002); and Donal Lowry, ed., *The South African War Reappraised* (New York: Manchester University Press, 2000).

15. James M. McPherson's superb works on the American Civil War, *For Cause and Comrades: Why Men Fought in the Civil War* (New York: Oxford University Press, 1997) and *What They Fought For, 1861–1865* (New York: Anchor Books, 1994), influenced the early stages of research on this project.

16. Buller was superceded by Roberts in the shake up that followed Black Week.

17. The British employed close to 450,000 troops in South Africa between 1 August 1899 and 31 May 1902. This figure includes men raised in Canada, Australia, New Zealand, and South Africa. It also includes the small number of men posted to garrisons in Natal and the Cape Colony prior to 1 August 1899. Frederick Maurice and M. H. Grant, *(Official) History of the War in South Africa, 1899–1902,* vol. 4 (London: Hurst and Blackwood, 1906–1910), app. 13.

18. Some historians may consider the use of the term "citizen-soldiers" in this book a bit awkward, perhaps even inaccurate, since technically Britons were subjects. But many at the time considered themselves to be citizens. See, for example, Edgar Wallace, *Unofficial Dispatches* (Cape Town: C. Struik, 1975), 55.

19. Most of the men who enlisted in January and February 1900, like most of the public, believed that hostilities in South Africa would be over by year's end. When this proved a false assumption, some were surprised and many were disappointed to learn that the government could keep them in service for the entire war. Although public pressure would have made this course of action political suicide, and the War Office took steps to get the men home as quickly as they could, most volunteers exceeded a one-year term of service.

20. At the battle of Paardeberg, Lord Kitchener attempted to force the Boers from their strongly entrenched position. The attack resulted in high casualties and discussion among British commanders to call off the attack and retreat. In the end, however, due to the overwhelming odds, Gen. Piet Cronjé and more than four thousand Transvaal and Free State burghers surrendered. What could have been yet another British failure turned into their biggest victory to date.

21. There were a few set-piece battles involving Volunteer forces, such as those at fought at Doornkop (29 May 1900) and Diamond Hill (11–12 June 1900).

22. After hearing the news of the British failure at Tweebosch, Secretary of State for War William St. John Brodrick wrote to Violet Cecil: "His [Methuen's] mounted troops bolted, and I have to begin the old driving & harrying to get some one made accountable. The Cabinet are quite out of patience with it & I really don't wonder." Brodrick to V. Cecil, 14 Mar. 1902, VM36/C176/136, Violet Milner Papers, as cited in Keith Terrance Surridge, *Managing the South African War, 1899–1902: Politicians v. Generals* (Woodbridge: Boydell, 1998), 150.

23. Some, like J. L. Garvin, have argued that the British defeat at the battle of Tweebosch enabled the Boers to make an honorable peace. J. L. Garvin, *The Life of Joseph Chamberlain* (London: Macmillan, 1934).

CHAPTER 1

1. John Holms, "Our Army and the People," *Nineteenth Century* 3 (1878): 47, as cited in Alan Ramsay Skelley, *The Victorian Army at Home: The Recruitment and Terms and Conditions of the British Regular, 1859–1899* (Montreal: McGill-Queen's University Press, 1977), 245.

2. Edward Cardwell served as Liberal secretary of state for war from 1868 to 1874 in William Gladstone's first cabinet. He was perhaps the most influential minister to hold that post in the nineteenth century. For a discussion of the Cardwell reforms, see Albert Tucker, "Army and Society in England, 1870–1900: A Reassessment of the Cardwell Reforms," *Journal of British Studies* 2 (1963): 110–41.

3. Edward M. Spiers, *The Late Victorian Army, 1868–1902* (London: St. Martin's, 1992), 143.

4. Nicholas Mansfield writes that for most of the working class, it was considered a disgrace to have a son who served in the Regular Army. Mansfield, *English Farmworkers and Local Patriotism, 1900–1930* (Burlington: Ashgate, 2001), 81.

5. William St. John Midleton, *Records & Reactions, 1856–1939* (New York: E. P. Dutton, 1939), 74.

6. T. H. Ward, *The Reign of Queen Victoria* (London: Smith, Elder, 1887), as cited in Brian Bond, "Recruiting the Victorian Army, 1870–92," *Victorian Studies* 5 (1962): 331.

7. See Ian F. W. Beckett, *The Amateur Military Tradition* (Manchester: Manchester University Press, 1991).

8. J. M. Mackenzie, *Propaganda and Empire: The Manipulation of British Public Opinion, 1880–1960* (New York: Manchester University Press, 1984), 2.

9. J. S. Bratton, "Of England, Home, and Duty: The Image of England in Victorian and Edwardian Juvenile Literature," in *Imperialism and Popular Culture*, ed. J. M. Mackenzie (New York: Manchester University Press, 1986), 74–75.

10. M. D. Blanch, "British Society and the War," in *The South African War: The Anglo-Boer War, 1899–1902*, ed. Peter Warwick and S. B. Spies (Harlow: Longman, 1980), 213.

11. See John Springhall, *Youth, Empire, and Society: British Youth Movements, 1883–1940* (Hamden, Conn.: Archon Books, 1977).

12. Ibid., 17.

13. Patrick Dunae, "New Grub Street for Boys," in *Imperialism and Juvenile Literature*, ed. Jeffrey Richards (New York: Manchester University Press, 1989), 22. For more on boys' papers, see Kelly Boyd, *Manliness and the Boys' Story Paper in Britain: A Cultural History, 1855–1940* (London: Palgrave Macmillan, 2003).

14. J. A. Hobson, *The Psychology of Jingoism* (London: Grant Richards, 1901), 2–3. See also Penny Summerfield, "Patriotism and Empire: Music-Hall Entertainment 1870–1914," in *Imperialism and Popular Culture*; Dave Russell, *Popular Music in England, 1840–1914: A Social History* (Kingston: McGill-Queen's University Press, 1987); and Jeffrey Richards, *Imperialism and Music: Britain, 1876–1953* (New York: Manchester University Press, 2001).

15. Peter Bailey, *Leisure and Class in Victorian England* (London: Routledge & Kegan Paul, 1978), 23.

16. Rudyard Kipling, *Something of Myself* (London: Macmillan, 1937), 150, as cited in Andrew S. Thompson, *Imperial Britain: The Empire in British Politics, c.1880–1932* (New York: Longman, 2000), 64.

17. H. L. Birkin, *History of the 3rd Regiment Imperial Yeomanry, 28-1-00 to 6-8-02* (Nottingham: J. J. Vice, 1905), introduction.

18. John Peck, *War, the Army, and Victorian Literature* (New York: St. Martin's, 1998), 141.

19. For a general discussion of military drill in late Victorian education, see Alan Penn, *Targeting Schools: Drill, Militarism, and Imperialism* (London: Woburn, 1999).

20. As cited in J. K. Dunlop, *The Development of the British Army, 1899–1914* (London: Methuen, 1938), 9.

21. The ballot was used as a means to fill vacancies in county militias. Each county parish was required to keep a list of all eighteen- to forty-five-year-old men eligible to serve. Those called up for service could enroll or elect to find or pay for a substitute.

22. Edward M. Spiers, *The Army and Society, 1815–1914* (New York: Longman, 1980), 163.

23. The strength of the Militia in the 1850s hovered around 100,000 men, roughly 20,000 less than the establishment. In 1860 the strength of the force dropped to 86,555. Royal Commission on the Militia and Volunteers, *Report, Minutes of Evidence, and Appendices,* apps. 31, 32, c.2064 (London: HMSO, 1904), 62, 68–71.

24. Peel returned to the post in 1866 and served for eight months in Derby's third government.

25. Hugh Childers served as the first of two secretaries of state for war in Gladstone's second government.

26. Marquess of Anglesey, *A History of the British Cavalry, 1816 to 1919,* vol. 1, *1816–1850* (London: Leo Cooper, 1973), 77.

27. Yeomanry establishments far exceeded actual strengths. In 1875 the establishment was 14,752 men; the strength was 11,907. In 1903 the establishment was 34,594; the strength, 25,488. Royal Commission on the Militia and Volunteers, *Report, Minutes of Evidence, and Appendices,* app. 31, c.2064, 63–65.

28. Marquess of Anglesey, *A History of the British Cavalry, 1816 to 1919,* vol. 2, *1851–1871* (London: Leo Cooper, 1975), 443.

29. Alfred Tennyson, "The War," *The Times (London),* 9 May 1859.

30. H. Cunningham, *The Volunteer Force: A Social and Political History, 1859–1908* (Hamden, Conn.: Archon Books, 1975), 11.

31. Disraeli served as Derby's chancellor of the exchequer. G. E. Buckle, *The Life of Benjamin Disraeli,* vol. 4 (New York: Macmillan, 1916), 226–30.

32. Ian Beckett provides an excellent account of the origins of the Volunteer force in *Riflemen Form: A Study of the Rifle Volunteer Movement, 1859–1908* (Aldershot: Ogilby Trusts, 1982), chap. 1.

33. War Office Circular, 12 May 1859, Volunteer Infantry, Research Press, http://www.researchpress.co.uk/volunteers/official/woc12may59.htm (accessed 15 May 2006).

34. Earl de Grey, later Lord Ripon, served as secretary of state for war when the Volunteer Act of 1863 was promulgated.

35. Cecil D. Eby, *The Road to Armageddon: The Martial Spirit in English Popular Literature, 1870–1914* (Durham, N.C.: Duke University Press, 1987), 16.

36. Rt. Hon Earl Brownlow, "The British Volunteer System," *North American Review* May 1900, reprinted, Volunteer Infantry, Research Press,

http://www.researchpress.co.uk/volunteers/volsystem190005nar.htm (accessed 15 May 2006).

37. Spiers, *Army and Society*, 166.

38. Glenn A Steppler, *Britons to Arms! The Story of the British Volunteer Soldier and the Volunteer Tradition in Leicestershire and Rutland* (Worcester: Alan Sutton, 1992), 36.

39. Beckett, *Riflemen Form*, 29.

40. Cunningham, *Volunteer Force*, 25.

41. O. Anderson, "The Growth of Christian Militarism in Mid-Victorian Britain," *English Historical Review* 86, no. 338 (1971): 46.

42. Paul Crook, *Darwinism, War, and History* (New York: Cambridge University Press, 1994), 47.

43. Hobson, *Psychology of Jingoism*, 1.

44. Daniel Pick, *War Machine: The Rationalisation of Slaughter in the Modern Age* (New Haven: Yale University Press, 1993), 111–13.

45. See H. Cunningham, "The Language of Patriotism, 1750–1914," *History Workshop* 12 (1981): 21–22.

46. From G. W. Hunt, "By Jingo," as cited in Christopher Pulling, *They Were Singing* (London: George G. Harrap, 1952), 77.

47. L. T. Hobhouse, *Democracy and Reaction* (London: Putnam, 1905), 173, as cited in C. Playne, *The Pre-War Mind in Britain* (London: George Allen & Unwin, 1928), 171.

48. H. Campbell-Bannerman to James Bryce, 29 Dec. 1903, as cited in Bernard Porter, *Critics of Empire: British Radical Attitudes to Colonialism in Africa, 1895–1914* (New York: St. Martin's, 1968), 76.

49. See Keith Terrance Surridge, *Managing the South African War, 1899–1902: Politicians v. Generals* (Woodbridge: Boydell, 1998).

50. Anderson, "Growth of Christian Militarism," 46–72.

51. See Andrew Porter, *Religion versus Empire? British Protestant Missionaries and Overseas Expansion, 1700–1914* (Manchester: University Press, 2004).

52. J. A Mangan, "Duty unto Death: English Masculinity and Militarism in the Age of the New Imperialism," in *Tribal Identities: Nationalism, Europe and Sport* (London: Frank Cass, 1996), 13–14.

53. John Wolffe, *God and Greater Britain: Religion and National Life in Britain and Ireland, 1843–1945* (New York: Routledge, 1994), 229.

54. Mackenzie, *Propaganda and Empire*, 228.

55. W. McG. Eager, *Making Men: The History of Boys' Clubs and Related Movements in Great Britain* (London: University of London Press, 1951), 321.

56. Springhall, *Youth, Empire, and Society*, 18.

57. Roger S. Peacock, *Pioneer of Boyhood: Story of Sir William A. Smith* (Glasgow: Boys' Brigade, 1954). 28.

58. John Springhall, "Building Character in the British Boy: The Attempt to Extend Christian Manliness to Working-Class Adolescents, 1880–1914," in *Manliness and Morality: Middle-Class Masculinity in Britain and America, 1800–1940*, ed. J. A. Mangan and J. Walvin (New York: St. Martin's, 1987), 55.

59. David Howie, *A History of the 1st Lanarkshire Rifle Volunteers* (Glasgow: 1887), 339, as cited in Springhall, *Youth, Empire, and Society,* 24.

60. J. A. R. Pimlott, *Toynbee Hall: Fifty Years of Social Progress, 1889–1934* (London: 1935), 78, as cited in Springhall, *Youth, Empire, and Society,* 72.

61. Springhall, *Youth, Empire, and Society,* 83.

62. J. A. Mangan, *The Games Ethic and Imperialism: Aspects of the Diffusion of an Ideal* (New York: Viking, 1986; rev. ed., London: Frank Cass, 1998), 27.

63. J. A. Mangan, "Images of Empire in the Late Victorian Public School," *Journal of Educational Administration and History* 12 (1980): 32.

64. Walter E. Houghton, *The Victorian Frame of Mind* (New Haven: Yale University Press, 1957), 242, as cited in Jeffrey Richards, "Spreading the Gospel of Self-Help: G. A. Henty and Samuel Smiles," *Journal of Popular Culture* 16, no. 2 (1982): 53.

65. Samuel Smiles, *The Autobiography of Samuel Smiles* (New York: Dutton, 1905), 394.

66. Tim Travers, *Samuel Smiles and the Victorian Work Ethic* (New York: Garland, 1987), 235.

67. Asa Briggs, *Victorian People: A Reassessment of Persons and Themes, 1851–1867,* rev. ed. (Chicago: University of Chicago Press, 1970), 127–28.

68. Ibid., 128.

69. See Stephen M. Miller, "In Support of the 'Imperial Mission'? Volunteering for the South African War," *Journal of Military History* 69, no. 3 (2005): 691–712.

70. Beckett, *Amateur Military Tradition,* 177.

71. Richards, *Imperialism and Music,* 213.

72. Charles Kingsley, *Alton Locke* (London: Macmillan, 1889), xxx, as cited in Cunningham, *Volunteer Force,* 28.

73. Andrew Wynter, "Our Sports and Pastimes," *Once a Week* 5 (1861): 151–53, as cited in Bailey, *Leisure and Class in Victorian England,* 61.

74. Stewart M. Ellis, ed., *A Mid-Victorian Pepys: Letters and Memoirs of Sir William Hardman* (London: C. Palmer, 1923), 26, as cited in Bailey, *Leisure and Class in Victorian England,* 61.

CHAPTER 2

1. *The Times (London),* 8 Sept. 1899, 3.

2. Although *The Times* and *The Daily Mail* were the most vocal in their support for the war, the majority of Britain's newspapers actively supported it as well. Notably, *The Manchester Guardian* and London's *Daily Chronicle,* along with smaller circulating newspapers such as *The Morning Leader, The Star,* and *Reynolds News,* opposed hostilities.

3. For more on Buller, see James B. Thomas, "Sir Redvers Buller in the Post-Cardwellian Army: A Study of the Rise and Fall of a Military Reputation" (Ph.D. diss., Texas A&M University, 1993).

4. The term "small wars" became the more-or-less official terminology for Britain's imperial conflicts during the Victorian period when Gen. N. G. Lyttelton, the chief of the general staff, endorsed Col. C. E. Callwell's book, *Small Wars: Their Principles and Practice,* and recommended it to all British army officers. *Small Wars* was first published in 1896, and a third edition, published ten years later, incorporated some of the lessons of the South African War.

5. Attendance at the British Staff College was seldom a popular career choice for would-be officers during the Victorian era. For more on the staff college, see Brian Bond, *The Victorian Army and the Staff College, 1854–1914* (London: Methuen, 1972).

6. *(London) Daily Mail,* 11 Oct. 1899, as cited in R. Postgate and A. Vallanie, *England Goes to Press* (New York: Bobbs-Merrill, 1937), 223; *(London) Daily Telegraph,* 22 Sept. 1899, 6.

7. For a recent account of the First Anglo-Boer War, see John Laband, *The Transvaal Rebellion* (New York: Pearson, 2005).

8. For a more detailed discussion of the causes of the second war, see A. N. Porter, *The Origins of the South African War: Joseph Chamberlain and the Diplomacy of Imperialism, 1895–99* (Manchester: Manchester University Press, 1980); and Iain R. Smith, *The Origins of the South African War, 1899–1902* (New York: Longman, 1996).

9. See Elizabeth Pakenham, *Jameson's Raid* (London: Weidenfeld and Nicolson, 1960).

10. A. Milner to J. Chamberlain, 4 June 1899, telegram 97, CO 879/56/572, Secret Papers Related to Affairs in South Africa, TNA.

11. J. Chamberlain to A. Milner, 2 Sept. 1899, telegram 337, ibid.

12. As J. A. Hobson later demonstrated, the press and the mining industry in Johannesburg were interconnected. Milner had very close relationships with both groups. Smith, *Origins of the South African War,* 214–15.

13. J. P. Fitzpatrick was an associate of the mineral interest, Wernher, Beit, & Company and worked with Milner to popularize Uitlander grievances.

14. *(London) Daily Mail,* 11 Oct. 1899, 4.

15. For his part in the Sudan campaign, Kitchener was rewarded with a peerage and took the title Lord Kitchener of Khartoum and of Aspall.

16. *The Times (London),* 22 Sept. 1899, 7.

17. Keith Terrance Surridge, *Managing the South African War, 1899–1902: Politicians v. Generals* (Woodbridge: Boydell, 1998), 41, 47.

18. *Pall Mall Gazette,* 13 Sept. 1899, 1.

19. "Report of His Majesty's Commissioners Appointed to Inquire into the Military Preparations and Other Military Matters Connected with the War in South Africa," 1904: cd 1790 xi, 14953. For more on Buller's role, see Lewis Butler, *Sir Redvers Buller* (London: Smith, Elder, 1909); and Thomas Pakenham, *The Boer War* (New York: Random House, 1979).

20. Halik Kochanski, *Sir Garnet Wolseley: Victorian Hero* (London: Hambledon, 1999), 239.

21. Bill Nasson, *The South African War, 1899–1902* (New York: Oxford, 1999), 90–91.

22. Stephen M. Miller, "Lord Methuen and the British Advance to Modder River," *Military History Journal* 10 (1996): 121–36.

23. For more on the British defeats of Black Week, see, for example, Byron Farwell, *The Great Anglo-Boer War* (New York: W. W. Norton, 1976), 101–39; Stephen M. Miller, *Lord Methuen and the British Army: Failure and Redemption in South Africa* (London: Frank Cass, 1999), 123–59; Nasson, *South African War,* 122–35; and Pakenham, *Boer War,* 208–51.

24. Byron Farwell, *Queen Victoria's Little Wars* (New York: W. W. Norton, 1972), app. 2.

25. L. S. Amery, *The Problem of the Army* (London: Edward Arnold, 1903), 184.

26. For a recent study of British perceptions of race and the military, see Heather Streets, *Martial Races: The Military, Race, and Masculinity in British Imperial Culture, 1875–1914* (Manchester: Manchester University Press, 2005).

27. Despite the end of the purchase system in 1871, the British officer corps continued to be dominated by the upper class. In 1912 the aristocracy and the landed gentry accounted for 41 percent of all commissions. Gwyn Harries-Jenkins, *The Army in Victorian Society* (Toronto: University of Toronto Press, 1977), 44.

28. Ivan Bloch, *The Future of War in Its Technical, Economic, and Political Relations; Is War Now Impossible?,* trans. R. C. Long (New York: Doubleday & McClure, 1899).

29. Lyddite proved to be highly overrated as Methuen, for one, found out at the battle of Magersfontein. Darrell Hall, *The Hall Handbook of the Anglo-Boer War,* ed. Fransjohan Pretorius and Gilbert Torlage (Pietermaritzburg: University of Natal Press, 1999), 41; Miller, *Lord Methuen,* 131–32.

30. The British estimated that there were 22,374 men between the ages of sixteen and sixty in the Orange Free State and 31,229 in the Transvaal available for service. *The War in South Africa: A German Official Account,* trans. W. H. Walters (New York: E. P. Dutton, 1904), 19.

31. Howard Bailes, "Military Aspects of the War," in *The South African War: The Anglo-Boer War 1899–1902,* ed. Peter Warwick and S. B. Spies (Harlow: Longman, 1980), 70; Nasson, *South African War,* 68; Fransjohan Pretorius, *The Anglo-Boer War, 1899–1902* (Cape Town: Struik, 1998), 14–16.

32. "Return of Military Forces in South Africa, 1899–1902," 1903: cd 990 lviii, 21; Frederick Maurice and M. H. Grant, *(Official) History of the War in South Africa, 1899–1902,* vol. 4 (London: Hurst and Blackwood, 1906–1910), app. 13.

33. The normal establishment for British forces in 1899–1900 was as follows: Regular Army, 176,309; reserves, 90,000; Militia, 129,572; Yeomanry, 11,891; and Volunteers, 264,833. "Army Estimates for 1900–1901," 1900: xlviii, 1.

34. Charles W. Dilke, *The British Army* (London: Chapman and Hall, 1888), 105.

35. Ibid., 217. H. Spenser Wilkinson, a leading advocate for Volunteer reform who later played a major role in shaping the 1904 report of the Royal

Commission on the Militia and Volunteers, also accentuated the weakness of the officers who commanded the auxiliary forces. Jay Luvaas, *The Education of an Army: British Military Thought, 1815–1940* (Chicago: University of Chicago Press, 1964), 253.

36. Dilke, *British Army,* 224–25.

37. J. K. Dunlop, *The Development of the British Army, 1899–1914* (London: Methuen, 1938), 104–105; P. S. Lake to H. Evelyn Wood, adj. gen., 23 Dec. 1899, WO 32/7866, TNA.

38. Dunlop, *Development of the British Army*, 42.

39. See chapter 1.

40. Between 1887 and 1899, Great Britain's population grew by more than 4 million and the size of the Yeomanry establishment shrunk from 14,405 to 11,891. John R. Harvey, *Records of the Norfolk Yeomanry Cavalry* (London: Jarrold & Sons, 1908), 334.

41. Le Roy-Lewis became inspector general of the auxiliary forces after the war. WO 32/7262, TNA.

42. Edward Stanhope, *The British Army and Our Defensive Position* (London: Kegan Paul, Trench, Trübner, 1892), 19–20.

43. *The British Army by a Lieutenant-Colonel in the British Army,* with an introduction by F. Maurice (London: Sampson Low, Marston, 1899).

44. Dunlop, *Development of the British Army,* 48.

45. Julian Symons, *Buller's Campaign* (London: Cresset, 1963), 93–94.

46. For an excellent discussion of Volunteer thought and that service's incorporation of modern technology, see Ian F. W. Beckett, *Riflemen Form: A Study of the Rifle Volunteer Movement, 1859–1908* (Aldershot: Ogilby Trusts, 1982), chap. 6.

47. Annual Returns of the Volunteer and Territorial Forces, 1895–1913.

48. S. H. Jeyes and F. D. How, *The Life of Sir Howard Vincent* (London: George Allen, 1912), 308.

49. Beckett, *Riflemen Form,* 165.

50. Dunlop, *Development of the British Army,* 94.

51. Charles Stonham and Benson Freeman, *Historical Records of the Middlesex Yeomanry, 1797–1927* (Chelsea: Regimental Committee, 1930), 88; John Paterson Papers, NAM.

52. Patrick Mileham, ed., *Clearly My Duty: The Letters of Sir John Gilmour* (East Linton: Tuckwell, 1996), 28 Nov. 1899; Henry Seton-Karr, *The Call to Arms, 1900–1901* (New York: Longmans, Green, 1902), 20.

53. Will Bennett, *Absent-Minded Beggars: Volunteers in the Boer War* (London: Leo Cooper, 1999), 9.

54. Despite an estimated cost of £850,000, the government decided to go ahead with the plan. This figure was based on the embodiment of thirty-six battalions. WO 32/6359, TNA.

55. E. C. Broughton, *A Continuation of the Historical Records of the 1st Regiment of Militia or Third West York Light Infantry now the Third Battalion York and Lancaster Regiment from 1875–1905* (London: William Clowes and Sons, 1906), 26.

56. Maj. Gen. Sir William Butler, the commander in chief of British forces in South Africa, was an important exception. Butler's opposition to Milner's policies led to accusations that he was a "pro-Boer." His Irish Catholic roots only added to the suspicion some had as to his true loyalties. Under much pressure, he resigned his post and left South Africa in September 1899. See William Butler, *Sir William Butler: An Autobiography* (London: Constable, 1911).

CHAPTER 3

1. Sidney C. Peel, *Trooper 8008 Imperial Yeomanry* (London: Edward Arnold, 1901), 1.

2. Parts of this chapter first appeared in *The Journal of Military History* 69 (2005): 691–712.

3. The pro-Boer Irish novelist George Moore called Black Week "the greatest event that happened since Thermopylae." D. P. McCracken, *The Irish Pro-Boers, 1877–1902* (Johannesburg: Perskor, 1989), 61–62.

4. Henry Seton-Karr, *The Call to Arms, 1900–1901* (New York: Longmans, Green, 1902), 2.

5. C. E. Playne, *The Pre-War Mind in Britain* (London: George Allen & Unwin, 1928), 188.

6. According to Reginald Brett, Second Viscount Esher, who later chaired the War Office (Reconstitution) Committee, the War Office opposed Roberts's appointment. Maurice V. Brett, ed., *Journals and Letters of Reginald, Viscount Esher,* 4 vols. (London: Nicholson and Watson, 1934–38), 1:252.

7. The British government also accepted offers from the empire, with colonial contingents raised in Canada, Australia, New Zealand, and South Africa. In addition, many British nationals went directly to South Africa to enlist in locally raised units. This book, however, is concerned solely with those Volunteer forces recruited in the British Isles.

8. Return of Military Forces, 1903: cd 892 lviii, 17; and cd 990 lviii, 21.

9. Although very supportive of the call to arms, some were still quite miffed over the way the government had responded to earlier offers of service. In their chronicle of the Twenty-ninth Company (Denbighshire) Imperial Yeomanry, Llewelyn Parry and B. Freeman write: "The Government, who had previously refused offers of service from several Yeomanry regiments in the earlier stages of the war, now turned to the Force they had so long snubbed and neglected, and which it was an open secret they wished to disband entirely." Parry and Freeman, eds., *Historical Records of the Denbighshire Hussars Imperial Yeomanry* (Wrexham: Woodall, Minshall, Thomas, 1909), 199.

10. Although *The Leeds Mercury* continued to oppose the war, it displayed tremendous support for the Volunteer Movement. See, for example, *The Leeds Mercury,* 18, 20, 21 Dec. 1899, 4.

11. Lovat had served in the Life Guards and was a major in the Fourth Volunteer Battalion Cameron Highlanders. Eventually, he received

permission to raise a force of approximately 250 men from the Scottish Highlands, which became known as Lovat's Scouts. Lovat used his influence to ensure that the men's jobs would be waiting for them when they returned from South Africa. Francis Lindley, *Lord Lovat: A Biography* (London: Hutchinson, 1935).

12. Newton met with Wolseley on 15 December. He was unofficially given the go ahead the next day. A public announcement followed on 20 December. CIV 1/10, City of London Imperial Yeomanry Papers, Corporation of London Records Office.

13. Proceedings of the Army Board for Mobilization Purposes, 18 Dec. 1899, WO 32/7869, TNA.

14. In a letter to his father (dated 20 December 1899), George Wyndham, the undersecretary of state for war, claimed authorship of the plan to raise the Imperial Yeomanry. "The 'Imperial Yeomanry' is my child. I invented it after lunch on Sunday and it is already a fine bantling. May it live and prosper. To bring it to birth has been a business. But I rejoice like the woman in the Bible over a man child that is born. Don't say it was my idea. It is not taken up officially. And I want no more." J. W. Mackail and Guy Wyndham, *Life and Letters of George Wyndham* (London: Hutchinson, 1915), 382.

15. Lansdowne did not sign the order until 24 December, and the creation of the Imperial Yeomanry did not become "official" until the proclamation of Special Army Order, 2 January 1900. That same day army orders brought the CIV and the Volunteer Service Corps into formation. The newly created Imperial Yeomanry Committee consisted of Lords Lucas, Valentia, Lonsdale, and Harris; Col. E. W. Beckett; and W. L. Bagot. Lord Chesham headed to South Africa in February and was later joined by Valentia and Bagot. *Auxiliary Forces for Service in South Africa* (London: HMSO, 1900).

16. H. L. Birkin, *History of the 3rd Regiment Imperial Yeomanry, 28–1-00 to 6–8-02* (Nottingham: J.J. Vice, 1905), introduction.

17. WO 100/120, TNA, as cited in William Spencer, *Records of the Militia and Volunteer Forces, 1757–1945,* rev. ed., Public Records Office Readers' Guide no. 3 (London: PRO Publications, 1997), 72–76.

18. J. Percy Fitzpatrick to H. A. Rogers, 8 Jan. 1900, in *FitzPatrick: South African Politician,* ed. A. H. Duminy and W. R. Guest (Johannesburg: McGraw-Hill, 1976), 250.

19. "Report on the Imperial Yeomanry in South Africa," WO 108/263, TNA.

20. Ibid.

21. "Proceedings of the Commander-in-Chief's Committee to Consider Questions Relating to Operations in South Africa," no. 536, WO 108/307, ibid.

22. Mackail and Wyndham, *Life and Letters of George Wyndham,* 383.

23. G. A. Brett, *A History of the South Wales Borderers and the Monmouthshire Regiment* (Pontypool: Hughes & Son, Griffin Press, 1956).

24. C. J. Hart, *The History of the 1st Volunteer Battalion: The Royal Warwickshire Regiment* (Birmingham: Midland Counties Herald, 1906), 228.

25. William Home, *With the Border Volunteers to Pretoria* (Hawick: W. & J. Kennedy, 1901), 2–3.

26. See chapter 2.

27. Herbert Wrigley Wilson, *With the Flag to Pretoria* (London: Harmsworth Bros., 1901), 230, as cited in Denis Judd and Keith Surridge, *The Boer War* (New York: Palgrave Macmillan, 2003), 67. Judd and Surridge argue that this was no exaggeration on Wilson's part.

28. Sixty-eight Militia battalions left Great Britain over the course of the war. Nine of these took over garrison duties in Malta, St. Helena, and Egypt. The rest served in South Africa. See J. K. Dunlop, *The Development of the British Army, 1899–1914* (London: Methuen, 1938), 90.

29. P. T. Ross, *A Yeoman's Letters* (London: Simpkins, Marshall, Hamilton, Kent, 1901), 179.

30. B. Porter, "The Pro-Boers in Britain," in *The South African War: The Anglo-Boer War, 1899–1902,* ed. Peter Warwick and S. B. Spies (Harlow: Longman, 1980), 239.

31. *Norfolk Daily Standard,* n.d., P. C. Jonas Papers, NAM.

32. *The Clarion,* 21 Oct. 1899, as cited in Paul Ward, *Red Flag and Union Jack: Englishness, Patriotism, and the British Left, 1881–1924* (London: Boydell, 1998), 60.

33. Michael Howard, *War and the Liberal Conscience* (London: Temple Smith, 1978), 69.

34. Anne Summers, "Militarism in Britain before the Great War," *History Workshop* 2 (1976): 107. Paul Laity has shown that peace associations could do nothing to stop the war and were very weak in the wake of the "extraordinary outburst" of patriotism. Laity, *The British Peace Movement, 1870–1914* (Oxford: Oxford University Press, 2002).

35. Music historians Lewis Winstock and Jeffrey Richards agree that "in 1899–1902 *God Save the Queen* had an appeal that has never been equaled." Winstock, *Songs and Music of the Redcoats: A History of the War Music of the British Army 1642–1902* (London: Stackpole, 1970), 255; Richards, *Imperialism and Music: Britain, 1876–1953* (New York: Manchester University Press, 2001), 94.

36. W .J. Reader, *At Duty's Call* (New York: St. Martin's, 1988), 10–11.

37. A. S. Orr, *Scottish Yeomanry in South Africa, 1900–1901* (Glasgow: James Hedderwick & Sons, 1901), 3–4.

38. Guy Scott and G. L. McDonnell, *The Record of the Mounted Infantry of the City Imperial Volunteers* (London: E. & F. N. Spon, 1902), 5–6.

39. Bernard Moeller, *Two Years at the Front with the Mounted Infantry* (London: Grant Richards, 1903), 1.

40. F. E. Charge to his father, 16 Apr. 1900, and published extract from *Worcestershire Echo,* 14 Apr. 1900, F. E. Charge Papers, WCM.

41. Alfred Marks, *The Churches and the South African War* (London: New Age Office, 1905), 4. Britain's churches generally supported the war effort, though there were a few notable and very vocal exceptions. See also John Wolffe, *God and Greater Britain: Religion and National Life in Britain and Ireland, 1843–1945* (New York: Routledge, 1994); and H. H. Hewison,

Hedge of Wild Almonds: South Africa, the 'Pro-Boers' & the Quaker Conscience, 1890–1910 (Portsmouth: Heinemann, 1989).

42. See, for example, H. Pelling, *Popular Politics and Society in Late Victorian Britain* (New York: St. Martin's, 1968); Robert Gray, *The Aristocracy of Labour in Nineteenth-Century Britain, c.1850–1900* (London: Macmillan, 1981); and Eric Hobsbawm, *The Age of Empire, 1875–1914* (New York: Vintage, 1989).

43. Hobsbawm, *Age of Empire,* 160–61.

44. Richard Price, *An Imperial War and the British Working Class: Working-Class Attitudes and Reactions to the Boer War, 1899–1902* (London: Routledge & Kegan Paul, 1972), 1.

45. Ibid., 105. Richard Shannon points out that despite Chamberlain's rhetoric, most contests in the 1900 election were fought over domestic issues. Low turnout and even apathy may not have been the result of voter indifference. More likely, it was the result of an election with a seemingly predetermined outcome in which neither major party invested much time or money. See Shannon, *The Age of Salisbury, 1881–1902* (New York: Longman, 1996), 509–12.

46. In *The Psychology of Jingoism* (London: Grant Richards, 1901), John Hobson argues that the societal conditions of late-nineteenth-century Great Britain had created an atmosphere in which the nation was more than ever subject to the influence of the "coarse patriotism" ladled out by the mass media and the music hall. Like a "contagion," a brutal form of jingoism spread to all classes. Mafeking night was an ugly, but predictable, occurrence. Likewise, Paula M. Krebs has more recently argued that Mafeking night was merely the product of the media's manipulation of the masses. "The date had been set and invitations issued by the lower-middle-class media." Krebs, *Gender, Race, and the Writing of Empire: Public Discourse and the Boer War* (New York: Cambridge University Press, 1999), 3.

47. Hobson, *Psychology of Jingoism,* 205.

48. Imperial Yeomanry recruits were paid at the attractive cavalry rate.

49. For a further discussion of seasonal unemployment, see Gareth Stedman Jones, *Outcast London* (New York: Pantheon, 1971).

50. Andrew S. Thompson, "The Language of Imperialism and the Meanings of Empire: Imperial Discourse in British Politics, 1895–1914," *Journal of British Studies* 36 (1997): 150.

51. Jon Lawrence, *Speaking for the People: Party, Language, and Popular Politics in England, 1867–1914* (New York: Cambridge University Press, 1998), 109.

52. Jeffrey Richards looked at music and the marketplace and concluded that working-class patriotism and its support for imperialism was widespread. *Imperialism and Music,* 2.

53. Bentley B. Gilbert, "Health and Politics," *Bulletin of the History of Medicine* 39 (1965), as cited in Matthew Hendley, "Help Us to Secure a Strong, Healthy, Prosperous, and Peaceful Britain," *Canadian Journal of History* 30 (1995): 268.

54. Just after the war, a royal commission determined that more than 70 percent of the Volunteer force came from the working class. Hugh Cunningham has shown that this group, for the most part, was steadily employed. *The Volunteer Force: A Social and Political History, 1859–1908* (Hamden, Conn.: Archon Books, 1975), 38–41.

55. Linda Colley, *Britons: Forging the Nation, 1707–1837* (New Haven: Yale University Press, 1992), 302.

56. Edward M. Spiers, *The Army and Society, 1815–1914* (New York: Longman, 1980), 44.

57. See Alan Ramsay Skelley, *The Victorian Army at Home: The Recruitment and Terms and Conditions of the British Regular, 1859–1899* (Montreal: McGill-Queen's University Press, 1977), 248.

58. Recruitment in the Regular Army increased significantly during the South African War. Few outside the working class would have ever considered a career in the army in peace or in wartime. M. D. Blanch, "British Society and the War," in *South African War*, ed. Peter Warwick and S. B. Spies, 226.

59. For a discussion on health issues and the British army during the South African War, see Frederick Maurice, "National Health: A Soldier's Study," *Contemporary Review* 83 (1903): 41–56; and (more recently) Hendley, "Help Us to Secure a Strong, Healthy, Prosperous, and Peaceful Britain," 261–88.

60. Imperial Yeomanry Attestation Forms, WO 128, TNA.

61. H. G. Mckenzie Rew, *Records of the Rough Riders (XXth Battalion) Imperial Yeomanry* (Bedford: Brown & Wilson, 1907), 4.

62. Harold Josling, *The Autobiography of a Military Great Coat* (London: Jarrold & Sons, 1907), 20.

63. See, for example, Price, *Imperial War and the British Working Class.*

64. Geoffrey Moore, *Pickman's Progress in the City Imperial Volunteers in South Africa, 1900* (Huntingdon: G. Moore, 1986), app. E.

65. "The British Volunteer (Ready When He's Wanted)," words by Harold Hardy, music by Stephen Richardson.

66. *Report on Raising, Organising, Equipping, and Despatching the City of London Imperial Volunteers to South Africa* (London: Blades, East, & Blades, 1900), 39–41; Moore, *Pickman's Progress,* app. E.

67. John H. Cooke, *5,000 Miles with the Cheshire Yeomanry in South Africa* (Warrington: Mackie, 1913) app.

68. Imperial Yeomanry Attestation Forms, WO 128, TNA.

69. This data was primarily collected from attestation forms held at the National Archives. Information on the Twenty-first Cheshire (Earl of Chester's) Company was taken from a muster roll in Cooke, *5,000 Miles with the Cheshire Yeomanry,* 5–16. The eighteen companies include the First Wiltshire, Fifth Warwickshire, Sixth Staffordshire, Seventh Leicestershire (Prince Albert's Own), Ninth Yorkshire, Tenth Nottinghamshire (Sherwood Rangers), Eleventh Yorkshire, Twelfth Nottinghamshire (South Notts), Thirteenth Shropshire, Fourteenth Northumberland, Seventeenth

Ayrshire (Earl of Carrick's Own), Twenty-second Cheshire (Earl of Chester's), Twenty-third Lancashire (Duke of Lancashire's Own), Twenty-fourth Westmorland and Cumberland, Twenty-ninth Denbighshire, and Forty-eighth North Somerset Company Imperial Yeomanry. WO 128, TNA. Some of the companies examined, like the Fourteenth Northumberland, which was recruited in Newcastle, were better represented by urban trades. Others, like the Tenth Nottinghamshire, recruited in Retford, had a significant number of rural trades.

70. Will Bennett, *Absent-Minded Beggars: Volunteers in the Boer War* (London: Leo Cooper, 1999), 14–17.

71. See, for example, Frederick Barnado, *An Active Life* (London: Bodley Head, 1963), 76; Josling, *Autobiography of a Military Great Coat,* 20; and Rew, *Records of the Rough Riders,* 4.

72. Although a small number of men for any number of reasons chose to join units away from their homes, Volunteer, Militia, and Imperial Yeomanry units recruited locally. A breakdown of auxiliary-force units supports these regional patterns. See Edward M. Spiers, *The Late Victorian Army, 1868–1902* (London: St. Martin's, 1992), 131; and Spencer, *Records of the Militia & Volunteers Forces.*

73. There have been significant contributions to the historiography of the South African War in the last few years. Very few of them, however, have discussed the auxiliary forces in detail. Bill Nasson's *The South African War* (New York: Oxford, 1999) has one of the more useful, albeit short, discussions on volunteer recruitment, synthesizing the arguments of Richard Price, Michael Blanch, Hugh Cunningham, and John M. Mackenzie. For two recent historiographical overviews, see A. Porter, "The South African War and the Historians," *African Affairs* 99 (2000): 633–48; and Nasson, "Waging Total War in South Africa: Some Centenary Writings on the Anglo-Boer War, 1899–1902," *Journal of Military History* 66 (2002): 813–28. Recent edited collections on the war include Greg Cuthbertson, Albert Grundlingh, and Mary-Lynn Suttie, eds., *Writing a Wider War: Rethinking Gender, Race, and Identity in the South African War, 1899–1902* (Athens: Ohio University Press, 2002); John Gooch, ed., *The Boer War: Direction, Experience, and Image* (London: Frank Cass, 2000); and Peter Dennis and Jeffrey Grey, eds., *The Boer War: Army, Nation, and Empire* (Canberra: Army History Unit, 2000). Greater interest in volunteer recruitment has been shown in Canadian, Australian, and New Zealand historiography. See, for example, Carman Miller, "Loyalty, Patriotism, and Resistance: Canada's Response to the Anglo-Boer War, 1899–1902," *South African Historical Review* 41 (2000): 312–23; Craig Wilcox, *Australia's Boer War: The War in South Africa, 1899–1902* (New York: Oxford, 2002); and Ian McGibbon and John Crawford, eds., *One Flag, One Queen, One Tongue: New Zealand and the South African War* (Auckland: Auckland University Press, 2003).

74. *Boys' Own Paper,* Dec. 1902, as cited in Guy Arnold, *Held Fast for England: G. A. Henty, Imperialist Boys' Writer* (London: Hamish Hamilton, 1980), 63.

75. See J. A. Mangan, "Duty unto Death: English Masculinity and Militarism in the Age of the New Imperialism," in *Tribal Identities: Nationalism, Europe, and Sport* (London: Frank Cass, 1996), 25.

76. See J. S. Bratton, "Of England, Home, and Duty: The Image of England in Victorian and Edwardian Juvenile Literature," in *Imperialism and Popular Culture,* ed. J. M. Mackenzie (New York: Manchester University Press, 1986).

77. Reader, *At Duty's Call.*

78. The music hall, in particular, acted as a powerful disseminator of imperialism and militaristic nationalism in late Victorian society. The Liberal economist and critic of empire J. A. Hobson called the culture emanating from it "the only 'popular' art of the present day." The music hall touched its audience in a way that literature and formal education could not. It was a community event. One was affected by both its message and by the audience's reaction to it. Attendance was considerable, and content was virtually uncensored. By the late 1880s and 1890s, the major themes of music-hall entertainment in both working- and middle-class establishments centered round "Tommy Atkins," "Jack Tar," and the empire. This fact was not accidental nor was it simply an attempt by owners to control the entertainment of its clientele. The evidence suggests that the owners simply gave the people what they wanted. Richard Price believes that Hobson overestimated the influence of the music hall on the sensibilities of the working class. In light of the recent scholarship of John M. Mackenzie, Penny Summerfield, and others, however, Hobson's emphasis seems to have been warranted. The music hall sent powerful messages to men who after Black Week would have to decide voluntarily whether they were going to participate in the South African War. Hobson, *Psychology of Jingoism,* 3; Mackenzie, *Propaganda and Empire: The Manipulation of British Public Opinion, 1880–1960* (New York: Manchester University Press, 1984); Summerfield, "Patriotism and Empire: Music-Hall Entertainment, 1870–1914," in *Imperialism and Popular Culture,* ed. J. M. Mackenzie (New York: Manchester University Press, 1986); Richards, *Imperialism and Music.*

79. Mackenzie, *Propaganda and Empire,* 6.

80. E. Manisty Papers, NAM. According to his grandson, Henry, Edward Manisty was not pressured by his father to volunteer. H. Manisty to S. Miller, 8 Sept. 2005.

81. Commissions in the CIV were highly prized. Indeed, there was great competition for all officer ranks in the Militia and the Imperial Yeomanry as well. Commissions, therefore, were generally obtained through influence.

82. H. E. Belfield to wife, 3 Aug. 1900, H. E. Belfield Papers, NAM.

83. Jarvis's memory must have been faulty. Terris was murdered in 1897.

84. Jarvis writes that he was overwhelmed by similar feelings in 1914. Pointedly, he contrasts the "care-free" mood of 1899 with the stark nature of 1914. C. S. Jarvis, *Half a Life* (London: John Murray, 1943), 58–59.

85. Josling, *Autobiography of a Military Great Coat,* 26.

86. Orr, *Scottish Yeomanry,* 1–3.

87. John Paterson Papers, NAM.

88. The most common theme of the sermons given at the town-hall reception for the volunteers was that of David fighting the Philistines. William Lamont, *Volunteer Memories* (Greenock: James McKelvie & Sons, 1911), 122.

89. Ibid., 123–25.

90. J. P. Sturrock, *The Fifes in South Africa* (Cupar-Fife: A. Westwood & Son, 1903), 5.

91. *Dundee Advertiser,* 28 Feb. 1900, as cited in ibid., 11–12.

92. Ibid., 10.

93. Unnamed Chester newspaper; as cited in Richard Verdin, *The Cheshire (Earl of Chester's) Yeomanry, 1898–1967* (Chester: Cheshire Yeomanry Association, 1971), 12.

94. *The Manchester Guardian,* 16 Jan. 1900, 8; 19 Jan. 1900, 6.

95. *The Leeds Mercury,* 5 Feb. 1900, 6.

96. *(London) Daily Mail,* 13 Jan. 1900, 3.

97. *The Times (London),* 15 Jan. 1900, 10.

98. *(London) Daily Mail,* 13 Jan. 1900, 3.

99. Ross, *Yeoman's Letters,* 180. Ross was a corporal in the Sixty-ninth Sussex Company Imperial Yeomanry.

100. Ibid.

101. Thomas F. Dewar, *With the Scottish Yeomanry* (Arbroath: T. Buncle, 1901), 28.

102. Barnado, *An Active Life,* 75.

103. Rennie Stevenson, *Through Rhodesia with the Sharpshooters* (London: John Macqueen, 1901), 9.

104. Ross, *Yeoman's Letters,* 180.

105. Jarvis, *Half a Life,* 64.

CHAPTER 4

1. *The Cossack Post: Journal of B Squadron, Paget's Horse, De La Rey's Farm, Lichtenberg, Transvaal, February to May 1901* (London: Junior Army and Navy Stores, 1901), 67.

2. Even the experienced volunteers, yeomanry, and, to a lesser extent, militiamen were subject to a much more intense process than they had encountered previously.

3. Regular Army recruitment, which is not the subject of this book, remained steady throughout the war. In addition, many men signed up for the auxiliary forces without the intention of foreign service.

4. Unknown author, "The Old 50th to the New," as cited in Sharrad Gilbert, *Rhodesia—and After* (London: Simpkin Marshall, Hamilton, Kent, 1901), 236–37.

5. See chapter 3, note 72.

6. Marquess of Anglesey, *A History of the British Cavalry, 1816 to 1919,* vol. 4, *1899–1913* (London: Leo Cooper, 1986), 92–93.

7. C. J. Hart, *The History of the 1st Volunteer Battalion: The Royal Warwickshire Regiment* (Birmingham: Midland Counties Herald, 1906), 228–31.

8. William Home, *With the Border Volunteers to Pretoria* (Harwick: W. & J. Kennedy, 1901), 1–2.

9. Godfrey Smith, *With the Scottish Rifle Volunteers at the Front* (Glasgow: William Hodge, 1901), 1–2.

10. Imperial Yeomanry Attestation Forms, WO 128, TNA.

11. M. F. Gage, ed., *Records of the Dorset Imperial Yeomanry, 1894–1905* (Sherborne: F. Bennett, 1906), 78–80.

12. H. G. Mckenzie Rew, *Records of the Rough Riders (XXth Battalion) Imperial Yeomanry* (Bedford: Brown & Wilson, 1907); Gage, *Records of the Dorset Imperial Yeomanry*, 4–7.

13. Frederick Barnado, *An Active Life* (London: Bodley Head, 1963), 76–77.

14. Surprisingly, he did not consider linen pajamas and champagne to be "useless." Diary, n.d., W. S. Power Papers, NAM.

15. Richard Verdin, *The Cheshire (Earl of Chester's) Yeomanry, 1898–1967* (Chester: Cheshire Yeomanry Association, 1971), 3–8.

16. See, for example, Francis M. Appleton, *The Volunteer Service Company (1st South Lancashire Regiment) in South Africa during the Boer War* (Warrington: Mackie, 1901); H. Graham, *The Annals of the Yeomanry Cavalry of Wiltshire; being a Complete History of the Prince of Wales' Own Royal Regiment*, 3 vols. (Devizes: Geo. Simpson, 1908); and Thomas Charles Wetton, *With Rundle's Eighth Division in South Africa* (London: Henry J. Drane, n.d.). The *Birmingham Daily Mail* and the *Birmingham Daily Post* helped raise a large reserve fund for volunteer families in need. The papers received contributions from more than fifty thousand "working families." Hart, *History of the 1st Volunteer Battalion*, 228–31.

17. Smith, *With the Scottish Rifle Volunteers*, 3.

18. Ayrshire newspaper clipping, n.d., John Paterson Papers, NAM.

19. Frank Fox, *The History of the Royal Gloucestershire Hussars Yeomanry, 1898–1922* (London: Philip Allan, 1923).

20. A. G. Garrish, *The Records of "I" Company: A Brief History of the East Surrey Volunteers' Service in the South African War* (London: Walbrook, 1901), 2–3.

21. H. S. Gaskell, *With Lord Methuen in South Africa* (London: Henry J. Drane, 1906), 1–10. C. S. Jarvis recalls that the two Montgomeryshire Imperial Yeomanry Companies departed while energetic crowds sang the Welsh national song, "Land of My Fathers." Jarvis, *Half a Life* (London: John Murray, 1943), 65–66.

22. A. S. Orr, *Scottish Yeomanry in South Africa, 1900–1901* (Glasgow: James Hedderwick & Sons, 1901), 2–3.

23. This was not the case with the second contingent of Imperial Yeomanry—men were sent to South Africa before the ink had time to dry on their attestation forms. This rapid deployment caused major problems. See chapter 6.

24. See Maurice Fitzgibbon, *Arts under Arms: An University Man in Khaki* (London: Longmans, Green, 1901).

25. The entire Thirteenth Battalion Imperial Yeomanry, which included the Forty-sixth Belfast "A," the Forty-seventh Duke of Cambridge's Own, the Fifty-fourth Belfast "B," and the Forty-fifth Companies, was captured by Gen. Piet De Wet at Lindley on 31 May 1900.

26. Michael Gallagher, *Mick Gallagher at the Front* (Liverpool: Mac's Sugar House, 1900), 7–8.

27. J. P. Sturrock, *The Fifes in South Africa* (Cupar-Fife: A. Westwood & Son, 1903), 7.

28. Paterson Papers, NAM.

29. Sidney C. Peel, *Trooper 8008 Imperial Yeomanry* (London: Edward Arnold, 1901), 6–8.

30. Gilbert, *Rhodesia*, 237. Sharrad Gilbert was in the Sixty-fifth (Leicestershire) Company Imperial Yeomanry. The Fiftieth, Sixtieth, Sixty-first, and Sixty-fifth Companies made up the Seventeenth Battalion Imperial Yeomanry.

31. Future novelist and Republican Erskine Childers, who served with a battery of the CIV, left London without fanfare just after midnight on 3 February 1900 amid a snowstorm. He notes with some jealousy, however, that everyone else was treated to parades. *In the Ranks of the C.I.V.* (London: Smith, Elder, 1900).

32. Graham, *Annals of the Yeomanry Cavalry of Wiltshire*, 3:68.

33. See, for example, Sgt. Harry Hopwood Papers (Second Volunteer Battalion Manchester Regiment), NAM; H. R. Lister Papers, NAM; and F. E. Charge Papers (Sixteenth Company Imperial Yeomanry), WCM.

34. "Diary of No. 8080, Pvt. J. W. Milne, First Service Company Volunteers, Gordon Highlanders (1900) during the Boer War," http://jwmilne.freeservers.com (accessed 17 May 2006).

35. *Worcestershire Echo*, 14 Apr. 1900.

36. H. L. Birkin held the rank of captain in the South Notts Hussars when his Imperial Yeomanry company was formed. Birkin, *History of the 3rd Regiment Imperial Yeomanry, 28–1-00 to 6–8-02* (Nottingham: J. J. Vice, 1905), viii.

37. As cited in Verdin, *Cheshire (Earl of Chester's) Yeomanry*, 11–12.

38. *The Manchester Guardian*, 11 Jan. 1900, 8.

39. *The Times (London)*, 15 Jan. 1900, 10.

40. *The Leeds Mercury*, 15 Jan. 1900, 6.

41. Frank Charge to his father, 16 Apr. 1900, Charge Papers, WCM.

42. Birkin, *History of the 3rd Regiment*, 2.

43. Ibid., 1. See also Orr, *Scottish Yeomanry*, 4–6.

44. Lionel Curtis, *With Milner in South Africa* (Oxford: Basil Blackwell, 1951), 25 Jan. 1900.

45. Charge to his father, 16 Apr. 1900.

46. There are a few accounts of pleasant accommodations, like that found in a letter from Trooper S. R. Pitt, Sixteenth (Worcestershire) Imperial Yeomanry, to his mother. The type of transport and the number of men

and horses aboard sometimes made all the difference: "In the mess there is everything for convenience, the tables all laid out in proper style, we sleep in hammocks that are very comfortable. The [SS *Kumara*] has been done up and everything is so clean and nice." Pitt to his mother, 8 Feb. 1900, S. R. Pitt Papers, WCM.

47. See, for example, Diary, 14 Jan. 1900, Lister Papers, NAM; T. B. Marson, *Scarlet and Khaki* (London: Jonathan Cape, 1930), 60–63; A. E. Pease, ed., *A Private Memoir of Sir Thomas Fowler* (London: William Clowes, 1905), 31; and William Corner, *The Story of the 34th Company (Middlesex) Imperial Yeomanry from the Point of View of Private No. 6243* (London: T. Fisher Unwin, 1902), 28 Feb. 1900.

48. Curtis, *With Milner in South Africa,* 25 Jan. 1900.

49. Home, *With the Border Volunteers,* 7.

50. Diary, 28 Feb. 1900, John Paterson Papers, NAM.

51. William Grant Papers, NAM.

52. W. S. Power to his cousin, 3 Mar. 1900, Power Papers, NAM.

53. Birkin, *History of the 3rd Regiment,* 4.

54. Diary, R. S. Britten Papers, NAM.

55. A. W. M. Atthill, *From Norwich to Lichtenburg via Pretoria* (Norwich: A. E. Soman, 1909).

56. Bernstein sailed on the SS *Erie* and was later attached to the Scottish Horse, a unit raised chiefly in Natal. Julius Bernstein Papers, NAM.

57. Home, *With the Border Volunteers,* 16–18.

58. Thomas Charles Wetton, *Reminiscences of the 34th Bn. Imperial Yeomanry* (London: Sidey and Bartlett, 1907), 29–33. For another account, see Home, *With the Border Volunteers,* 16–17.

59. Wetton does not explain how he convinced the crew that he was a veteran of the crossing, nor does he comment on whether he participated in the initiation ritual this second time. Probably to avoid the wrath of his comrades, he watched from the sidelines. Wetton, *Reminiscences.*

60. H. R. Lister to his mother, 28 Jan. 1900, Lister Papers, NAM.

61. "Diary of No. 8080."

62. Ada Thomson, *Memorials of Charles Dixon Kimber* (London: James Nisbet, 1902), 18.

63. J. Barclay Lloyd, *One Thousand Miles with the C.I.V.* (London: Methuen, 1901), 25.

64. Sturrock, *Fifes in South Africa,* 19.

65. C. S. Awdry to his father, 19 Mar. 1900, C. S. Awdry Papers, NAM.

66. Sturrock, *Fifes in South Africa,* 19.

67. Fitzgibbon, *Arts under Arms,* 16–17; S. R. Pitt to his mother, 8 Feb. 1900, Pitt Papers, WCM.

68. Grant Papers, NAM.

69. Ibid.

70. Frank Charge to his father, 18 Apr. 1900, Charge Papers, WCM.

71. Brian Alt, *Brian Alt* (London: Ballantyne, Hanson, 1900), 10.

72. Garrish, *Records of "I" Company,* 4; Peel, *Trooper 8008,* 12–13.

73. Pitt to his mother, 22 Feb. 1900, Pitt Papers, WCM.

74. Lister to his mother, 28 Jan. 1900, Lister Papers, NAM.

75. After serving in the Honorourable Artillery Company for eight years, Bernard Moeller volunteered for the mounted infantry section of the CIV in December 1899. He was killed two years later in South Africa. Moeller, *Two Years at the Front with the Mounted Infantry* (London: Grant Richards, 1903), 4.

76. John Patterson to his brother, 2 Mar. 1900, Paterson Papers, NAM.

77. Diary, 21 Feb. 1900, Hopwood Papers, NAM.

78. According to H. Rew, the men of the Twentieth Battalion Imperial Yeomanry, who sailed on the *Canada* in April 1900, were not allowed to purchase fruit at Las Palmas. If his information is correct, this seems to be an exception to the rule. *Records of the Rough Riders*, 7–8.

79. J. Patterson to his brother, 2 Mar. 1900.

80. Peel, *Trooper 8008*, 11–13.

81. Patrick Mileham, ed., *Clearly My Duty: The Letters of Sir John Gilmour* (East Linton: Tuckwell, 1996), 6 Mar. 1900.

82. Although many quips in letters and diaries suggest that the inoculation was not successful, Wright's 1901 study suggests that it was. But it was not until World War I that the immunization was fully appreciated. See J. C. de Villiers, "The Medical Aspect of the Anglo-Boer War, 1899–1902," Part 2, *Military History Journal* [Bloemfontein] 6 (June 1984).

83. Georgiana Howe, ed., *The Imperial Yeomanry Hospitals in South Africa*, 3 vols. (London: Humphreys, 1902), 2:5.

84. Rew, *Records of the Rough Riders*, 8–10.

85. Home, *With the Border Volunteers*, 17–19.

86. Barnado returned to South Africa and served as a doctor for several months until the end of the war. Barnado, *An Active Life*, 77–78.

87. Ibid.

88. Karl B. Spurgin, *On Active Service with the Northumberland and Durham Yeomen, under Lord Methuen* (London: Walter Scott, 1902), 8.

89. Pease, *Private Memoir of Sir Thomas Fowler*, 31.

90. There was even a collision involving the *Winkfield* and the RMSS *Mexican*.

91. Frank Charge to his father, 3 May 1900, Charge Papers, WCM.

CHAPTER 5

1. William Home, *With the Border Volunteers to Pretoria* (Hawick: W. & J. Kennedy, 1901), 50.

2. Meynell Hunt, *With the Warwickshire Yeomanry in South Africa* (Birmingham: Cornish Brothers, 1902), 35.

3. Parts of this chapter and chapter 6 were published in the *Journal of the Society for Army Historical Research* 84 (2006): 158–74.

4. Bill Nasson, *The South African War, 1899–1902* (New York: Oxford, 1999), 183.

5. Thomas Pakenham, *The Boer War* (New York: Random House, 1979), 258.

6. Diary, 30 Jan. 1900, H. R. Lister Papers, NAM.

7. Diary, 11 Mar. 1900, Harry Hopwood Papers, NAM.

8. Thomas Charles Wetton, *With Rundle's Eighth Division in South Africa* (London: Henry J. Drane, n.d.), 56.

9. Frank Stephenson to home, 17 Mar. 1901, Frank Stephenson Papers, NAM.

10. I have not been able to verify whether Charge accurately identified the men he saw as Zulu. Frank Charge to his father, 8 May 1900, F. E. Charge Papers, WCM.

11. W. S. Power to his cousin, 16 Feb. 1900, W. S. Power Papers, NAM.

12. For more on the 1901 epidemic and the politics of segregation in South Africa, see M. Swanson, "The Sanitation Syndrome: Bubonic Plague and Urban Native Policy in the Cape Colony, 1900–1909," *Journal of African History* 8, no. 3 (1977): 387–410; and Vivian Bickford-Smith, *Ethnic Pride and Racial Prejudice in Victorian Cape Town* (London: Cambridge University Press, 1995).

13. Hugo Beaumont Burnaby to parents, 25 Mar. 1900, Hugo Burnaby Papers, LHCMA; Bernard Moeller, *Two Years at the Front with the Mounted Infantry* (London: Grant Richards, 1903), 10–12.

14. Wetton, *With Rundle's Eighth Division*, 56–57.

15. The second contingent of Imperial Yeomanry was rushed to South Africa in 1901 without much preparation. The War Office expected that their training would take place in these camps and in the field. As a result, many companies stayed at Maitland Camp for more than a week.

16. H. G. Mckenzie Rew, *Records of the Rough Riders (XXth Battalion) Imperial Yeomanry* (Bedford: Brown & Wilson, 1907), 10.

17. H. L. Birkin, *History of the 3rd Regiment Imperial Yeomanry, 28-1-00 to 6-8-02* (Nottingham: J. J. Vice, 1905), 5.

18. Sidney C. Peel, *Trooper 8008 Imperial Yeomanry* (London: Edward Arnold, 1901), 16.

19. Ada Thomson, *Memorials of Charles Dixon Kimber* (London: James Nisbet, 1902), 22.

20. Peel, *Trooper 8008*, 17.

21. Rew, *Records of the Rough Riders*, 10–12; Birkin, *History of the 3rd Regiment*, 4–5.

22. W. S. Power to his cousin, 28 Feb. 1900, Power Papers, NAM.

23. Not all onlookers observed the situation through the same lens as Lieutenant Power. Capt. Richard Gubbins, working with remounts near the Orange River Camp, was quite impressed with the adaptability of the Volunteer Mounted Infantry. "It's great fun," he wrote, "watching them on unbroken Argentine ponies and new saddles, but bad as they are at present, it's wonderful how soon they pick it up." R. Gubbins to unnamed recipient, 4 Feb. 1900, Richard Gubbins Papers, NAM.

24. John Paterson to his brother, 23 Mar. 1900, John Paterson Papers, NAM.

25. Home, *With the Border Volunteers*, 23.

26. Likewise, among the detractors of the Imperial Yeomanry, the initials "I.Y." referred to "I am Yours" in reference to their alleged propensity for surrendering. Diary, n.d., Jourdain Papers, NAM.

27. Some of the CIV Mounted Infantry took part in the battle. The foot infantry, however, did not leave Cape Town until 20 February and were sent toward Bloemfontein. Maj. Gen. Henry MacKinnon, who commanded the CIV, noted in his journal that he rarely saw his Mounted Infantry. W. H. Mackinnon, *The Journal of the C.I.V. in South Africa* (London: John Murray, 1901), 168. See also Will Bennett, *Absent-Minded Beggars: Volunteers in the Boer War* (London: Leo Cooper, 1999), 44–46.

28. See Nasson, *South African War*; Keith Terrance Surridge, *Managing the South African War, 1899–1902: Politicians v. Generals* (Woodbridge: Boydell, 1998); and Stephen M. Miller, *Lord Methuen and the British Army: Failure and Redemption in South Africa* (London: Frank Cass, 1999).

29. Fransjohan Pretorius, *The Great Escape of the Boer Pimpernel Christiaan de Wet: The Making of a Legend*, trans. Stephen Hofstätter (Pietermaritzburg: University of Natal Press, 2001), 8–9.

30. Under Roberts's command, farm burning had already begun in earnest, but it was under Kitchener that it became an essential part of a systematic policy of counterinsurgency.

31. Godfrey Smith, *With the Scottish Rifle Volunteers at the Front* (Glasgow: William Hodge, 1901), 16.

32. Home, *With the Border Volunteers*, 81.

33. Diary, 13 Apr. 1901, William Grant Papers, NAM.

34. E. Day-Lewis to parents, 11 June 1901, Edward Day-Lewis Papers, NAM.

35. Although Day-Lewis did not fully appreciate black participation in this encounter at the time, a month later, after one of the African scouts was killed in a similar action, he paid for the man's tombstone. E. Day-Lewis to parents, 31 July 1901, Day-Lewis Papers, NAM.

36. "Pom-pom" was the onomatopoeic nickname of the 37-mm Vickers-Maxim. Diary, 20 Apr. 1900, P. C. Jonas Papers, NAM.

37. J. Barclay Lloyd, *One Thousand Miles with the C.I.V.* (London: Methuen, 1901), 154.

38. Ibid., 161–62. The bond between war and sport had been established and firmly planted in late Victorian culture by public-school advocates. Henry Newbolt's poem "Vitai Lamapada" remains a stunning example of this equation. See John Lowerson, *Sport and the English Middle Classes, 1870–1914* (New York: Manchester University Press, 1993); J. A. Mangan, *Athleticism in the Victorian and Edwardian Public School* (New York: Cambridge University Press, 1981); and Mangan, *The Games Ethic and Imperialism: Aspects of the Diffusion of an Ideal* (New York: Viking, 1986; rev. ed., London: Frank Cass, 1998).

39. Cronjé's decision was influenced by the loss of his draught cattle on 18 February. He did not want to abandon his wagon laager. Fransjohan Pretorius, *Life on Commando during the Anglo-Boer War, 1899–1902* (Cape Town: Human & Rousseau, 1999), 200.

40. Roberts wrote to Lt. Gen. Thomas Kelly-Kenny, "consider that Lord Kitchener is with you for the purpose of communicating to you my orders." L. S. Amery, ed., *The Times History of the War in South Africa, 1899–1902,* 7 vols. (London: Sampson Low, Marston, 1900–1909), 3:419.

41. Diary, 27 Feb. 1900, Lister Papers, NAM.

42. Mackinnon, *Journal of the C.I.V.*, 78.

43. Pakenham, *Boer War,* 451.

44. Barclay Lloyd, *One Thousand Miles with the C.I.V.*, 237.

45. Miller, *Lord Methuen,* 184–86; Ex-Lt. of Gen. de Villebois-Mareuil [D'Etechegoyen], *Ten Months in the Field with the Boers* (London: William Heinemann, 1901), 131. For more information on Villebois-Maneuil, see Roy Macnab, *The French Colonel: Villebois-Mareuil and the Boers, 1899–1900* (London: Oxford University Press, 1975).

46. H. S. Gaskell, *With Lord Methuen in South Africa* (London: Henry J. Drane, 1906), 56.

47. A. W. A. Pollock, *With Seven Generals in the Boer War* (London: Skeffington & Son, 1900), 207; Birkin, *History of the 3rd Regiment,* 16.

48. Diary, 9 Apr. 1900, R. S. Britten Papers, NAM.

49. A. S. Orr, *Scottish Yeomanry in South Africa, 1900–1901* (Glasgow: James Hedderwick & Sons, 1901), 28.

50. Ibid. 29.

51. Diary, 27 June 1900, Hopwood Papers, NAM.

52. Diary, 28 July 1900, ibid.

53. Diary, 3 Aug. 1900, ibid.

54. Diary, 31 Aug. 1900, ibid.

CHAPTER 6

1. Q.L., *The Yeomanry Cavalry of Worcestershire, 1794–1913* (Devizes: G. Simpson, 1914), 146.

2. W.S. Power to his cousin, 6 June 1900, W. S. Power Papers, NAM.

3. Charles Stride to his parents, 12 June 1900, C. Stride Papers, NAM.

4. *The Cossack Post: Journal of B Squadron, Paget's Horse, De La Rey's Farm, Lichtenberg, Transvaal, February to May 1901* (London: Junior Army and Navy Stores, 1901), 48.

5. Bill Nasson, *The South African War, 1899–1902* (New York: Oxford, 1999), 181; Thomas Pakenham, *The Boer War* (New York: Random House, 1979), 455.

6. Roberts left Maj. Gen. H. E. Colvile to pacify the eastern Orange Free State (known as the Orange River Colony after its annexation on 28 May 1900) as the British advanced on Pretoria. Colvile, however, did not have adequate resources to deal with several Boer commandos still functioning in the area. A miscalculation by him led to the isolation and abandonment of the Thirteenth Battalion Imperial Yeomanry at Lindley. On 31 May 1900 the commander of that unit, Lt. Col. B. E. Spragge, surrendered. Spragge was later cleared of any wrongdoing by a court of enquiry. "Finding of a Court of Enquiry Held at Barberton on 25th September, 1900 to Investigate

the Circumstances under which Lieutenant-Colonel B. E. Spragge, D. S. O. XIIIth Battalion Imperial Yeomanry and Others, Became Prisoners of War," 1901: cd470 xlvii, 557; Stephen M. Miller, *Lord Methuen and the British Army: Failure and Redemption in South Africa* (London: Frank Cass, 1999), 188–89. Fransjohan Pretorius argues that the defeat at Lindley was a major blow to British prestige and helped solidify support behind M. T. Steyn, the president of the Free State, for the continuation of the war. Pretorius, *The Great Escape of the Boer Pimpernel Christiaan de Wet: The Making of a Legend,* trans. Stephen Hofstätter (Pietermaritzburg: University of Natal Press, 2001), 12.

7. Julius Bernstein to his uncle, 25 Mar. 1901, Julius Bernstein Papers, NAM.

8. Hugo Beaumont Burnaby to parents, 1 May 1900, Hugo Burnaby Papers, LHCMA.

9. Burnaby to parents, 28 May 1900, ibid.

10. Thomas Charles Wetton, *With Rundle's Eighth Division in South Africa* (London: Henry J. Drane, n.d.), 124.

11. W. S. Power to his cousin, 29 May 1900, Power Papers, NAM.

12. P. T. Ross, *A Yeoman's Letters* (London: Simpkin, Marshall, Hamilton, Kent, 1901), 32.

13. John Paterson to his brother, 27 Apr. 1900, John Paterson Papers, NAM.

14. W. H. Mackinnon, *The Journal of the C.I.V. in South Africa* (London: John Murray, 1901), 168.

15. Ibid., 102.

16. H. S. Gaskell, *With Lord Methuen in South Africa* (London: Henry J. Drane, 1906), 47.

17. John Paterson to his brother, 24 May 1900, Paterson Papers, NAM.

18. L. A. Bethell, *Outpost Duties as Learnt in South Africa* (London: William Clowes and Sons, 1903), 6.

19. Karl B. Spurgin, *On Active Service with the Northumberland and Durham Yeomen, under Lord Methuen* (London: Walter Scott, 1902), 54.

20. J. Stuart Hills to unnamed recipient, 30 July 1900, City of London Imperial Volunteers Papers, GL.

21. J. Barclay Lloyd, *One Thousand Miles with the C.I.V.* (London: Methuen, 1901), 100–105.

22. Ross, *Yeoman's Letters*, 25.

23. Q.L., *Yeomanry Cavalry of Worcestershire*, 141.

24. Diary, 25 Apr.1901, William Grant Papers, NAM.

25. Diary, 16 July 1900, Harry Hopwood Papers, NAM.

26. Ross, *Yeoman's Letters*, 10.

27. See note 6. Elphinstone and his brother, Kenneth, were among those captured at Lindley. Lancelot H. Elphinstone to his parents, 8 May 1900, L. H. Elphinstone Papers, NAM.

28. Alt was killed at Diamond Hill on 12 June 1900. Brian Alt, *Brian Alt* (London: Ballantyne, Hanson, 1900).

29. C. S. Awdry to his father, 24 May 1901, C. S. Awdry Papers, NAM; Harold Josling, *The Autobiography of a Military Great Coat* (London: Jarrold & Sons, 1907), 70–75.

30. John Paterson to his brother, 27 Apr. 1900, Paterson Papers, NAM; Spurgin, *On Active Service*, 18–19.

31. Rounders was an old English sport played with bats and balls and two teams of no more than nine. American baseball has its roots in the sport. See, for example, Francis M. Appleton, *The Volunteer Service Company (1st South Lancashire Regiment) in South Africa during the Boer War* (Warrington: Mackie, 1901); R. S. Britten Papers, NAM; and Meynell Hunt, *With the Warwickshire Yeomanry in South Africa* (Birmingham: Cornish Brothers, 1902).

32. Lister also describes as "sport" several degrading activities to which the regiment's African porters and scouts were subjected. This included the "bun and treacle competition for niggers," in which each man had to attack with his mouth a "damper" tied on a string and covered with sugar and water. "His difficulties were much enhanced by having flour chucked in his face and more sugar and water poured over it at times." Lister continues, "they seemed to enjoy it immensely, strange to say!" Diary, 12 Apr. 1900, H. R. Lister Papers, NAM.

33. House was a game played with numbered blocks.

34. Diary, 16 Apr. 1900, Hopwood Papers, NAM.

35. Godfrey Smith, *With the Scottish Rifle Volunteers at the Front* (Glasgow: William Hodge, 1901), 38–39.

36. C. E. Callwell, *Small Wars: Their Principles and Practice*, 3rd ed. (London: HMSO, 1906; reprint, Lincoln: University of Nebraska Press, 1996), 35–36.

37. The farm-burning policy was supported by Lord Salisbury and his government. See Andrew Roberts, *Salisbury: Victorian Titan* (London: Weidenfeld and Nicolson, 1999), 767. Although Roberts was certain the war would end once the Boer armies were destroyed and their industrial and political centers captured, Lord Milner was far from confident. Milner was also much more concerned than Roberts about the political ramifications after the war of the military policies employed during it. See Keith Terrance Surridge, *Managing the South African War, 1899–1902: Politicians v. Generals* (Woodbridge: Boydell, 1998), chap. 4.

38. The first metal blockhouses were introduced in January 1901. The structure was supported by wooden posts, stones, and sand and was connected to circular and radiating trenches for defensive purposes in the event of a Boer attack. Wire entanglements, complete with empty tins, which acted as rudimentary alarm systems, connected multiple blockhouses. Prefabricated metal units were introduced the following month. Emanoel Lee, *To the Bitter End: A Photographic History of the Boer War, 1899–1902* (New York: Penguin, 1985), 157–58.

39. Between 1900 and 1902, the British built about fifty camps, which eventually housed more than 150,000 men, women, and children. This

number includes more than 40,000 black refugees as well. The location of the camps, often set far from water sources and rail lines, resulted in long and arduous journeys for the prisoners and refugees. Shelter was scarce and of poor quality; food, or as the social reformer Emily Hobhouse put it, the "starvation ration," was insufficient; and fuel was supplied irregularly. Sanitation conditions were horrendous, which led to high death rates. Conditions only got better late in the war thanks to pressure placed on the British government by Hobhouse and others. Historians estimate that as many as 28,000 Boers and more than 14,000 blacks died in the concentration camps. For more on these camps, see S. B. Spies, *Methods of Barbarism* (Cape Town: Human and Rousseau, 1977); Fransjohan Pretorius, ed., *Scorched Earth* (Cape Town: Human & Rousseau, 2001); and Jonathan F. Vance, ed., *The Encyclopedia of Prisoners of War and Internment* (Denver: ABC-CLIO, 2000), s.v. "The Boer War," by Stephen M. Miller.

40. William Home, *With the Border Volunteers to Pretoria* (Hawick: W. & J. Kennedy, 1901), 50–2.

41. Frank Stephenson to home, 18 Oct. 1901, Frank Stephenson Papers, NAM.

42. Burnaby to parents, 28 June 1901, Burnaby Papers, LHCMA.

43. C. S. Awdry to his mother, 21 Sept. 1900, Awdry Papers, NAM.

44. G. F. A. Reece to his family, 18 May 1901, G. F. A. Reece Papers, NAM.

45. G. F. A. Reece to his family, 4 Dec. 1901, ibid.

46. Seasonal weather patterns naturally affected the volunteers' attitudes toward the South African landscape. But I found no examples of a volunteer commenting on the landscape or the weather in a seasonal context. As first-time visitors to South Africa, many probably did not expect to see changes. See, for example, Diary, 9 Sept. 1900, Hopwood Papers, NAM.

47. Bernard Moeller, *Two Years at the Front with the Mounted Infantry* (London: Grant Richards, 1903), 45.

48. H. E. Belfield to his wife, 24 July 1900, H. E. Belfield Papers, NAM.

49. W. Steel Brownlie, *The Proud Trooper* (London: Collins, 1964), 154.

50. Q.L., *Yeomanry Cavalry of Worcestershire*, 141.

51. Frank Stephenson to home, 14 Apr. 1901, Stephenson Papers, NAM.

52. I found no published accounts written by British volunteers that mentioned the execution of prisoners.

53. The best-known case of shooting prisoners was the subject of Bruce Beresford's 1980 film, *Breaker Morant,* and George Witton's 1907 book, *Scapegoats of the Empire.* Most recently, the story of Morant and the Bushveldt Carbineers has been retold in Nick Bleszynski, *Shoot Straight, You Bastards* (Melbourne: Random House, 2002).

54. Diary, 12 Apr. 1900, Lister Papers, NAM.

55. W. A. W. Lawson, Third Baron Burnham, to Syb, 9 Apr. 1900, Burnham Papers, LHCMA.

56. W. S. Power to his cousin, 11 July 1900, Power Papers, NAM.

57. Frederick Barnado, *An Active Life* (London: Bodley Head, 1963), 78–90.

58. Patrick Mileham, ed., *Clearly My Duty: The Letters of Sir John Gilmour* (East Linton: Tuckwell, 1996), 3 July 1900.

59. C. S. Awdry to his father, 6 June 1900, Awdry Papers, NAM.

60. Frank Charge to his father, 19 June 1900, F. E. Charge Papers, WCM.

61. Frank Charge to his father, 8 May 1900, ibid.

62. G. F. A. Reece to his family, 29 Aug. 1901, Reece Papers, NAM.

63. Sidney C. Peel, *Trooper 8008 Imperial Yeomanry* (London: Edward Arnold, 1901), 111.

64. Kimber managed to escape in July 1900. A year later, while on mounted patrol, he was shot and killed at a farmstead along the road to Ventersdorp. Ada Thomson, *Memorials of Charles Dixon Kimber* (London: James Nisbet, 1902), 43.

65. L. Curtis to his mother, 13 Mar. 1900, CIV Papers, GL.

66. "Kaffir" is a derogatory term that many volunteers used in their letters, memoirs, and published accounts to describe all black, and often multiracial, South Africans.

67. Peel, *Trooper 8008*, 50–75.

68. Frank Stephenson to home, 21 Apr. 1901, Stephenson Papers, NAM.

69. Gaskell, *With Lord Methuen in South Africa*, 22–23.

70. Smith, *With the Scottish Rifle Volunteers*, 30.

71. A. G. Garrish, *The Records of "I" Company. A Brief History of the East Surrey Volunteers' Service in the South African War* (London: Walbrook, 1901), 98.

72. Sharrad Gilbert, *Rhodesia—and After* (London: Simpkin Marshall, Hamilton, Kent, 1901), 20–27.

73. For the role of black South Africans in the war, see Peter Warwick, *Black People and the South African War* (Johannesburg: Ravan, 1983); and Bill Nasson, *Abraham Esau's War: A Black South African War in the Cape, 1899–1902* (New York: Cambridge University Press, 1991).

74. See chapter 5.

75. Diary, n.d., P. C. Jonas Papers, NAM.

76. Attitudes toward English-speaking South Africans were mixed, though they tended to be positive. As for Jewish South Africans, soldiers usually identified them with the mining or merchant communities and held them in general contempt. Anti-Semitic comments are found in many volunteer accounts of the war.

77. Ross, *Yeoman's Letters*, 18–19; Spurgin, *On Active Service*, 172–75; C. Stride to his parents, 20 Dec. 1900, Stride Papers, NAM; "Diary of No. 8080, Pvt. J. W. Milne, First Service Company Volunteers, Gordon Highlanders (1900) during the Boer War," http://jwmilne.freeservers.com (accessed 17 May 2006).

78. A "spruit" is a wash or a small stream that flows only during the rainy season. Wetton, *With Rundle's Eighth Division*, 59–60.

79. Garrish, *Records of "I" Company*, 11.

80. Moeller, *Two Years at the Front*, 36.

81. John Paterson to his brother, 27 Apr. and 5 May 1900, Paterson Papers, NAM.

82. Frank Charge to his father, 17 July and 31 Aug. 1900, Charge Papers, WCM.

83. Lionel Curtis, *With Milner in South Africa* (Oxford: Basil Blackwell, 1951), 1 Mar. 1900.

84. John Paterson to his brother, 3 Apr. and 5 May 1900, Paterson Papers, NAM.

85. "Diary of No. 8080."

86. Mileham, *Clearly My Duty,* 20 Mar., 1 and 6 Apr. 1900.

87. Smith, *With the Scottish Rifle Volunteers,* 10.

88. J. P. Sturrock, *The Fifes in South Africa* (Cupar-Fife: A. Westwood & Son, 1903), 52.

89. W. S. Power to his cousin, 14 Apr. 1900, Power Papers, NAM; Peel, *Trooper 8008,* 71; Gilbert, *Rhodesia,* 14.

90. Home, *With the Border Volunteers,* 90–99.

91. Brian Alt, *Brian Alt* (London: Ballantyne, Hanson, 1900), 25.

92. Gaskell, *With Lord Methuen in South Africa,* 48–50.

93. C. S. Awdry to his mother, 14 May 1900, Awdry Papers, NAM.

94. W. S. Power to his cousin, 28 Mar. 1900, Power Papers, NAM.

95. Barclay Lloyd, *One Thousand Miles with the C.I.V.,* 237–39.

96. H. B. Burnaby to parents, 10 June 1900, Burnaby Papers, LHCMA.

97. Gilbert, *Rhodesia,* 58.

98. Appleton, *Volunteer Service Company,* 24 June 1900.

99. William Corner, *The Story of the 34th Company (Middlesex) Imperial Yeomanry from the Point of View of Private No. 6243* (London: T. Fisher Unwin, 1902), 163.

100. L. Curtis to his mother, 17 June 1900, CIV Papers, GL.

101. Frank Charge to his father, 8 May 1901, Charge Papers, WCM.

102. Diary, n.d., Jonas Papers, NAM.

103. W. A. W. Lawson, Third Baron Burnham, to Syb, 5 Apr. 1900, Burnham Papers, LHCMA.

104. C. S. Awdry to his father, 1 May 1900, Awdry Papers, NAM.

105. C. S. Awdry to his mother, 1 Apr. 1901, ibid.

106. I could find only one reference in which a volunteer, in this case Bernard Moeller, thought about requesting a transfer to another unit in South Africa that he believed was more actively engaged with the enemy. See Moeller, *Two Years at the Front,* 87. Of course, volunteers did transfer to other units, particularly to the South African Constabulary. In December 1900 twenty of Sir John Gilmour's sixty men applied to join the constabulary. Mileham, *Clearly My Duty,* 1 Dec. 1900.

107. Great Britain was one of eight countries that sent troops to China to suppress the Boxer Rebellion in May 1900. See, for example, C. S. Awdry to his father, 21 July 1900, Awdry Papers, NAM.

108. H. B. Burnaby to parents, 23 Feb. 1902, Burnaby Papers, LHCMA.

109. Josling, *Autobiography of a Military Great Coat,* 75–78.

110. G. F. A. Reece to his family, 18 May 1901, Reece Papers, NAM.

111. A. E. Pease, ed., *A Private Memoir of Sir Thomas Fowler* (London: William Clowes, 1905), 96.

112. Spurgin, *On Active Service,* 42.

113. John Paterson to his brother, 3 June 1900, Paterson Papers, NAM. Paterson is most likely referring to the Bakgatla. For a discussion of their participation, see Bernard Mbenga, "The Role of the Bakgatla of the Pilanesberg in the South African War," in *Writing a Wider War: Rethinking Gender, Race, and Identity in the South African War, 1899–1902,* ed. Greg Cuthbertson, Albert Grundlingh, and Mary-Lynn Suttie (Athens: Ohio University Press, 2002).

114. W. S. Power to his cousin, 12 June 1900, Power Papers, NAM.

115. Frank Stephenson to home, 14 Apr. 1901, Stephenson Papers, NAM.

116. Diary, 13 May 1901, Joseph Duncalf Papers, NAM.

117. Diary, 6 July 1901, ibid.

118. Spurgin, *On Active Service,* 57.

119. See, for example, Thomas F. Dewar, *With the Scottish Yeomanry* (Arbroath: T. Buncle, 1901), Oct. 1900.

120. Ross, *Yeoman's Letters,* 130.

121. Peel, *Trooper 8008,* 25.

122. W. R. Birdwood, *Khaki and Gown: An Autobiography* (London: Ward, Locke, 1941), 119.

123. H. G. Mckenzie Rew, *Records of the Rough Riders (XXth Battalion) Imperial Yeomanry* (Bedford: Brown & Wilson, 1907), 12.

124. Gilbert, *Rhodesia,* 58–60.

125. Diary, 20 Sept. 1900, Hopwood Papers, NAM.

126. Georgiana Howe, ed., *The Imperial Yeomanry Hospitals in South Africa,* 3 vols. (London: Humphreys, 1902), 2:25–31.

127. "Report of His Majesty's Commissioners Appointed to Inquire into the Military Preparations and Other Military Matters Connected with the War in South Africa," 1904: cd 1792 xlii, 258, as cited in Pakenham, *Boer War,* 607.

128. Frank Charge to his father, 1 June 1900, Charge Papers, WCM.

129. For a recent discussion on health issues and the concentration camps, see Elizabeth van Heyningen, "Women and Disease: The Clash of Medical Cultures in the Concentration Camps of the South African War," in Cuthbertson, Grundlingh, and Suttie, *Writing a Wider War,* 186–212.

130. Nasson, *South African War,* 279.

131. According to Col. A. G. Lucas, a member of the Imperial Yeomanry Committee, the average strength of an Imperial Yeomanry company was thirty-five by the summer of 1901. See Imperial Yeomanry, *Report of the Deputy Adjutant-General of the Force and New Battalions for the Imperial Yeomanry in South Africa. Supplementary to the Report Submitted on the 15th May, 1901* (London: Harrison and Sons, 1903), 13, as cited in Will Bennett, *Absent-Minded Beggars: Volunteers in the Boer War* (London: Leo Cooper, 1999), 82.

132. A. W. M. Atthill, *From Norwich to Lichtenburg via Pretoria* (Norwich: A. E. Soman, 1909), 30–34.

133. Ross, *Yeoman's Letters,* 157.

134. See, for example, Sturrock, *Fifes in South Africa*, 110–20; Smith, *With the Scottish Rifle Volunteers*, 82–85; and H. B. Burnaby to parents, 27 June 1900, Burnaby Papers, LHCMA.

135. Mileham, *Clearly My Duty*, 18 Nov. 1900.

136. The term "absent beggars" is a direct reference to Rudyard Kipling's very successful poem and patriotic call for service, "Absent-Minded Baggar." Ross is obviously frustrated that his government does not seem to show the same interest in the volunteers that it did when the men were being recruited. Ross, *Yeoman's Letters*, as cited in Bennett, *Absent-Minded Beggars*, 77.

137. C. S. Awdry to his father, 27 Dec. 1900, Awdry Papers, NAM.

138. Pease, *Private Memoir of Sir Thomas Fowler*, 99.

139. Bill Nasson writes that the war was publicly declared as good as over. Nasson, *South African War*, 191.

140. Anonymous letter to *Standard*, 11 Dec. 1900, Britten Papers, NAM. C. S Jarvis writes that many of the men in his company of Imperial Yeomanry, raised in Montgomeryshire, believed that they had signed up only for six months. They were mistaken. Jarvis, *Half a Life* (London: John Murray, 1943), 111.

141. Sturrock, *Fifes in South Africa*, 60–80.

142. They were all reprimanded for this action. Corner, *Story of the 34th Company*, 371.

143. W. A. W. Lawson, Third Baron Burnham, to Syb, 1 Feb. 1901, Burnham Papers, LHCMA.

144. Brodrick replaced Lansdowne in November 1900.

145. W. St. John Brodrick to Lord Kitchener, 15 Dec. 1900, PRO 30/57/22, TNA.

146. Lord Roberts to Lord Kitchener, 18 Jan. 1901, PRO 30/57/20, ibid.

147. Lord Kitchener to W. St. John Brodrick, 15 Mar. 1901, PRO 30/57/22, ibid.

148. The class of the men also changed with an increase of full-time and part-time workers and a decrease of middle-class men volunteering to serve. Ian F. W. Beckett, *Riflemen Form: A Study of the Rifle Volunteer Movement, 1859–1908* (Aldershot: Ogilby Trusts, 1982), 214–16.

149. *Cossack Post*, 188–89. Paget's Horse was raised in London and comprised the Fifty-first, Fifty-second, Sixty-eighth, and Seventy-third Companies Imperial Yeomanry.

150. Lord Roberts to Lord Kitchener, 21 Nov. 1901, PRO 30/57/20, TNA.

151. Frank Charge to his father, 21 Mar. 1901, Charge Papers, WCM.

152. Frank Charge to his father, 6 July 1900, ibid.

CHAPTER 7

1. Rudyard Kipling, "The Lesson," *The Times (London)*, 29 July 1901, as cited in Elleke Boehmer, ed., *Empire Writing: An Anthology of Colonial Literature, 1870–1918* (New York: Oxford University Press, 1998), 294.

2. Sidney C. Peel, *Trooper 8008 Imperial Yeomanry* (London: Edward Arnold, 1901), vii.

3. *The Times (London),* 12 July 1902, 7.

4. Kitchener was accompanied by Gens. Sir John French and Sir Ian Hamilton and Col. Sir Harry Rawlinson.

5. *The Times (London),* 14 July 1902, 6.

6. Ibid.

7. Diary, T. W. Lemmon Papers, NAM; C. J. Hart, *The History of the 1st Volunteer Battalion: The Royal Warwickshire Regiment* (Birmingham: Midland Counties Herald, 1906).

8. The other members of the regiment had either died, settled in South Africa, or previously returned due to disease or expired time of service. *The Times (London),* 20 June 1902, 12.

9. Brian Gardner, *Allenby of Arabia* (New York: Coward-McCann, 1965), 50; PRO 30/57/22, Kitchener Papers, TNA, as cited in Will Bennett, *Absent-Minded Beggars: Volunteers in the Boer War* (London: Leo Cooper, 1999), 193.

10. Copy of telegram, 14 Mar. 1902, W. R. Birdwood Papers, NAM.

11. W. A. W. Lawson, Third Baron Burnham, to Syb, 21 Mar. and 11 Apr. 1901, Burnham Papers, LHCMA.

12. Hertzog later formed the National Party and served as the Union of South Africa's prime minister from 1924 to 1939.

13. L. S. Amery, ed., *The Times History of the War in South Africa, 1899–1902,* 7 vols. (London: Sampson Low, Marston, 1900–1909), 5:80–81.

14. Six percent of the second contingent of Imperial Yeomanry was sent home almost immediately at Kitchener's request. The Gipps Committee, which convened in late 1901 to examine the second contingent, found this figure to be reasonable. A. Hastings Stewart, the medical examiner in London for the Imperial Yeomanry Committee and the Special Corps, testified that the medical services were overwhelmed by the numbers of would-be recruits. With four hundred men coming in every day for examinations, there was not even time to ask them to take off their boots for foot inspections. "Report of Sir R. Gipps Committee on the Imperial Yeomanry of 1901," WO 108/107, TNA.

15. J. K. Dunlop, *The Development of the British Army, 1899–1914* (London: Methuen, 1938), 112–17.

16. Wm. St. John Brodrick to Kitchener, 6 July 1901, PRO 30/57/22, TNA.

17. Roberts to Kitchener, 31 Jan. 1902, PRO 30/57/20, ibid.

18. Of course, Regular Army, Militia, and Volunteer units also suffered setbacks during the war. For example, the Berkshire Regiment, Volunteer Service Company, surrendered at Holfontein to only fifty Boers without a shot fired. Although their commanding officer, Captain Ewen, was acquitted by a court-martial for wrongfully surrendering his post, he was "convicted of being taken as a prisoner for lack of precaution." Roberts to Lansdowne, 18 Nov. 1900, WO 108/411, TNA.

19. Julius Bernstein to his uncle, 22 July 1901, Julius Bernstein Papers, NAM.

20. André Wessels, ed., *Anglo-Boer War Diary of Herbert Gwynne Howell* (Pretoria: Human Sciences Research Council, 1986), 155–56.

21. Amery, *Times History of the War,* 5:438.

22. Gen. Sir Henry de Beauvoir de Lisle, "My Narrative of the South African War, 1899–1902," H. de Lisle Papers, LHCMA, 86.

23. George Arthur, *Life of Lord Kitchener* (London: Macmillan, 1920), 5

24. See, for example, Kitchener to Brodrick, 20 Apr. 1902, PRO 30/57/22, Kitchener Papers, TNA.

25. Wessels, *Anglo-Boer War Diary,* 172. Amery disagrees with this assessment, believing the Imperial Yeomanry acted courageously and, considering the circumstances, performed better than should have been expected. Amery, *Times History of the War,* 5:498–99.

26. Stephen M. Miller, *Lord Methuen and the British Army: Failure and Redemption in South Africa* (London: Frank Cass, 1999), 235n.

27. Q.L, *The Yeomanry Cavalry of Worcestershire, 1794–1913* (Devizes: G. Simpson, 1914), 158.

28. Philip Magnus, *Kitchener: Portrait of an Imperialist* (New York: E. P. Dutton, 1959), 187.

29. Wm. St. John Brodrick to Kitchener, 15 Mar. 1902, PRO 30/57/22, Kitchener Papers, TNA.

30. Wm. St. John Brodrick to Kitchener, 16 Mar. 1902, ibid.

31. Frank Stephenson to home, 18 Oct. 1901, Frank Stephenson Papers, NAM.

32. Henry A. Adderley, *History of the Warwickshire Yeomanry Cavalry* (Warwick: W. H. Smith & Son, 1912), conclusion.

33. Dundonald played a critical but contentious role in the restructuring of the Canadian militia after the war.

34. Douglas Dundonald, *My Army Life* (London: Edward Arnold, 1926), 187.

35. South Africa Despatches, vol. 1, 1 Nov. 1899–1 Aug. 1900, WO 108/380, TNA.

36. Roberts to Lansdowne, 7 June 1900, WO 108/410, ibid.

37. Miscellaneous CIV Papers, NAM.

38. A. W. A. Pollock, *With Seven Generals in the Boer War* (London: Skeffington & Son, 1900), 206–207.

39. *Report of the Deputy Adjutant-General of the Force Regarding the Raising of Drafts and New Battalions for the Imperial Yeomanry in South Africa. Supplementary to the Report Submitted on the 15th May, 1901* (London: Harrison & Sons, 1902), app. 4.

40. Duncan Doolittle, *A Soldier's Hero* (Narragansett, R.I.: Anawan, 1991), 219.

41. R. Gubbins to unnamed recipient, 2 Aug. 1900, Richard Gubbins Papers, NAM; W. S. Power to his cousin, 25 Sept. 1900, W. S. Power Papers, NAM; Diary, 10 Sept. 1900, Harry Hopwood Papers, NAM.

42. Wessels, *Anglo-Boer War Diary,* 98, 155–56.

43. Eric Rosanthal, *General De Wet,* 2nd ed. (Cape Town: Simondium, 1968), 122.

44. Amery, *Times History of the War,* 5:426–27.

45. "Report of Sir R. Gipps Committee on the Imperial Yeomanry of 1901," WO 108/107, TNA.

46. William Home, *With the Border Volunteers to Pretoria* (Hawick: W. & J. Kennedy, 1901), 176–77.

AFTERMATH

1. Fred Cape, "The Tin Gee-Gee," rev. and sung by Mel B. Spurr (London: T. B. Marns and F. D. Hunter, 1890–99), as cited in P. T. Ross, *A Yeoman's Letters* (London: Simpkin, Marshall, Hamilton, Kent, 1901), 157.

2. Sir H. Campbell-Bannerman to Sir R. Knox, 23 Oct. 1900, H. Campbell-Bannerman Papers, 41221, Manuscript Collections, British Library, London.

3. See, for example, H. Birchenough, "Our Last Effort for a Voluntary Army: A Civilian View," *The Nineteenth Century and After* 49 (1901): 545–54; and Lowell J. Satre, "St. John Brodrick and Army Reform, 1901–1903," *Journal of British Studies* 15 (1976): 117–39.

4. Frederick Maurice, ed., *Soldier, Artist, Sportsman: The Life of General Lord Rawlinson of Trent* (New York: Houghton Mifflin, 1928), 78–82.

5. See, for example, Ian F. W. Beckett, "Arnold-Forster and the Volunteers," in *Politicians and Defence*, ed. I. F. W. Beckett and J. Gooch (Manchester: Manchester University Press, 1981), 47–68; and H. O. Arnold-Forster, *The Army in 1906: A Policy and Vindication* (New York: E. P. Dutton, 1906).

6. R. B. Haldane, *Army Reform and other Addresses* (London: T. Fisher Unwin, 1907), 32. See also John Gooch, "Haldane and the 'National Army,'" in Beckett and Gooch, *Politicians and Defence*, 47–68.

7. Edward M. Spiers, *The Army and Society, 1815–1914* (New York: Longman, 1980), 279.

8. For an important discussion of the Territorial Force, see Peter Dennis, *The Territorial Army, 1906–1940* (Wolfeboro, N.H.: Boydell, 1987).

9. Ironically, the Territorial Force was not tested in 1914 when World War I erupted because Kitchener, then secretary of state for war, chose to raise additional troops through a public call to arms. Spiers, *Army and Society*, 281.

10. G. R. Searle, *The Quest for National Efficiency* (Berkeley: University of California Press, 1971), 39.

11. Matthew Hendley, "Help Us to Secure a Strong, Healthy, Prosperous, and Peaceful Britain," *Canadian Journal of History* 30 (1995): 261–89.

12. Frederick Maurice, "Where to Get Men," *Contemporary Review* 81 (1902): 78–79.

13. Hendley, "Help Us to Secure a Strong, Healthy, Prosperous, and Peaceful Britain," 270.

14. For further discussions of the conscription debate, see R. J. Q. Adams and Philip P. Poirier, *The Conscription Controversy in Great Britain, 1900–18* ([Columbus]: Ohio State University Press, 1987); and T. Ropp, "Conscription in Great Britain, 1900–1914," *Military Affairs* 20 (1956): 71–76.

15. "Lord Ebrington's Committee to Consider a Revised Edition of Regulations for the Imperial Yeomanry," 17 July 1902, WO 32/7270, TNA; 23 Apr. 1902, WO 32/6453, ibid.

16. Lord Esher to H.R.H. Edward VII, 11 July 1903, in *Journals and Letters of Reginald, Viscount Esher,* 4 vols., ed. Maurice V. Brett (London: Nicholson and Watson, 1934–38), 1:417.

17. The Royal Commission on the War in South Africa, *Report, Minutes of Evidence, and Appendices,* Report (London: HMSO, 1903), 73.

18. Ibid., 64.

19. Ibid., 66.

20. Ibid., 71–72.

21. Ibid., 73.

22. Ibid.

23. Lord Esher to Lord Knollys, n.d., in Brett, *Journals and Letters,* 2:185.

24. The Royal Commission on the Militia and Volunteers, *Report, Minutes of Evidence, and Appendices,* Report (London: HMSO, 1904), 5.

25. Ibid., app. 8 (12).

26. Ibid., Report, 9.

27. Ibid., 16.

28. Spiers, *Army and Society*, 255.

29. Royal Commission on the Militia and Volunteers, *Report, Minutes of Evidence, and Appendices,* app. 11 (16–25).

30. Edward George Villiers Stanley, Seventeenth Earl of Derby, the son of one of the commissioners, served as director general of recruitment in 1915. He was a fierce opponent of conscription. For a discussion of the Norfolk Commission, see Ian F. W. Beckett, *Riflemen Form: A Study of the Rifle Volunteer Movement, 1859–1908* (Aldershot: Ogilby Trusts, 1982), chap. 8.

31. Amery, who once referred to the Militia and Volunteers as an "entirely unorganized mob," supported universal training for sixteen- and seventeen-year-olds, followed by one or two years of Militia service. He strongly condemned Brodrick's vision but did advocate for Arnold-Forster's policies. L. S. Amery, *My Political Life* (London: Hutchinson, 1953), 199.

32. *The Cossack Post: Journal of B Squadron, Paget's Horse, De La Rey's Farm, Lichtenberg, Transvaal, February to May 1901* (London: Junior Army and Navy Stores, 1901), 188–89.

BIBLIOGRAPHY

ARCHIVES AND MANUSCRIPT COLLECTIONS

Corporation of London Records Office
City of London Imperial Volunteers Papers

Guildhall Library, London
City of London Imperial Volunteers Papers

Imperial War Museum, London
French Papers

Liddell Hart Centre for Military Archives, King's College, University of London
Aston Papers
Hugo Burnaby Papers
Burnham Papers
De Lisle Papers
Hamilton Papers
Lawson Papers

Manuscript Collections, British Library, London
Balfour Papers
Campbell-Bannerman Papers

The National Archives, Kew
CAB 37 Cabinet Records, General Papers
CAB 41 Cabinet Records, Letters to the Monarch
PRO 30/57 Kitchener Papers
WO 32 War Office, Miscellaneous Papers on the South African War
WO 108 War Office, South African War Papers
WO 114 War Office, Annual Returns
WO 128 War Office, Attestation and Discharge Papers for the Imperial Yeomanry
WO 136 War Office, Colvin Papers

National Army Museum, London (Chelsea)
Awdry Papers
Belcher Papers
Belfield Papers
Bernstein Papers
Birdwood Papers
Brammer Papers
Britten Papers
Cadell Papers
Day-Lewis Papers
Douse Papers
Duncalf Papers
Elphinstone Papers
Grant Papers
Gubbins Papers
Hopwood Papers
Jonas Papers
Jordain Papers
Lemmon Papers
Lister Papers
Manisty Papers
Maurice Papers
Neale Papers
Niccolls Papers
Paterson Papers
Power Papers
Putland Papers
Reece Papers
Roberts Papers
Stephenson Papers
Stride Papers
Ward Papers
Warre Papers
Various clippings and Scrapbooks

Wiltshire Records Office, Trowbridge
Methuen Papers

Worcester City Museum, Worcester
Charge Papers
Pitt Papers

PARLIAMENTARY PAPERS AND PUBLISHED REPORTS

Act to Amend Reserve Forces Act of 1882.
1900: 276 iv, 313.
Act to Amend Volunteer Act of 1863.
1900: 286 v, 575.
Annual Returns of the Volunteer and Territorial Forces, 1895–1913.
Auxiliary Forces for Service in South Africa. London: HMSO, 1900.
Bill to Amend Law Relating to Militia and Yeomanry.
1901: iii, 463.
1902: iii, 517.
Regulations for the Imperial Yeomanry. London: Harrison and Sons, 1902.
"Report from Lt. Gen. Lord Methuen on the Action that Took Place near Tweebosch on 7th March, 1902."
1902: cd 967 lxix, 287.
Report of the Deputy Adjutant-General of the Force Regarding the Raising of Drafts and New Battalions for the Imperial Yeomanry in South Africa. Supplementary to the Report Submitted on the 15th May, 1901. London: Harrison & Sons, 1902.
"Report of His Majesty's Commissioners Appointed to Inquire into the Military Preparations and Other Military Matters Connected with the War in South Africa."
1904: cd 1789 xl, 1; cd 1790 xi, 325; cd 1791 xli, 1; cd 1792 xlii, 1.
Reports on the Raising, Organising, Equipping and Despatching the City of London Imperial Volunteers to South Africa. London : Blades, East, & Blades, 1900.
Return of Establishment of Each Regiment of Militia in the United Kingdom, 1899.
1900: cd 89 xlix, 221.
Return of Military Forces.
1900: cd 421 xlix, 277.
1902: cd 462 xxxix, 639; cd 578 xxxix, 643.
1903: cd 892 lviii, 17; cd 990 lviii, 21.
Return of the Number of Companies of Imperial Yeomanry Formed, 1900.
1900: 115 xlix, 425.
Royal Commission on the Militia and Volunteers. *Report, Minutes of Evidence, and Appendices.* c.2061–64. London: HMSO, 1904.
Strength of Volunteer Service Corps and Drafts.
1901: cd 610 xi, 173.

CONTEMPORARY BOOKS

Adderley, Henry A. *History of the Warwickshire Yeomanry Cavalry.* Warwick: W. H. Smith & Son, 1912.

Alt, Brian. *Brian Alt.* London: Ballantyne, Hanson, 1900.

Amery, L. S. *My Political Life.* London: Hutchinson, 1953.

———. *The Problem of the Army.* London: Edward Arnold, 1903.

———, ed. *The Times History of the War in South Africa, 1899–1902.* 7 vols. London: Sampson Low, Marston, 1900–1909.

Appleton, Francis M. *The Volunteer Service Company (1st South Lancashire Regiment) in South Africa during the Boer War.* Warrington: Mackie, 1901.

Arnold-Forster, Hugh Oakeley. *The Army in 1906: A Policy and Vindication.* New York: E. P. Dutton, 1906.

———. *Army Letters, 1897–98.* London: Edward Arnold, 1898.

———. *The War Office, the Army, and the Empire: A Review of the Military Situation in 1900.* London: Cassell, 1900.

Arnold-Forster, Mary. *The Right Honourable Hugh Oakeley Arnold-Forster: A Memoir.* London: Edward Arnold, 1910.

Atlay, J. B. *Lord Haliburton.* Toronto: William Briggs, 1909.

Atthill, A. W. M. *From Norwich to Lichtenburg via Pretoria.* Norwich: A. E. Soman, 1909.

Barclay Lloyd, J. *One Thousand Miles with the C.I.V.* London: Methuen, 1901.

Barnado, Frederick. *An Active Life.* London: Bodley Head, 1963.

Berry, Robert Potter. *A History of the Formation and Development of the Volunteer Infantry.* London: Simpkin, Marshall, Hamilton, Kent, 1903.

Bethell, L. A. *Outpost Duties as Learnt in South Africa.* London: William Clowes and Sons, 1903.

Biddulph, Robert. *Lord Caldwell at the War Office.* London: Murray, 1904.

Birdwood, W. R. *Khaki and Gown: An Autobiography.* London: Ward, Locke, 1941.

Birkin, H. L. *History of the 3rd Regiment Imperial Yeomanry, 28–1-00 to 6–8-02.* Nottingham: J. J. Vice, 1905.

Brett, G. A. *A History of the 2nd Battalion The Monmouthshire Regiment.* Pontypool: Hughes & Son, Griffin Press, 1933.

Brett, Maurice V., ed. *Journals and Letters of Reginald, Viscount Esher.* 4 vols. London: Nicholson and Watson, 1934–38.

Brookfield, Arthur Montagu. *Annals of a Chequered Life.* London: John Murray, 1930.

Burgoyne, Gerald. *The Fife & Forfar Imperial Yeomanry and Its Predecessors.* Cupar-Fife: J. & G. Innes, 1904.

Burn-Murdoch, J. H. *With Lumsden's Horse Agin the Boers.* Taunton: Barnicott & Pearce, 1901.

Butler, William. *Sir William Butler: An Autobiography.* London: Constable, 1911.

Cairnes, W. E. *An Absent Minded War.* London: John Milne, 1900.

Callwell, C. E. *Small Wars: Their Principles and Practice.* 3rd ed. London: HMSO, 1906. Reprint, Lincoln: University of Nebraska Press, Bison Books, 1996.

Conan Doyle, Arthur. *The Great Boer War.* 16th ed. London: Thomas Nelson & Sons, 1903.

Cooke, John H. *5,000 Miles with the Cheshire Yeomanry in South Africa.* Warrington: Mackie, 1913.

Corner, William. *The Story of the 34th Company (Middlesex) Imperial Yeomanry from the Point of View of Private No. 6243.* London: T. Fisher Unwin, 1902.

The Cossack Post: Journal of B Squadron, Paget's Horse, De La Rey's Farm, Lichtenberg, Transvaal, February to May 1901. London: Junior Army and Navy Stores, 1901.

Cottesloe, Thomas Francis Fremantle. *The Englishman and the Rifle.* London: Jenkins, 1946.

Cunliffe, Foster H. E. *History of the Boer War.* London: Methuen, 1901–1904.

Curtis, Lionel. *With Milner in South Africa.* Oxford: Basil Blackwell, 1951.

Dennison, C. G. *A Fight to a Finish.* London: Longmans, Green, 1904.

Dewar, Thomas F. *With the Scottish Yeomanry.* Arbroath: T. Buncle, 1901.

Dilke, Charles W. *The British Army.* London: Chapman and Hall, 1888.

Dundonald, Douglas. *My Army Life.* London: Edward Arnold, 1926.

Dunlop, J. K. *The Development of the British Army, 1899–1914.* London: Methuen, 1938.

Eaton, Francis W. *History of the 3rd Regiment Imperial Yeomanry, in South Africa.* N.p., 1909.

Edmeades, J. F. *Some Historical Records of the West Kent (Q.O.) Yeomanry.* London: Andrew Melrose, 1909.

Fayle, C. E. *The New Patriotism: A Study in Social Obligations.* London: Harrison and Sons, 1914.

Field, H. John. *Toward a Programme of Imperial Life: The British Empire at the Turn of the Century.* Contributions in Comparative Colonial Studies, ed. Robin Winks, no. 9. Westport, Conn.: Greenwood, 1982.

Fisher, W. G. *The History of Somerset Yeomanry, Volunteer, and Territorial Units.* Taunton: Goodman, 1924.

Fitzgibbon, Maurice. *Arts under Arms: An University Man in Khaki.* London: Longmans, Green, 1901.

Fuller, J. F. C. *The Last of the Gentlemen's Wars.* London: Faber and Faber, 1937.

———. *Training Soldiers for War.* London: Hugh Rees, 1914.

Gage, M. F., ed. *Records of the Dorset Imperial Yeomanry, 1894–1905.* Sherborne: F. Bennett, 1906.

Gallagher, Michael. *Mick Gallagher at the Front.* Liverpool: Mac's Sugar House, 1900.

Garrish, A. G. *The Records of "I" Company: A Brief History of the East Surrey Volunteers' Service in the South African War.* London: Walbrook, 1901.

Gaskell, H. S. *With Lord Methuen in South Africa.* London: Henry J. Drane, 1906.

Gibbon, F. P. *William A. Smith of the Boys' Brigade.* London: Collins' Clear-Type Press, 1934.

Gilbert, Sharrad. *Rhodesia—and After.* London: Simpkin Marshall, Hamilton, Kent, 1901.

Gladstone, E. W. *The Shropshire Yeomanry, 1795–1945.* London: Whitethorn, 1953.

Graham, H. *The Annals of the Yeomanry Cavalry of Wiltshire; being a Complete History of the Prince of Wales' Own Royal Regiment.* 3 vols. Devizes: Geo. Simpson, 1908.

Grierson, J. M. *Records of the Scottish Volunteer Force, 1859–1908.* Edinburgh: Wm. Blackwood & Sons, 1909.

Haldane, R. B. *Army Reform and other Addresses.* London: T. Fisher Unwin, 1907.

Hales, A. G. *Campaign Pictures of the War in South Africa 1898–1900: Letters to the Front.* London: Cassell, 1900.

Hart, C. J. *The History of the 1st Volunteer Battalion: The Royal Warwickshire Regiment.* Birmingham: Midland Counties Herald, 1906.

Henderson, G. F. R. *The Science of War.* London: Longmans, Green, 1912.

Hobson, J. A. *The Psychology of Jingoism.* London: Grant Richards, 1901.

———. *Imperialism: A Study.* Rev. ed. London: Murray, 1905. Reprint, Ann Arbor: University of Michigan Press, 1965.

Home, William. *With the Border Volunteers to Pretoria.* Hawick: W. & J. Kennedy, 1901.

Howe, Georgiana, ed. *The Imperial Yeomanry Hospitals in South Africa.* 3 vols. London: Humphreys, 1902.

Howland, Frederick Hoppin. *The Chase of De Wet.* Providence: Preston & Rounds, 1901.

Hunt, Meynell. *With the Warwickshire Yeomanry in South Africa.* Birmingham: Cornish Brothers, 1902.

Jarvis, C. S. *Half a Life.* London: John Murray, 1943.

Jeyes, S. H. and F. D. How. *The Life of Sir Howard Vincent.* London: George Allen, 1912.

Josling, Harold. *The Autobiography of a Military Great Coat.* London: Jarrold & Sons, 1907.

Lamont, William. *Volunteer Memories.* Greenock: James McKelvie & Sons, 1911.

Mackail, J. W., and Guy Wyndham. *Life and Letters of George Wyndham.* London: Hutchinson, 1915.

Mackinnon, W. H. *The Journal of the C.I.V. in South Africa.* London: John Murray, 1901.

MacLean, A. H. *Public Schools and the War in South Africa.* London: Edward Stanford, 1903.

Marks, Alfred. *The Churches and the South African War.* London: New Age Office, 1905.

Marson, T. B. *Scarlet and Khaki.* London: Jonathan Cape, 1930.

Maude, Alymer. *War and Patriotism.* London: A. Bonner, 1900.

Maurice, Frederick, ed. *Soldier, Artist, Sportsman: The Life of General Lord Rawlinson of Trent.* New York: Houghton Mifflin, 1928.

Maurice, Frederick, and George Arthur. *The Life of Lord Wolseley.* New York: Doubleday, Page, 1924.

Maurice, Frederick, and M. H. Grant. *(Official) History of the War in South Africa, 1899–1902.* Vol. 4. London: Hurst and Blackwood, 1906–1910.

Midleton, William St. John. *Records & Reactions, 1856–1939.* New York: E. P. Dutton, 1939.

Moeller, Bernard. *Two Years at the Front with the Mounted Infantry.* London: Grant Richards, 1903.

Orr, A. S. *Scottish Yeomanry in South Africa, 1900–1901.* Glasgow: James Hedderwick & Sons, 1901.

Parr, Henry. *The Further Training and Employment of Mounted Infantry and Yeomanry.* 3rd ed. London: Gale & Polden, 1902.

Peacock, Roger S. *Pioneer of Boyhood: Story of Sir William A. Smith.* Glasgow: Boys' Brigade, 1954.

Pease, A. E., ed. *A Private Memoir of Sir Thomas Fowler.* London: William Clowes, 1905.

Peel, Sidney C. *Trooper 8008 Imperial Yeomanry.* London: Edward Arnold, 1901.

Playne, C. E. *The Pre-War Mind in Britain.* London: George Allen & Unwin, 1928.

Pollock, A. W. A. *With Seven Generals in the Boer War.* London: Skeffington & Son, 1900.

Q.L. *The Yeomanry Cavalry of Worcestershire, 1794–1913.* Devizes: G. Simpson, 1914.

Rew, H. G. Mckenzie. *Records of the Rough Riders (XXth Battalion) Imperial Yeomanry.* Bedford: Brown & Wilson, 1907.

Rosebery, Archibald Primrose. *Questions of Empire.* New York: A. L. Humphreys, 1900.

Ross, P. T. *A Yeoman's Letters.* London: Simpkin, Marshall, Hamilton, Kent, 1901.

Scott, Guy, and G. L. McDonnell, *The Record of the Mounted Infantry of the City Imperial Volunteers.* London: E. & F. N. Spon, 1902.

Seeley, John R. *The Expansion of England.* Boston: Roberts Brothers, 1883.

Seton-Karr, Henry. *The Call to Arms, 1900–1901.* New York: Longmans, Green, 1902.

Simpson, R. J. S. *The Medical History of the War in South Africa.* London: HMSO, 1911.

Smith, Godfrey. *With the Scottish Rifle Volunteers at the Front.* Glasgow: William Hodge, 1901.

Spender, J. A. *The Life of The Right Hon. Sir Henry Campbell-Bannerman.* New York: Houghton Mifflin, 1924. Reprint, New York: Kraus Reprint, 1968.

Spurgin, Karl B. *On Active Service with the Northumberland and Durham Yeomen, under Lord Methuen.* London: Walter Scott, 1902.

Stanhope, Edward. *The British Army and Our Defensive Position.* London: Kegan Paul, Trench, Trübner, 1892.

Sturrock, J. P. *The Fifes in South Africa.* Cupar-Fife: A. Westwood & Son, 1903.

Thomson, Ada. *Memorials of Charles Dixon Kimber.* London: James Nisbet, 1902.

Tullibardine, K. M. (Atholl). *A Military History of Perthshire, 1899–1902.* Perth: R. A. and J. Hay, 1908.

Turner, Alfred E. *Sixty Years of a Soldier's Life.* London: Methuen, 1912.

Wetton, Thomas Charles. *Reminiscences of the 34th Bn. Imperial Yeomanry.* London: Sidey and Bartlett, 1907.

———. *With Rundle's Eighth Division in South Africa.* London: Henry J. Drane, n.d.

White, Arnold. *Efficiency and Empire.* London: Methuen, 1901. Reprint, ed. with an introduction and notes by G. R. Searle, Brighton: Harvester Press, 1973.

Wilkinson, H. Spenser. *Lessons of the War.* Philadelphia: J. B. Lippincott, 1900.

———. *Volunteers and National Defense.* Westminster: Archibald Constable, 1896.

Williams, Basil, and Erskine Childers. *The H.A.C. in South Africa.* London: Smith, Elder, 1903.

Wylly, C. H. *Historical Records of the 1st King's Own Stafford Militia, now 3rd and 4th Battalions South Staffordshire Regiment.* Lichfield : A. C. Lomax, 1902.

Wynn, R. W. W., and Benson Freeman. *The Historical Records of the Yeomanry and Volunteers of Montgomeryshire, 1803–1908.* Oswestry: Woodhall, Minshall, Thomas, 1909.

CONTEMPORARY JOURNAL AND MAGAZINE ARTICLES

Birchenough, H. "Our Last Effort for a Voluntary Army: A Civilian View." *The Nineteenth Century and After* 49 (1901): 545–54.

Hale, Lonsdale. "Our Peace Training for War. Guilty or Not Guilty?" *Nineteenth Century* 47 (1900): 227–43.

Maurice, Frederick. "National Health: A Soldier's Study." *Contemporary Review* 83 (1903): 41–56.

———. "Where to Get Men." *Contemporary Review* 81 (1902): 78–86.

Russell, F. "Our Last Effort for a Voluntary Army: A Military View." *The Nineteenth Century and After* 49 (1901): 555–65.

Whigham, H. J. "The Fighting with Methuen's Division: Belmont, Gras Pan, and Modder River." *Scribner's Magazine* 27 (March 1900): 259–72.

MODERN BOOKS

Adams, R. J. Q., and Philip P. Poirier. *The Conscription Controversy in Great Britain, 1900–18.* [Columbus]: Ohio State University Press, 1987.

Anderson, Gregory. *Victorian Clerks.* Manchester: Manchester University Press, 1976.

Anglesey, Marquess of. *A History of the British Cavalry, 1816 to 1919*. Vol. 4, *1899–1913*. London: Leo Cooper, 1986.

Arnold, Guy. *Held Fast for England: G. A. Henty, Imperialist Boys' Writer*. London: Hamish Hamilton, 1980.

Attridge, Steve. *Nationalism, Imperialism, and Identity in Late Victorian Culture: Civil and Military Worlds*. London: Palgrave, 2003.

Babington, Anthony. *Military Intervention in Britain: From the Gordon Riots to the Gibraltar Incident*. New York: Routledge, 1990.

Bailey, Peter. *Leisure and Class in Victorian England*. London: Routledge & Kegan Paul, 1978.

Banton, Michael. *Racial Theories*. London: Cambridge University Press, 1987.

Bebbington, D. W. *The Nonconformist Conscience: Chapel and Politics, 1870–1914*. Boston: George Allen & Unwin, 1982.

Beckett, Ian F. W. *The Amateur Military Tradition*. Manchester: Manchester University Press, 1991.

———. *Call to Arms: The Story of Bucks' Citizen Soldiers from Their Origins to Date*. Buckingham: Barracuda, 1985.

———. *Riflemen Form: A Study of the Rifle Volunteer Movement, 1859–1908*. Aldershot: Ogilby Trusts, 1982.

Belfield, Eversley. *The Boer War*. Hamden, Conn.: Archon Books, 1975; Reprint, London: Leo Cooper, 1993.

Bennett, Will. *Absent-Minded Beggars: Volunteers in the Boer War*. London: Leo Cooper, 1999.

Benson, John. *The Working Class in Britain, 1850–1939*. New York: Longman, 1989.

Bolt, Christine. *Victorian Attitudes to Race*. London: Routledge & Kegan Paul, 1971.

Bratton, J. S. *The Impact of Victorian Children's Fiction*. London: Croon Helm, 1981.

Breuilly, John. *Nationalism and the State*. New York: St. Martin's, 1982.

Briggs, Asa. *A Social History of England*. New York: Penguin, 1983.

Brown, Lucy. *Victorian News and Newspapers*. Oxford: Clarendon, 1985.

Brownlie, W. Steel. *The Proud Trooper*. London: Collins, 1964.

Burke, Peter. *The Siege of O'Okiep*. Bloemfontein: War Museum of the Boer Republics, 1995.

Cammack, Diana. *The Rand at War, 1899–1902: The Witwatersrand and the Anglo-Boer War*. Berkeley: University of California Press, 1990.

Clarke, I. F. *Voices Prophesying War, 1763–1984*. New York: Oxford University Press, 1966.

Colls, Robert, and Philip Dodd. *Englishness: Politics and Culture, 1880–1920*. London: Croon Helm, 1986.

Cousins, Geoffrey. *The Defenders: A History of the British Volunteer*. London: Frederick Muller, 1968.

Crossick, Geoffrey, ed. *The Lower Middle Class in Britain, 1870–1914*. New York: St. Martin's, 1977.

Cunningham, Hugh. *The Volunteer Force: A Social and Political History, 1859–1908*. Hamden, Conn.: Archon Books, 1975.

Cuthberton, Greg, Albert Grundlingh, and Mary-Lynn Suttie, eds. *Writing a Wider War: Rethinking Gender, Race, and Identity in the South African War, 1899–1902.* Athens: Ohio University Press, 2002.

Davey, Arthur. *The British Pro-Boers, 1877–1902.* Cape Town: Tafelberg, 1978.

Dennis, Peter, and Jeffrey Grey, eds. *The Boer War: Army, Nation, and Empire.* Canberra: Army History Unit, 2000.

Duminy, A. H., and W. R. Guest, eds. *FitzPatrick: South African Politician.* Johannesburg: McGraw-Hill, 1976.

Eager, W. McG. *Making Men: The History of Boys' Clubs and Related Movements in Great Britain.* London: University of London Press, 1951.

Eby, Cecil D. *The Road to Armageddon: The Martial Spirit in English Popular Literature, 1870–1914.* Durham, N.C.: Duke University Press, 1987.

Eldridge, C. C. *Victorian Imperialism.* Atlantic Highlands, N.J.: Humanities Press, 1978.

Ensor, R. C. K. *England, 1870–1914.* Oxford: Clarendon, 1936.

Farwell, Byron. *The Great Anglo-Boer War.* New York: W. W. Norton, 1976.

Fraser, W. Hamish. *The Coming of the Mass Market, 1850–1914.* London: Macmillan, 1981.

Gilbert, A. D. *Religion and Society in Industrial England.* New York: Longman, 1976.

Gillis, John R. *Youth and History.* New York: Academic Press, 1974.

Gooch, John, ed. *The Boer War: Direction, Experience, and Image.* London: Frank Cass, 2000.

Gourvish, T. R., and A. O'Day, eds. *Later Victorian Britain, 1867–1900.* New York: St. Martin's, 1988.

Grainger, J. H. *Patriotisms: Britain, 1900–1939.* London: Routledge and Kegan Paul, 1986.

Gray, Robert. *The Aristocracy of Labour in Nineteenth-Century Britain, c.1850–1900.* London: Macmillan, 1981.

Harries-Jenkins, Gwyn. *The Army in Victorian Society.* Toronto: University of Toronto Press, 1977.

Harrison, J. F. C. *Late Victorian Britain, 1875–1901.* New York: Routledge, 1991.

Hewison, H. H. *Hedge of Wild Almonds: South Africa, the 'Pro-Boers,' & the Quaker Conscience, 1890–1910.* Portsmouth: Heinemann, 1989.

Horrall, Andrew. *Popular Culture in London, c.1890–1918.* New York: Manchester University Press, 1998.

Jackson, Patrick. *The Last of the Whigs: A Political Biography of Lord Hartington, Later Eighth Duke Devonshire (1833–1908).* Rutherford, N.J.: Fairleigh Dickinson University Press, 1994.

Jones, Gareth Stedman. *Outcast London.* New York: Pantheon, 1971.

Jones, P. d'A. *The Christian Socialist Revival, 1877–1914: Religion, Class, and Social Conscience in Late-Victorian England.* Princeton: Princeton University Press, 1968.

Judd, Denis, and Keith Surridge. *The Boer War.* New York: Palgrave Macmillan, 2003.

Kennedy, Paul, and Anthony Nicholls, eds. *Nationalist and Racialist Movements in Britain and Germany before 1914.* London: Macmillan, 1981.

Koss, Stephen. *The Pro-Boers.* Chicago: University of Chicago Press, 1973.

Krebs, Paula M. *Gender, Race, and the Writing of Empire: Public Discourse and the Boer War.* New York: Cambridge University Press, 1999.

Kruger, Rayne. *Good-Bye Dolly Gray.* New York: J. B. Lippincott, 1960.

Laity, Paul. *The British Peace Movement, 1870–1914.* Oxford: Oxford University Press, 2002.

Lowerson, John. *Sport and the English Middle Classes, 1870–1914.* New York: Manchester University Press, 1993.

Lowry, Donal, ed. *The South African War Reappraised.* New York: Manchester University Press, 2000.

Mackenzie, J. M., ed. *Imperialism and Popular Culture.* New York: Manchester University Press, 1986.

———, ed. *Popular Imperialism and the Military, 1850–1950.* Manchester: Manchester University Press, 1992.

———. *Propaganda and Empire: The Manipulation of British Public Opinion, 1880–1960.* New York: Manchester University Press, 1984.

Magnus, Philip. *Kitchener: Portrait of an Imperialist.* New York: E. P. Dutton, 1959.

Mangan, J. A. *Athleticism in the Victorian and Edwardian Public School.* New York: Cambridge University Press, 1981.

———, ed. *"Benefits Bestowed"? Education and British Imperialism.* New York: St. Martin's, 1988.

———. *The Games Ethic and Imperialism: Aspects of the Diffusion of an Ideal.* New York: Viking, 1986. Rev. ed., London: Frank Cass, 1998.

Mangan, J. A., and J. Walvin, eds. *Manliness and Morality: Middle-Class Masculinity in Britain and America, 1800–1940.* New York: St. Martin's, 1987.

Mansfield, Nicholas. *English Farmworkers and Local Patriotism, 1900–1930.* Burlington: Ashgate, 2001.

Marsh, Jan. *Back to the Land.* New York: Quartet Books, 1982.

Meacham, Standish. *A Life Apart: The English Working Class, 1890–1914.* Cambridge, Mass.: Harvard University Press, 1977.

Mileham, Patrick, ed. *Clearly My Duty: The Letters of Sir John Gilmour.* East Linton: Tuckwell, 1996.

Miller, Stephen. *Lord Methuen and the British Army: Failure and Redemption in South Africa.* London: Frank Cass, 1999.

Mingay, G. E., ed. *The Victorian Countryside.* Boston: Routledge & Kegan Paul, 1981.

Moore, Geoffrey. *Pickman's Progress in the City Imperial Volunteers in South Africa, 1900.* Huntingdon: G. Moore, 1986.

Morris, A. J. A. *The Scaremongers.* London: Routledge & Kegan Paul, 1984.

Nasson, Bill. *Abraham Esau's War: A Black South African War in the Cape, 1899–1902.* New York: Cambridge University Press, 1991.

———. *The South African War, 1899–1902.* New York: Oxford, 1999.

Omissi, David, and Andrew S. Thompson, eds. *The Impact of the South African War.* New York: Palgrave, 2002.

Pakenham, Thomas. *The Boer War.* New York: Random House, 1979.

Peck, John. *War, the Army, and Victorian Literature.* New York: St. Martin's, 1998.

Pelling, H. *Popular Politics and Society in Late Victorian Britain.* New York: St. Martin's, 1968.

Penn, Alan. *Targeting Schools: Drill, Militarism, and Imperialism.* London: Woburn, 1999.

Pick, Daniel. *War Machine: The Rationalisation of Slaughter in the Modern Age.* New Haven: Yale University Press, 1993.

Porter, Bernard. *Critics of Empire: British Radical Attitudes to Colonialism in Africa, 1895–1914.* New York: St. Martin's, 1968.

Porter, A. N. *The Origins of the South African War: Joseph Chamberlain and the Diplomacy of Imperialism, 1895–99.* Manchester: Manchester University Press, 1980.

Pretorius, Fransjohan. *The Great Escape of the Boer Pimpernel Christiaan de Wet: The Making of a Legend.* Translated by Stephen Hofstätter. Pietermaritzburg: University of Natal Press, 2001.

———. *Life on Commando during the Anglo-Boer War, 1899–1902.* Cape Town: Human & Rousseau, 1999.

Price, Richard. *An Imperial War and the British Working Class: Working-Class Attitudes and Reactions to the Boer War, 1899–1902.* London: Routledge & Kegan Paul, 1972.

Read, Donald, ed. *Edwardian England.* London: Croon Helm, 1982.

Reader, W. J. *At Duty's Call.* New York: St. Martin's, 1988.

Reckitt, B. N. *The Lindley Affair: A Diary of the Boer War.* Hull: A. Brown & Sons, 1972.

Rich, Paul B. *Race and Empire in British Politics.* New York: Cambridge University Press, 1986.

Richards, Jeffrey, ed. *Imperialism and Juvenile Literature.* New York: Manchester University Press, 1989.

———. *Imperialism and Music: Britain, 1876–1953.* New York: Manchester University Press, 2001.

Roberts, Andrew. *Salisbury: Victorian Titan.* London: Weidenfeld and Nicolson, 1999.

Robinson, Ronald, and John Gallagher, with Alice Denny. *Africa and the Victorians.* 2nd ed. London: Macmillan, 1981.

Rosenthal, Michael. *The Character Factory: Baden-Powell and the Origins of the Boy Scout Movement.* New York: Pantheon Books, 1986.

Russell, Dave. *Popular Music in England, 1840–1914: A Social History.* Kingston: McGill-Queen's University Press, 1987.

Samuel, Raphael, ed. *Patriotism: The Making and Unmaking of British National Identity.* London: Routledge, 1989.

Searle, G. R. *The Quest for National Efficiency.* Berkeley: University of California Press, 1971.

Semmel, Bernard. *Imperialism and Social Reform: English Social-Imperial Thought, 1895–1914.* New York: George Allen & Unwin, 1960. Reprint, Garden City, N.J.: Anchor Books, 1968.

Shannon, Richard. *The Age of Salisbury, 1881–1902.* New York: Longman, 1996.

Skelley, Alan Ramsay. *The Victorian Army at Home: The Recruitment and Terms and Conditions of the British Regular, 1859–1899.* Montreal: McGill-Queen's University Press, 1977.

Smith, Iain R. *The Origins of the South African War, 1899–1902.* New York: Longman, 1996.

Spencer, William. *Records of the Militia and Volunteer Forces, 1757–1945.* Rev. ed., Public Records Office Readers' Guide No. 3. London: PRO Publications, 1997.

Spiers, Edward M. *The Army and Society, 1815–1914.* New York: Longman, 1980.

———. *Haldane: An Army Reformer.* Edinburgh: Edinburgh University Press, 1980.

———. *The Late Victorian Army, 1868–1902.* London: St. Martin's, 1992.

Spies, S. B. *Methods of Barbarism.* Cape Town: Human and Rousseau, 1977.

Springhall, John. *Youth, Empire and Society: British Youth Movements, 1883–1940.* Hamden, Conn.: Archon Books, 1977.

Steele, David. *Lord Salisbury: A Political Biography.* New York: Routledge, 2001.

Steppler, Glenn A. *Britons to Arms! The Story of the British Volunteer Soldier and the Volunteer Tradition in Leicestershire and Rutland.* Worcester: Alan Sutton, 1992.

Summers, A. *Angels and Citizens: British Women as Military Nurses, 1854–1914.* New York: Routledge & Kegan Paul, 1988.

Surridge, Keith Terrance. *Managing the South African War, 1899–1902: Politicians v. Generals.* Woodbridge: Boydell, 1998.

Symons, Julian. *Buller's Campaign.* London: Cresset, 1963.

Thompson, Andrew S. *Imperial Britain: The Empire in British Politics, c.1880–1932.* New York: Longman, 2000.

Van Wyck Smith, M. *Drummer Hodge: The Poetry of the Anglo-Boer War, 1899–1902.* Oxford: Clarendon, 1978.

Verdin, Richard. *The Cheshire (Earl of Chester's) Yeomanry, 1898–1967.* Chester: Cheshire Yeomanry Association, 1971.

Waller, P. J. *Town, City, and Nation: England, 1850–1914.* New York: Oxford University Press, 1983.

Walvin, James. *Leisure and Society, 1830–1950.* New York: Longman, 1978.

Ward, Paul. *Red Flag and Union Jack: Englishness, Patriotism, and the British Left, 1881–1924.* London: Boydell, 1998.

Warwick, Peter, and S. B. Spies. *The South African War: The Anglo-Boer War, 1899–1902.* Harlow: Longman, 1980.

Wessels, André, ed. *Anglo-Boer War Diary of Herbert Gwynne Howell.* Pretoria: Human Sciences Research Council, 1986.

Wolffe, John. *God and Greater Britain: Religion and National Life in Britain and Ireland, 1843–1945.* New York: Routledge, 1994.

MODERN JOURNAL ARTICLES

Anderson, O. "The Growth of Christian Militarism in Mid-Victorian Britain." *English Historical Review* 86, no. 338 (1971): 46–72.

Bailes, Howard. "Patterns of Thought in the Late Victorian Army." *Journal of Strategic Studies* 4 (1981): 29–45.

Beckett, Ian F. W. "Arnold-Forster and the Volunteers." In *Politicians and Defence,* eds. I. F. W. Beckett and J. Gooch, 47–68. Manchester: Manchester University Press, 1981.

———. "Early Historians and the South African War." *Sandhurst Journal of Military Studies* 1 (1990): 15–32.

———. "The Problems of Military Discipline in the Volunteer Force, 1859–1899." *Journal of the Society for Army Historical Research* 56, no. 226 (1978): 66–78.

Best, Geoffrey. "Militarism and the Victorian Public School." In *The Victorian Public School,* eds. B. Simon and I. Bradley, 129–46. Dublin: Gill and Macmillan, 1975.

Blanch, Michael. "Imperialism, Nationalism, and Organized Youth." In *Working-Class Culture,* eds. J. Clarke, C. Critcher, and R. Johnson, 103–120. New York: St. Martin's, 1979.

Bond, Brian. "Recruiting the Victorian Army, 1870–92." *Victorian Studies* 5 (1962): 331–38.

Cunningham, H. "The Language of Patriotism, 1750–1914." *History Workshop* 12 (1981): 8–33.

Dunae, Patrick A. "'Boys' Literature and the Idea of the Empire, 1870–1914." *Victorian Studies* 24 (1980): 105–21.

Gooch, John. "Attitudes to War in Late Victorian and Edwardian England." In *War and Society: A Yearbook of Military History,* eds. B. Bond and I. Roy, 88–102. New York: Holmes & Meier, 1975.

———. "Haldane and the 'National Army.'" In *Politicians and Defence,* eds. I. F. W. Beckett and J. Gooch, 69–86. Manchester: Manchester University Press, 1981.

Gourvish, T. R. "The Standard of Living, 1890–1914." In *The Edwardian Age: Conflict and Stability, 1900–1914,* ed. A. O'Day, 13–34. Hamden, Conn.: Archon Books, 1979.

Hendley, Matthew. "Help Us to Secure a Strong, Healthy, Prosperous, and Peaceful Britain." *Canadian Journal of History* 30 (1995): 261–88.

Hurt, J. S. "Drill, Discipline, and the Elementary School Etho." In *Popular Education and Socialization in the Nineteenth Century,* ed. Phillip McCann, 167–93. London: Methuen, 1977.

Hyslop, Jonathan. "A Scottish Socialist Reads Carlyle in Johannesburg Prison, June 1900: Reflections on the Literary Culture of the Imperial

Working Class." *Journal of Southern African Studies* 29 (2003): 639–55.

Mangan, J. A "Duty unto Death: English Masculinity and Militarism in the Age of the New Imperialism." In *Tribal Identities: Nationalism, Europe, and Sport,* ed. J. A. Mangan, 10–38. London: Frank Cass, 1996.

Marks, Shula. "British Nursing and the South African War." In *Writing a Wider War,* eds. G. Cuthbertson, A. Grundlingh, and M. Suttie, 159–85. Athens: Ohio University Press, 2002.

Merriwether, Jeffrey. "The Intricacies of War Office Administration: Civilians, Soldiers, and the Opening of the South African War, October–December 1899." *Archives* 28 (2003): 48–68.

Miller, Stephen. "In Support of the 'Imperial Mission'? Volunteering for the South African War." *Journal of Military History* 69, no. 3 (2005): 691–713.

———. "Slogging across the Veld: British Volunteers and the Guerrilla Phase of the South African War. " *Journal of the Society for Army Historical Research* 84 (2006): 158–74.

Morton, Patricia. "Another Victorian Paradox: Anti-Militarism in a Jingoistic Society." *Historical Reflections* 5, no. 2 (1981): 169–89.

Preston, A. W. "British Military Thought, 1856–90." *Army Quarterly and Defence Journal* 89 (1964): 57–74.

Satre, Lowell J. "St. John Brodrick and Army Reform, 1901–1903." *Journal of British Studies* 15 (1976): 117–39.

Summers, Anne. "Militarism in Britain before the Great War." *History Workshop* 2 (1976): 104–23.

Surridge, Keith. "'All You Soldiers Are What We Call Pro-Boer': The Military Critique of the South African War, 1899–1902." *History* 82 (1997): 582–600.

Talbot, Philip. "The English Yeomanry in the Nineteenth Century and the Great Boer War." *Journal of the Society for Army Historical Research* 79 (2001): 45–62.

Tucker, Albert. "Army and Society in England, 1870–1900: A Reassessment of the Cardwell Reforms." *Journal of British Studies* 2 (1963): 110–41.

———. "The Issue of Army Reform in the Unionist Government, 1903–5." *Historical Journal* 9 (1966): 90–100.

Wilkinson, Glen R. "'The Blessings of War': The Depiction of Military Force in Edwardian Newspapers." *Journal of Contemporary History* 33 (1998): 97–115.

NEWSPAPERS AND MILITARY JOURNALS

Athenaeum, The (London)
Blackwood's Edinburgh Magazine
Contemporary Review (London)
Daily News (London)

Edinburgh Review
Fortnightly Review (London)
Illustrated London News
Journal of the Royal United Service Institution (London)
Leeds Mercury
Manchester Guardian
Natal Mercury
Nineteenth Century (and After) (London)
Punch (London)
Quarterly Review (London)
Review of Reviews (London)
Spectator, The (London)
Times, The (London)
United Service Gazette and Naval and Military Chronicle (London)

Index

Page numbers in italics refer to illustrations.